THE ROMAN CATHOLIC CHURCH
IN ENGLAND AND WALES

Other books by E. E. Reynolds include

The Field is Won: the Life and
    Death of St. Thomas More
Saint John Fisher
Thomas More and Erasmus
The Trial of Thomas More
Margaret Roper
etc.

THE
ROMAN CATHOLIC CHURCH
IN ENGLAND AND WALES

A SHORT HISTORY

By

E. E. Reynolds

ANTHONY CLARKE BOOKS
WHEATHAMPSTEAD – HERTFORDSHIRE

© E. E. Reynolds 1973
First published 1973

ANTHONY CLARKE BOOKS
WHEATHAMPSTEAD — HERTFORDSHIRE

SBN: 85650 025 9

Made and Printed in Great Britain by
Robert MacLehose & Co Ltd, The University Press, Glasgow

Contents

Maps

Preface

THERE are a number of good ecclesiastical histories of England, but from the Reformation onwards they become histories of the Church of England. This is the correct line for authors to follow whose interest is the development of the Anglican Church.

It seemed to me that there is a place for a history of the Roman Catholic Church in England and Wales from the earliest times to the present so that it could be read as a continuous story.

The need for keeping within the limits of an ordinary volume has meant that some topics have been dealt with more briefly than I should like, but I hope that nothing of importance has been omitted. As this book is intended for the general reader I have not cumbered it with a multitude of references to sources and other authorities. An Appendix suggests further reading for those who would like to go more deeply into the subject.

E.E.R.

CHAPTER I

To the coming of St. Augustine

It is not known when or by what means Christianity first reached Britain. Bede in his *History of the Church of England*, written in the eighth century, refers to a Lucius, 'King of the Britons', who wrote to Pope Eleutherus (A.D. 171?) asking to be made a Christian. This Lucius is otherwise unknown and there may have been a confusion with Lucius, King of Edessa, whose capital was named Britium. The later story that Joseph of Arimathea founded Glastonbury, is even more suspect; it was not recorded until the twelfth century. The probability is that Christianity was first preached in this country by missionaries from Gaul during the second century, but further than that it is not safe to speculate.

There is evidence of Christianity, or, it would be more correct to say, of Christians, during the Roman Occupation which ended at the beginning of the fifth century. At Silchester (the Roman Calleva) there is a small Christian basilica, and some Christian wall-paintings have been uncovered in a house-church at Lullingstone in Kent. Other indications are given by mosaics, by emblems on tombstones, and by other archaeological finds. The proto-martyr of Britain, St. Alban, suffered in the third century. His story was inevitably embellished in the re-telling. The basic fact seems to have been that he was a native of Verulamium, not necessarily a soldier, who was a convert. His attempt to shield a priest was frustrated and he was executed on a hill outside the town for refusing to burn incense to the Roman gods. Two other martyrs of the same period, Aaron and Julius, are little more than names; both suffered at Caerleon (the Roman Isca) in Monmouthshire.

We get on to firm ground with the knowledge that three bishops from Britain attended the Council at Arles in the year 314, and three were at the Council of Ariminum in 359. The names of the three bishops at Arles are given as Eborius of York, Restitutus of London, and Adelphius, probably of Lincoln. They had with them Sacerdos, a presbyter, and Arminius, a deacon. The names 'Eborius' and 'Sacerdos' are doubtful. 'Eboracum' (York) suggests 'Eborius', and 'Sacerdos' might apply to any cleric. The presence of British bishops tells us two things; first that there was an organised Church in Britain, and, secondly, that they were orthodox, as they accepted the Creed of Nicaea. No other traces of this early Church in this country are discernible.

One glimpse of the fifth-century Church we owe to the British heretic Pelagius, a monk who did not promulgate his opinions in his native land, but settled in Rome about the year 400. He denied the doctrine of original sin; he granted that in the forgiveness of sin there is an element of grace, but man, he argued, has freedom of choice between right and wrong and can make or mar his spiritual life by his own will. Disciples of his came to Britain and gained adherents to this teaching. St. Germanus, bishop of Auxerre and St. Lupus of Troyes were sent by Pope Celestine (422–32) to counter the influence of Pelagius. They came over in the year 429 and met the heretics in conference at Veralamium (St. Alban's) and routed them in argument. Soon afterwards a force of Saxon and Pictish raiders attacked the Britons who asked for help from Germanus. He went with the army and instructed the soldiers to cry out 'Alleluia!' at the sight of the enemy who were dismayed and fled. Pelagianism, however, was not completely eradicated, and ten years later Germanus answered another call to Britain, and this time he succeeded and the heretics were banished.

These incidents tell us that the Church was well established in the fifth century and was in contact with the Church in Gaul. They also presage the tragic days that were to come, for the Saxons whom Germanus helped to repulse were the forerunners of a seemingly unending and irresistible flood of pagan invaders from across the North Sea.

From the middle of the fifth century to the end of the sixth, Britain was subjected to the onslaughts of Jutes, Angles and Saxons. It meant the end of Britain but the beginning of England. It was not a coordinated invasion, but a series of attacks by various tribes; these were not tip-and-run raids, as the invaders were looking for fresh lands in which to settle. The result, for some time, was a welter of small kingdoms, if, indeed, many of these settlements deserved that name. There were a few enclaves of British, such as Elmet, west of York, that held out as independent communities. The inhabitants of some British settlements were massacred; churches and monasteries were sacked and destroyed. While some of the surviving inhabitants were absorbed and in later years intermarried with their conquerors, others retreated westwards until they found refuge in Wales and Cornwall, or, crossing the Channel, reached Armorica (Brittany). Some found new homes in Strathclyde, west of the Pennines from the Mersey to the Clyde, so reaching up into what we know as the Lowlands of Scotland. The picture of what happened to the original inhabitants lacks precise detail. There are no records, and archaeology does not shed much light; place-names are suggestive but by no means determinative. Thus we do not know what proportion of the population was absorbed by the invaders, of whose total numbers we are also ignorant. What does seem clear is that the British who escaped from the occupied territory made no attempts to convert their neighbouring supplanters; nor is this surprising as the bitter hatred between the defeated British and the conquering Anglo-Saxons made contacts impossible.

3

While the British Church was being despoiled, the Celtic Church gathered strength. Early in the fifth century Ninian, a Strathclyde Briton, went to Rome where he was ordained priest and consecrated a bishop by the Pope. On his return, Ninian built a church of stone, the Candida Casa, from which is derived the name of Whithorn (White-house) in Galloway. From there Ninian and his companions began the conversion of the Picts. A more successful assault on paganism was carried out by St. Patrick in Ireland during the period 432 to 463. He was born in west Britain about the year 390, but the place of his birth is a matter of dispute. He was of Romano-British origin; his father was a decurion (a local official) and his grandfather was a priest. About 403 Patrick was carried off by Irish raiders and, after six years of bondage, he escaped and got to Gaul, and so back home. He had an irresistible vocation for the conversion of the Irish. He went to the famous monastery of Lérins (off Cannes) to be trained for the priesthood, and after that he served at Auxerre under Bishop Germanus for some years. In 431 St. Palladius had been sent to Ireland as a missionary, but he was so discouraged that he left after a year and went to Scotland where he died. St. Germanus consecrated Patrick bishop in place of Palladius. St. Patrick's wonderful ministry of thirty years cannot be described here; Ireland's unwavering Catholicism is his memorial.

The renewal of the Church in Wales owed much in the sixth century to St. Illtud who founded an influential monastery at Llantwit Major (Llanilltud Fawr in Welsh) on the Glamorgan coast. It is said that Illtud was trained by St. Germanus, but he remains a shadowy figure. A contemporary was Dyfrig (Dubricius) and among those trained by St. Illtud were St. Samson, St. Gildas, and, possibly, St. Dewi (David). Later centres of learning and evangelisation were the Bangors: Bangor Fawr on the Menai Straits and Bangor Iscoed (Bangor-on-Dee). The latter is said to have been the earliest monastery founded in Britain. St. Petroc, a Welshman, evangelised Cornwall.

It was also in the sixth century that St. Columba founded

the monastery on the island of Iona. He was of royal Irish descent, but, after some years of missionary labours in his native land, he left in the year 563 with twelve companions for western Scotland[1] which had been settled by the Irish.

The long and involved story of the Anglo-Saxon conquest must be read in the history books. It is like a kaleidoscope, with kings (or chieftains) rising and falling and with over-lordship changing hands as power passed from one region to another. The disposition about the year 600 was as follows: Ethelbert of Kent exercised some degree of suprem-acy over Wessex and Sussex south of the Thames, over Essex and East Anglia and over Mercia. The last was a 'kingdom' of variable boundaries covering the Midlands as far as the Severn and up to Chester. Northumbria (east of the Pennines down to the Humber) was independent; the southern part was called Deira (roughly Yorkshire) and the northern part, Bernicia. The whole of the west from the Clyde down to the south coast of Cornwall remained Celtic-British.

The Anglo-Saxons were heathen but they had no system-atised religion — one might say, no theology — and their pantheon was a rather confused galaxy of gods and goddesses; their number and variety were considerable and differed from tribe to tribe; settlements were often isolated and this prevented any one system predominating. The fact that some of these pagan deities are perpetuated in the names we give to the days of the week is evidence of the grip paganism must have had on the English. Tuesday is from Tiw, one of the war gods; Wednesday from Woden, the chief of the gods and the ancestor, it was claimed, of the English kings; Thursday is from Thor or Thunor, the thunderer, and Friday is from Frig, the goddess of fertility. A temple of tim-ber would be built where the king had his high seat, but a landowner would have his own temple. This custom was carried into Christian times when the local lord would build his own church and engage the priest. What may be called

[1] Up to the tenth century the name 'Scotia' referred to Ireland alone. Only slowly did the name come to be applied to the northern part of Great Britain as the Irish settled there.

5

official worship at the temples was in the main a matter of sacrificing cattle followed by the sprinkling of blood and a feast on the meat. It should be noticed that there was nothing here of what we understand by 'worship', a service of prayer and praise. More ancient than these temple sacrifices were the people's fertility rites for the increase of herds and an abundant harvest. There were a number of special festivals during the year, as in May when the whole community would welcome the return of the fertility spirit, or go in processions through the fields to appease the spirits who could grant or withhold fruitfulness. There again there was no universal pattern; each settlement, living very much on its own, developed its local ways of conciliating, not worshipping, the gods and spirits.

Such was the religious situation towards the end of the sixth century. Paganism had overcome Christianity in England[1] as far west as the Severn. Wales and Cornwall were steadily being won for the Church, but this must not be thought of as a uniform picture. In remote places sacrifices would still be made to the pagan gods and the Christianity of the converted was not always entirely freed from heathen customs and traditional conceptions. Some linger on to-day as popular superstitions. The initiative that led to the conversion of the English did not come from the west, nor from the residual British Church, nor from Gaul which had its own troubles with barbarian invaders; the initiative came from Rome.

How the thoughts of St. Gregory the Great were turned towards England is a well-known story. He noticed in the Roman slave-market some boys 'of white skin and comely countenance and hair also of excellent beauty' as Bede described them. Gregory asked of what nation they were. 'Angles,' he was told. 'Not Angles, but Angels,' he declared. He was distressed to learn that they were heathens. He was a Roman of patrician birth who had early shown his administrative and diplomatic gifts in the service of both City and

[1] It is convenient to use the terms 'England' and 'English' though premature at this stage if we think they denote one, united nation.

Church. He gave up his rich inheritance and founded the monastery of St. Andrew's on the Caelian Hill. The church of San Gregorio Magno occupies the site and contains his episcopal throne. When the call to England came to him, he set off with some of his monks but the Pope summoned him to return as his services in Rome were too valuable. Gregory himself became Pope in the year 590 and six years later he was able to plan the mission to England. Meanwhile he had been gathering what news he could of the country and its rulers. As leader of his group of evangelists he appointed Augustine, the prior of the monastery. There seem to have been about forty of them. They left Rome in 596 and probably went by sea to the coast of Provence; there they had to face the six-hundred-mile journey northwards through the kingdom of the Franks. The monks became discouraged when they were warned of the savagery of the Anglo-Saxons — a reputation that lingered from the early days of their invasion. We cannot blame the monks for their reluctance to go forward; England was a heathen island of which not much was known and where a strange language was spoken. They therefore persuaded Augustine to return to Rome to get the Pope's permission for them to give up the mission. While their leader was absent, the monks probably were received at the monastery of Lérins. Here we have an indication of Augustine's character; he was not a forceful leader of men. Gregory reassured him and gave him letters of introduction to bishops through whose dioceses they would pass on their way north. With this renewed command, the monks went forward and they landed at Ebbsfleet in the Isle of Thanet just before Easter in the year 597.

Ethelbert, the most powerful of the English kings of that period had married Bertha, a daughter of King Charibert of Paris. She was a Christian, and one condition of the marriage was that she should have freedom of worship, and she brought with her a chaplain named Liudhard. Ethelbert gave her a church which dated back to Roman times; it was dedicated to St. Martin of Tours when it was reconse-

7

crated. The present church, which stands outside the old royal city on the road to Sandwich, is partly built of Roman brick. It may be that Queen Bertha wrote to Pope Gregory; certainly her presence as a devout Christian must have predisposed some of the Kentish leaders to regard her religion with good will, but she did not succeed in converting the king. He was not, however, antagonistic to the newly arrived missioners. Had they landed on the south coast of Sussex they might have had a hostile reception.

Augustine had with him some interpreters from the land of the Franks. He sent one of them to the king to announce that he brought good news from Rome which offered men the everlasting joys of heaven. Ethelbert, in reply, told the monks to remain where they were until he had decided what to do; meantime they would be provided for. Some days later, the king came to the island with some of his noblemen and councillors and there, in the open, he heard what Augustine had to say. 'In the open' because he feared that if they were sorcerers they could do most harm under a roof. They came to him in procession, as Bede tells us, 'carrying before them in place of a banner a cross of silver[1] and the image of the Lord Saviour painted on a table,[2] and singing the litanies.' The king welcomed them and listened carefully to Augustine's 'good news'. 'The words and promises you give us are fair,' said Ethelbert, 'but yet, for that they are strange and uncertain, I cannot rashly assent unto them, forsaking those things which this long time I have observed with all the English people.' However, he made no objection to their trying to win converts. He invited them to Canterbury and let them occupy some land near the present church of St. Alfege. The missioners crossed from the island to Richborough and then took the fifteen-mile road to Canterbury. As they neared that city, they formed into procession and chanted the Rogation antiphon, 'We beseech

---

[1] The crucifix was not yet in common use. Until about the 12th century, Our Lord was shown alive, robed and crowned as reigning from the Cross. Our modern horrific renderings would have been discordant.

[2] 'Table' here means a panel of wood.

8

thee, Lord, in all thy mercy, that thy fury and anger may be taken from this city and from thy holy house, because we have sinned. Alleluia.'

They worshipped at St. Martin's church which, for this reason, has been well called the Mother Church of England. Ethelbert himself received instruction and was baptised on Whit Sunday, 2nd June 597. He would submit to the rite then used for adult baptism: the priest would blow in his face to expel the devil, then place salt on the mouth as a symbol of the covenant with God, and finally immerse the king three times in the water — this would be in a neighbouring stream. In a letter from Pope Gregory to the Patriarch of Alexandria it is stated that some ten thousand of Ethelbert's subjects had been baptised by Christmas Day of that year. This kind of wholesale baptism seems questionable to us, and, we ask, were all these men and women fully instructed in their new faith, and did they really understand it? These questions cannot be answered. It may, however, be noted that Ethelbert did not immediately embrace the faith. On such an important matter he would have consulted his witan, and once he had gained the approval of his councillors the rest of the people would follow since the tie between king, leaders and people was a very close one based on long tribal tradition. It must be admitted that if the king renounced his religion, the majority of his people would follow his example. At the same time there would no doubt be a nucleus of firm believers who would remain faithful to their Christian belief.

CHAPTER 2

St. Augustine of Canterbury

As Augustine had not received episcopal orders before landing in Kent, he went, in accordance with Pope Gregory's instructions, to Gaul in the autumn of 597 to Archbishop Virgilius of Arles who consecrated Augustine as 'Archbishop of the English' on the 16th November. There was, in effect, no English nation at that period, so it may be claimed that the conception of one people was a religious one before it could become a political reality.

It was at this period that Augustine sent two of his monks, Laurentius and Peter, to Rome to report on the progress of the mission, to ask for further help, and to put before the Pope some of the problems that had arisen. In these questions we may see another indication of Augustine's character. He was not the man to make bold decisions on his own authority, or at least not at that stage; his consecration as archbishop probably gave him greater confidence since it meant a defined authority rather than the vague leadership of a group of missionary monks. Slowness and difficulty of communication with Rome meant inevitable delays in settling doubtful points; actually Augustine had to wait nearly two years before he got the Pope's replies. Gregory had been seriously ill and he was beset with many problems so that he could not give immediate attention to Augustine's troubles; moreover he may have had some difficulty in finding suitable recruits for the English mission. In company with Laurentius and Peter, on their return with Gregory's letters, were several more monks including Mellitus, Justus and Paulinus; it was a notable company, for three of them were to be successors to Augustine in the see of Canterbury, and Paulinus was to be bishop of York and, later, bishop of Rochester.

While they were on their way to England, a messenger from Pope Gregory caught them up with another letter asking for news of them and sending further advice to Augustine. The monks also had with them letters to King Ethelbert and Queen Bertha thanking them for their hospitality to the monks; there were letters to eleven Gallic bishops commending the monks to their care. Gregory also sent gifts to the English church; these included chalices, altarcloths and vestments, relics of the martyrs, and a number of liturgical and other books.[1] To Augustine himself the Pope sent the pallium, which at that time was a vestment that had associations with Imperial Rome; it was bestowed by the popes on archbishops to mark them as direct representatives of the Holy See.[2]

The answers to Augustine's questions on the divisions of the offerings of the faithful, on marriage, on theft from churches, on ceremonial purity and on the consecration of bishops need not detain us. Other questions, however, have a wider interest. At that time there was no uniform liturgy throughout the Church. The fundamental principles of the Mass were, of course, always preserved, but there were local variations in the prayers used and in some details of ritual. Augustine asked for guidance as to which custom he

[1] It is thought that a copy of the Gospels at Corpus Christi College, Cam-Cambridge, is one of the manuscript books sent by Gregory.

[2] Later it took the stylised form of a narrow band giving a Y-shape in front and behind as it hangs over the shoulders of the archbishop. It is made from the wool of lambs reared at St. Agnes, Rome, and then placed on the tomb of St. Peter before presentation. It is displayed in the arms of the see of Canterbury.

should follow. Gregory told him to select whatever he found suitable for 'the Church of the English.' 'Choose then,' he wrote, 'out of each Church that that is godly, that is religious, that is right in any of them, and these being gathered as it were in a bundle, deliver unto them and inure the minds of the English thereunto.' He pointed out that 'the things are not to be loved for the place, but the place is to be loved for the good things that are in it.'

A problem that faced Augustine, and indeed that faces every missionary, was what policy to adopt towards pagan and superstitious practices. Here Gregory showed a large-mindedness and a common-sense that unfortunately were not always followed by his successors. Where pagan temples were in a reasonable state of repair, they should not be demolished but purified and adapted as churches. As to the traditional pagan festivals, these too should, if possible, be assimilated and Christianised. 'For it is doubtless impossible to cut off all abuses at once from rough hearts, seeing that he too that laboureth to climb up into a high place, goeth upward by steps and paces but not by leaps.' So it was that the Teutonic Yule-tide of twelve days was sanctified as Christmastide, and the festival of Eostre, the goddess of spring, kept at the vernal equinox, gave its name to our Easter.

In his report to Gregory, Augustine seems to have referred perhaps with some complacency to miracles he had worked. The Pope did not question the fact or minimise the importance of this sign of divine favour, but he warned Augustine against the danger of 'mounting pride of thy heart. And whatsoever grace thou hast either received or shalt receive to work miracles, think that they have been granted not unto thee but unto them for whose salvation they have been bestowed upon thee.'

Augustine was troubled about his relations with the Gallic and Celtic-British bishops. Gregory made it clear that the Archbishop of the English had no authority outside his own country, though he should maintain the friendliest relations with the bishops of the kingdom of the Franks, 'for thou canst not thrust the sickle of thy judgment into the corn that seemeth to have been committed to other men's charges.' As to the Celtic-British bishops, 'we commit them into the charge of thy brotherliness, that the unlearned may be instructed, the weak by good persuasions be strengthened, the forward be corrected by authority.' From this it is clear that Gregory had no idea of the complexity of the situation with which Augustine was faced.

It is convenient to use the term Celtic (or Celtic-British) Church to distinguish it from Augustine's work of laying the foundations of an English Church. We must, however, bear in mind the fact that the differences between them were not on matters of doctrine, for all accepted the Nicene Creed; nor was there any question of the authority of the Holy See. There was the geographical separation; the whole of heathen England lay between Canterbury and the Severn, but this was not an insuperable obstacle. The basic difference was that the Celtic-British Christians inevitably distrusted the Anglo-Saxons, and for more than a century before the landing of Augustine, the Celtic Church had gone forward steadily with the conversion of West Britain, that is Wales and Cornwall, and had refused to have anything to do with the conquerors who had driven many of them into the west. St. Aldhem (d. 709), bishop of Sherborne, recorded that the British priests beyond the Severn would not worship with Saxons nor would they have any social dealings with them. The newcomers from Rome, who seemed to claim a measure of superior authority, were regarded with suspicion. It was a very human situation that called for the greatest tact in its handling. Unfortunately Augustine lacked this gift. He, a Roman, had gained the confidence of an Anglo-Saxon King and he had no direct knowledge of the British.

The isolation and self-containment of the Celtic Church had resulted in the adoption of some usages that were peculiar, and it was on these that dissension arose, not, let it be repeated, on doctrine. The differences were on secondary matters, but these, as we all know, can inflame tempers just as much as disagreements on great principles.

The first problem was the dating of Easter. This involved astronomical and other calculations that cannot be set out here.[1] The Celts followed an earlier system that had been superseded by Rome by what was considered a more accurate way of reckoning. As a result there could be a difference of a week or more in the observation of Easter.

A second difference was in the form of the clerical tonsure. The Roman practice was to shave the crown of the head; the Celtic custom was to shave from ear to ear over the head and allow the back hair to grow.

The Celtic clergy were allowed to marry, whereas only those below the subdiaconate could marry according to Roman regulations. Abbacies in the Celtic Church, contrary to Roman practice, were hereditary. Moreover the status of bishops was dissimilar. Evangelisation in Celtic lands was carried out from monasteries. Some of the monks would lead an ascetic life of prayer, but others would spread the Gospel in the neighbourhood or even farther afield. Each monastery would have its bishop, who, in addition to his faculties for consecration, would be engaged in preaching; he was under the authority of the abbot. The Roman system was based on dioceses, in each of which the bishop would be the supreme authority.

We do not know how Augustine got into touch with the Celtic Church. Communications could not have been easy while the country was still disturbed and rival kings and chiefs were at war with one another. He managed to have a meeting with some Celtic bishops in 602 or 603 at a place, according to Bede, 'called in the English tongue *Augustine's ac*, that is, Augustine's oak, being on the borders of the Hwiccas and West Saxons.' The Hwiccas were Anglo-Saxon tribes occupying Gloucestershire, Warwickshire and Worcestershire; the West Saxons had by this time reached Somerset. Two sites have been claimed for this meeting: the first is the oak near Down-Ampney in the south-east of Gloucestershire, and the second is Aust on the southern

[1] The least technical explanation will be found in an Excursus at the end of C. Plummer's edition of Bede.

shore of the estuary of the Severn in the same county. This
first attempt at unifying the Celtic and English Churches
did not succeed. The British bishops said they could not
agree with Augustine's views 'without the consent and leave
of their own people.' So a second meeting was arranged. We
are not told where this was held; it was probably farther
north on the Welsh border perhaps near Chester. In addition
to seven bishops, many of the monks attended from Bangor
Iscoed, the chief centre of learning. The story was that the
bishops consulted a holy hermit as to what policy they should
follow. He replied that if Augustine was a man of God,
they should follow him, and they would know this by his
conduct; if he stood up to receive them, then 'he is the servant
of Christ,' but if he remained seated, then they should reject
him. Augustine did remain seated when the British party
approached him; they therefore declared that they could not
accept him as archbishop nor could they agree to his demands.
This hardly credible story may be based on the fact that
Augustine, in accordance with the custom of a Roman
presiding magistrate, remained seated. In his demands he
was ready to compromise on the lesser differences; he asked
for three changes; first they should accept the Roman date
for Easter; secondly, they should baptise according to the
Roman custom,[1] and thirdly they should join with him
in evangelising the Anglo-Saxons. It was probably this last
request that angered the British bishops; they would have
nothing to do with their conquerors. The bitterness of a
defeated people, driven from their homeland, made reconciliation impossible; time alone could assuage such
feelings. Augustine warned them that 'if they would not
preach to the English nation the way of life, they should
through their hands suffer the vengeance of death.' When,
in the year 613, King Ethelfrith of Northumbria inflicted
a crushing defeat on the Welsh at Chester and massacred
many hundreds of the monks of Bangor Iscoed, some saw
in this the fulfilment of Augustine's warning. Writing in
731, Bede declared that 'unto this day the Briton's

---

[1] It is not known how the Celtic form of baptism differed from the Roman.

custom is to make light of the faith and religion of the English, nor to have any more communications with them than with pagans.' So Augustine failed to bring about a united Church in Britain, but for that he could not be blamed.

Pope Gregory's scheme for the organisation of the English Church was impracticable; he seems to have been thinking in terms of the days when Britain was part of the Roman Empire; he evidently had no idea of how the Anglo-Saxon conquest had disrupted the old society. Under Gregory's plan the country was to be divided into two provinces, the southern with the metropolitan see at London, and the northern at York. When Augustine landed, London was in the territory of the East Saxons, and, although he appointed a bishop, Mellitus, and Ethelbert founded a church there dedicated to St. Paul, the position proved unstable, and, for this reason, Canterbury maintained its seniority and thus became the metropolitan see of the south. It was not until some years after Augustine's death that it proved possible to send a bishop to York; here, as in London, the conditions were unfavourable for a permanent establishment, and the bishop, Paulinus, had to leave Northumbria. Both Mellitus and Paulinus were in the second party of monks sent by Gregory; this suggests that he chose his men with care.

Augustine was also instructed to consecrate twelve bishops for the southern province, and the metropolitan of York was to do the same. During his lifetime, Augustine was to be the senior metropolitan, but after his death the two provinces were to be independent of one another and the two archbishops equal in dignity, but the senior by ordination was to be regarded as first in rank. This rather awkward provision was to lead to prolonged disputes as to the relative status of the two archbishops; in the twelfth century it was decided that the Archbishop of Canterbury should be Primate of all Britain without prejudice to the authority of his fellow archbishop.

It was not possible for Augustine during his lifetime to carry out the papal scheme even in the southern province.

Each Anglo-Saxon kingdom had to be converted as a separate operation before a bishop could take effective charge. Justus was consecrated Bishop of Rochester by Augustine. His work was conditioned by the support of King Ethelbert who evidently took his new religion seriously. He provided the site for St. Paul's in London and for the church of St. Andrew in Rochester; he even moved his palace from Canterbury to Reculver so that a church could be built within the city itself. Up to then the Christians had two small churches both outside the city — St. Martin's, and a second dedicated to St. Pancras, the boy-martyr of Rome. Bede tells us that Augustine restored and enlarged a ruined church that had been built by Romano-British Christians. The new church, dedicated 'in the name of the Holy Saviour, Jesus Christ our God and Lord,' was the foundation of the Cathedral of Christ Church. Bede adds, 'and there he made a house for him and his successors.' There was probably a school attached to the church. Outside the walls Augustine built a monastery dedicated to SS. Peter and Paul, but it later became known as St. Augustine's. It was here that he wished to be buried according to the Roman custom of having cemeteries outside the towns.

St. Augustine died on 26th May, probably in 605, a year after the death of St. Gregory the Great. The first Archbishop of Canterbury was temporarily buried near his monastery which had not yet been completed. When it was finished, the body was reinterred in the northern porch or chapel. At the same time were translated the bodies of Queen Bertha (the date of her death is uncertain), and of her chaplain Luidhard; they were reburied in the southern porch which was dedicated to St. Martin. Ethelbert died in 616 after a reign of fifty-six years; he too was buried in the St. Martin's porch. He was popularly canonised. So, to quote Dean Stanley, 'somewhere in the field around the ruins of the Abbey, his bones with those of Bertha and Augustine, probably still repose.'

As a man, St. Augustine remains a shadowy figure. Unfortunately none of his monks thought to make a record of his life, so we lack those personal details that are so valuable in trying to visualise him. There was at first a lack of self-confidence which is shown by the meticulous questions he put to the Pope; but he was plunged into a kind of society that was strange to him, not only its language but the ideas that framed society. He certainly showed courage in twice making the hazardous journey across the breadth of England to meet the Celtic-British bishops. He used his own discretion in not making London the metropolitan see. It may be said that he was not a dynamic leader; had he been so, his mission would probably have foundered at the outset. By his quieter manner and his obvious sincerity he won and retained the confidence and regard of King Ethelbert, a man of great qualities as a ruler who would not easily be deceived. Within a few years of his conversion, the king issued a set of laws which protected the Church as well as giving a code for the kingdom. Augustine may have had some influence in framing this earliest body of laws to be written in English. We must bear in mind that his work was crowded into a period of only seven or eight years. He did not found the English Church on the sand; in defiance of the storms that were soon to beat upon it, Canterbury remained.

CHAPTER 3

Ebb and flow

SHORTLY before his death, Augustine consecrated Laurentius, one of his original companions, as his successor. Strictly speaking this was uncanonical, but the dying archbishop must have feared the effects of an interregnum that could result from the delay, which might be of many months, before instructions came from Rome, Moreover he would know that Eadbald, Ethelbert's eldest son, had refused to be baptised, and he might, as king, overturn his father's work.

While Ethelbert was alive, the new archbishop had the king's steady support. Laurentius tried again to persuade the Celtic-British bishops to join with the English Church in the evangelisation of the heathen, but his efforts were rebuffed. How bitter was the feeling was shown when an Irish bishop named Dagan 'would not,' to quote a letter from Laurentius, 'eat with us, but would not so much as take his meat in the same house.'

Ethelbert did not try to force Christianity on the kings who recognised him as overlord. He had been able to establish a London bishopric, but his influence did not go further. Redwald of East Anglia had been converted while on a visit to Ethelbert, but, on his return home, he met with strong opposition; he compromised by putting up a Christian altar side by side with a heathen altar in one of the temples.[1]

On his accession in 616, Eadbald married his step-mother, King Ethelbert's second queen. This was in accordance with tribal custom but it was a declaration of his paganism. It was at this difficult period that Bishop Mellitus was forced to leave London. Saebert, king of the East Saxons, was a nephew of Ethelbert; he was converted and had agreed to the foundation of St. Paul's. He died soon afterwards and was succeeded by his three sons who were nominal Christians but had relapsed into paganism on their father's death. When they presented themselves for communion at St. Paul's, Bishop Mellitus refused to give them 'the white bread.' They therefore drove him out of London.

Rochester was inevitably affected by the paganism of Eadbald. Bishop Justus found it difficult to maintain his position there and he conferred with Mellitus and the archbishop on their future prospects. Justus and Mellitus withdrew to France in the hope of better times, and Laurentius was to have followed them, but a vision gave him the courage to make one more effort to save the mission. St. Peter appeared to him in a dream and chided him for lack of faith in thinking of deserting the English Church. It was now St. Peter's turn to say, 'Quo vadis?' Laurentius, as a penance, scourged himself. In a later legend it was said that St. Peter himself administered the scourging. What happened is best told in Bede's words. Laurentius 'came straightway to the king early in the morning, and, loosening his garments, showed him how sore he was beaten and how pitifully his flesh was torn. The king, much amazed therat, enquired who durst be so bold as to whip and scourge such a man; and when he heard that for his own salvation's sake the bishop had suffered so grievous beatings of the apostle of Christ, he feared greatly; and so having cursed all worship of idols, and renouncing his unlawful marriage, he embraced the faith of Christ, and being baptised, he endeavoured to

[1] The persistence of paganism is shown by the Sutton Hoo Ship barrow which has been dated thirty years after Redwald's death.

consider and befriend the cause of the Church in all points to his uttermost power. He sent also into France and called home Mellitus and Justus, commanding them to return to their churches and give instruction freely; and they returned again the year after their departure; and Justus went back to Rochester where he was bishop, but, as for Mellitus, the Londoners would not receive him for bishop, choosing rather to obey idolatrous high priests; for Eadbald was not a king of so great a power as was his father.'

Laurentius died in the year 619 and was succeeded by Mellitus; he was in poor health and during his five years at Canterbury little seems to have been done to spread the Gospel beyond Kent; it was doubtless a time for holding and consolidating the somewhat precarious position of the Church rather than for attempting more venturesome missionary work. Fortunately King Eadbald proved a steadfast Christian and he was a builder of churches. He corresponded with Pope Boniface V (619–25), who wrote to both Laurentius and Mellitus to encourage them; he also wrote to Archbishop Justus who succeeded Mellitus in 624. With this letter he sent the pallium to be worn 'only in the celebration of the most holy mysteries.' Justus was the last of the bishops who had been consecrated by Augustine. He himself consecrated Romanus as Bishop of Rochester. Justus was archbishop for only three years but before his death in the year 627, he had the joy of knowing that at last there was an extension of the Church outside Kent. The story of how this came about is a typical illustration of how religion was closely associated with kingship.

Edwin of Northumbria had been driven out of his father's kingdom of Deira (Yorkshire), and after an adventurous and wandering youth he gained the support of Redwald of East Anglia, who, as we have seen, had accepted Christianity in a dubious manner. With Redwald's help, Edwin not only won back Deira but also Bernicia to the north and so became king of the whole of Northumbria. He wished to marry Ethelberga, the sister of Eadbald of Kent, but Eadbald refused to allow her, a Christian, to marry a heathen. When

Edwin promised that she would have full freedom of worship, Eadbald gave his consent. Archbishop Justus consecrated one of his companions, Paulinus, as bishop and he went north with Ethelberga as her chaplain. Bede described him as 'tall, with a slight stoop, black hair, a thin face, an aquiline nose, an aspect at once venerable and awe-striking.' With him was a deacon named James, 'a man of great zeal and fame in Christ's Church.'

Although he allowed his daughter Eanfled to be baptised, King Edwin did not at once become a Christian; he was a man of thoughtful disposition and only acted with deliberation. Even when he felt strongly drawn to the Church he would not make his decision until he had consulted his witan. He may have had in mind the confusion caused by King Redwald who did not discuss his contemplated conversion with his wife and council. Bede's account of the debate is too long to give here, but one passage has rightly become famous and deserves quotation. One of the thanes is speaking.

'Such seemeth to me, my Lord, the present life of men here in earth (for the comparison of our uncertain time to live), as if a sparrow should come to the house and very swiftly flit through; which entereth in at one window and straightway passeth out through another, while you sit at dinner with your ealdormen and thanes in winter-time; the parlour being then made warm with the fire kindled in the midst thereof, but all the places abroad being troubled with raging tempests or winter rain and snow. Right for a time it be within the house, it feeleth no smart of the winter storm, but after a very short space of fair weather that lasteth but for a moment, it soon passeth again from winter to winter and escapeth your sight. So the life of man appeareth here for a little season, but what followeth or what hath gone before, that surely we know not. Wherefore if this new learning hath brought us any better surety, methink it is worthy to be followed.'

The outcome was that the witan decided to follow 'this new teaching' and a general conversion followed. Edwin himself was baptised in the small timber church which had been built at York for his queen; afterwards he had it replaced by a building of stone; such was the modest forerunner of the great Minster.

Edwin ruled for six years as a Christian. By his military prowess he had become the most powerful king in Britain; his own Northumbria stretched from the Forth to the Humber and his overlordship covered most of the country outside Wales, Cornwall, and Kent. An alliance between Cadwallon of North Wales and King Penda of Mercia defeated Edwin at Heathfield near Doncaster in 633; Edwin was slain. Under Cadwallon, Northumbria lapsed into paganism. Paulinus with the widowed queen Ethelberga left York and fled to Kent. His companion, the deacon James, remained in Northumbria, 'who living long after in that church by teaching and baptising saved many from the old enemy.' He lived for many years in a village in Swale Dale.

On his return to Kent, Paulinus became Bishop of Rochester, a see that had been vacant for six years. He died there in 644. Queen Ethelberga founded an abbey at Lyminge (half-way between Ashford and Dover) and there she died a few years after Paulinus. She, King Edwin, and Paulinus were popularly canonised.

The progress of the Church in East Anglia was irregular. As we have seen, it began in confusion, but the seed had been sown. Redwald was succeeded by his son Eorpwald who was a Christian, but he was murdered, and for several years East Anglia relapsed into paganism. In 631 Sigbert, a son-in-law of Redwald, became king; he had spent some years of exile in France and had given his time to learning as well as to religion. Archbishop Honorius, who had succeeded Justus at Canterbury in 627, consecrated a Burgundian priest named Felix as bishop and sent him to Sigbert who gave him Dunwich[1] as his episcopal see. Felix was later joined by an Irish monk named Fursey. Together they carried out an effective mission. This revival of Christianity in East Anglia can be set against the disaster in Northumbria,

---

[1] Little is left of Dunwich owing to inundation by the sea.

but here too paganism had only a temporary revival.

There was a movement also in Wessex which, early in the seventh century, meant the part of England south of the Thames from Hampshire to Somerset. The mission there was independent of Canterbury; it was the work of St. Birinus. Not very much is known of him. He may have been a Roman of Germanic origin. He had a vocation for missionary work and Pope Honorius I suggested Britain as his field. Birinus, who was consecrated bishop before he left Rome, had the intention of evangelising the heart of the country, but when he landed in 634 he found that the West Saxons were so sunk in paganism that his duty lay in their territory. He converted King Cynegils who gave him Dorchester on the Thames as his episcopal seat. Birinus laboured in Wessex for some fifteen years and accomplished a lasting work. As far as records go, he seems to have had no contact with Canterbury.

When Edwin won back his kingdom, Oswald and Oswy, the sons of the defeated Ethelfrith, fled northwards and found refuge in Iona where they spent an exile of seventeen years; both became devout Christians under the direction of the community that had been established there by St. Columba. After Edwin's death at the battle of Heathfield (633), the brothers determined to win back the lands their father had ruled. For a year Cadwallon carried out a reign of terror in Northumbria. Oswald and Oswy with a small army 'but fenced with the faith of Christ', to quote Bede, met the forces of Cadwallon in 634 at Heavenfield near the Roman Wall. Oswald erected a cross as a sign that his soldiers put their trust in the 'almighty, living and true God.' Cadwallon's army was defeated and he was slain. For eight years Oswald reigned over Northumbria and extended his power beyond his own kingdom.

His first concern was to restore the Christian Church. It was natural that he should turn to Iona for help and not to Canterbury. The island community sent him a monk named Aidan who was to prove a great apostle. Oswald gave him Lindisfarne (Holy Isle) and Aidan there established

a missionary monastery. Bede gives this account of how
Aidan and his monks re-evangelised Northumbria. 'Aidan
did chiefly commend his doctrine to all men, because the
learning which he taught was correspondent to the life he
led with his brethren. . . He was wont to travel abroad
through all places both in towns and country, not riding on
horseback but walking on foot.' He and his monks tramped
long distances in their work of bringing the people back to
Christ. Oswald gave him full suppport, and, it is said, acted
as Aidan's interpreter until the monk had learned to speak
English.

Penda of Mercia and his Welsh allies were still at enmity
with Northumbria and at the battle of Masereld in 642
(perhaps near Oswestry), Oswald was slain. His brother
Oswy succeeded him and eventually defeated Penda at
Winwaed Field in 655. This was a decisive victory for it
marked the end of British-Welsh intervention in north
England; from that time the Welsh have been a separate
people. Oswy reigned until 671; for the last sixteen years he
was king of all Northumbria, a period long enough to ensure
the firm establishment of the Church.

Aidan died in 651. Not the least of his good works was the
training of young men who could go out into the mission
field or pursue their studies at Lindisfarne. Among his
notable disciples were the brothers Cedd and Chad who
evangelised Mercia; Cedd also worked in Essex and did
much to revive Christianity there. As companion they had
Diuma who became the first bishop in Mercia. A later
student at Lindisfarne was Wilfrid of Ripon of whom we
shall hear more.

The state of the Church in England towards the end of the
seventh century was confused; the advance of Christianity
was not by orderly progress from the landing of Augustine
onwards; there was no concerted plan. This reflected the
constantly shifting political situation. As we have seen,
much depended on who was king at any one time in any
particular territory. The marriage of a pagan king to a
Christian princess could be a decisive factor. Yet, in spite

of the ups and downs of the kingdoms, we can see an overall expansion going on. We can distinguish three lines of advance. First came Augustine in Canterbury (597) reaching out to Rochester and London. This mission was not a beginning from scratch. There had been a British Church, but most of its adherents had been driven westwards and would have no dealings with their conquerors. There were also some contacts with Gaul (France). With Augustine can be associated the short-lived missions of Paulinus (625) to York and of Felix (631) to East Anglia. Secondly came the independent and eventually fruitful mission of Birinus (635) who came to Wessex direct from Rome and not through Canterbury. Thirdly came the advance from the north. Aidan (635) and his monks from Lindisfarne evangelised Northumbria; Diuma and Cedd went to Mercia (653) and Cedd, later, to Essex.

It will be noted that Canterbury was the least venturesome of the missions. It may be that the kings of other territories were suspicious of Kent which had exerted so much authority under Ethelbert. Kent, the most stable of the kingdoms, remained Christian, save for a short set-back during the early years of Eadbald's reign. Honorius succeeded Justus as archbishop in 627 and ruled the see for twenty-six years. Some believe that he had been one of Augustine's companions, but, if so, he must have been very aged at the time of his death. He consecrated Ithamar to succeed Paulinus at Rochester; this was a notable action as Ithamar was the first native of England to become a bishop. In his turn Ithamar consecrated Frithona (who took the name of Deusdedit) to be archbishop in 655. The Pope had given special permission for such otherwise irregular consecrations to avoid the delay needed for getting approval from Rome. The Pope was informed at once, and sent the pallium to signify his consent. Deusdedit, who was a West Saxon and so the first native archbishop, ruled at Canterbury for ten years; the year of his death, 664, was a crucial one in the history of the English Church, and it was probably the death of the archbishop that explains why Canterbury was not represented at the Synod of Whitby of that year which we must now consider.

We have seen how the Celtic-British and English Churches differed in some of their customs and how St. Augustine had twice tried to bring about an agreement. Sixty years later another effort was made to reconcile differences, but the initiative did not come from the Church but from the State, and arose from a practical, almost domestic, difficulty. One of the problems was the date of Easter. King Oswy followed the Celtic reckoning, but his queen, as she had been brought up in Kent, kept the Roman calendar. This could mean that while the king was celebrating Easter, his queen was still keeping the Lenten fast. So Oswy called a conference in 664 to settle this and other differences. It met at the monastery founded by him at Whitby (Strean-aeshalch); it was a double monastery with separate communities of men and women under the Abbess Hilda, a great-niece of King Edwin. The discussion on the date of Easter was opened by Bishop Colman of Lindisfarne in favour of the Celtic observance. He was opposed by Wilfrid, formerly of Lindisfarne, who had recently been to Rome and had spent some time in France. Bede gives us their speeches, but there would be no point here in going over this long-forgotten dispute. It was Oswy who had the final word. 'Peter', he said, 'is the keeper of the door and of the keys. I will neither enter into strife and controversy with him, nor will I condone any who do.' He thus brushed aside all the learned arguments based on astronomical and other grounds. A parallel could be drawn between the Council of Nicaea in 325 and the Synod of Whitby in 664. In both, the decision, almost an arbitrary one, lay with the presiding monarch who desired unity in the Church. But whereas Constantine was concerned with doctrine, Oswy had to settle more mundane issues as the dispute was not a theological one.

Too much has sometimes been claimed for the Synod of Whitby. It took time for its decisions to be accepted by the Celtic Church. The Welsh Church did not adopt the Roman Easter until a century later, and some of the distinctive Celtic usages lingered until the Norman Conquest. The importance of Whitby is that it freed the log-jam that had been piling up; it was afterwards only a matter of time for uniformity of usage to be established throughout the Church in Britain. Canterbury played no part at Whitby. The aged deacon James was present but nearly forty years had passed since he had left Canterbury for York with Paulinus. It might have seemed that the Church would be divided not only between Celt and Saxon but between north and south. Five years after the Synod, Theodore of Tarsus arrived as Archbishop of Canterbury; his work was to consolidate the Church in England as one community under Rome, as it was to remain for more than eight centuries.

A NOTE ON CANONISATION

There are many British, Celtic and Anglo-Saxon saints including a number of the kings and queens. Some of these ascriptions may seem surprising to us, but this may be because the records are often scanty and in consequence we do not know the full circumstances. We can be equally surprised at what appears to be the omission of some who, to us at least, seem as deserving of canonisation as the others. A notable instance is that of King Alfred of Wessex.

In the earliest days of the Church, only martyrs were canonised; later it was felt that the same tribute should be given to those who had suffered great persecution for the faith but had not been put to death; finally, those who bore witness to the faith by the holiness of their lives were also so honoured. For more than a thousand years there was no formal process of canonisation by the popes; indeed the majority of the saints in the Roman Martyrology have not been canonised in the sense in which we now use the term. Generally, but not always, the local bishop gave his approval. They became saints by common consent of the laity based upon popular acclaim and immemorial cultus. The process — if anything so informal can be called such — began locally with the people, as, indeed, it still does. The pope does not institute an inquiry on his own impulse. The present procedure for canonisation was not established until the seventeenth century.

CHAPTER 4

The Golden Age of the Saxon Church

KING Erconberht of Kent died in the same year, 664, as Archbishop Deusdedit. Egbert, the new king, continued the Christian tradition now established in the royal line of Kent. King Oswy of Northumbria took a direct interest in the appointment of a new archbishop; this was in further-ance of his policy at Whitby, and his concern for the succes-sion at Canterbury marks an important stage in the history of the Roman Church in England. It also has significance as a step towards the formation of an English people, for such collaboration between Northumbria and Kent was something new. Had Oswy concentrated on the promotion of Christianity in his own kingdom alone, he could have made York the centre of a separate church organisation. The two kings chose a native-born Canterbury priest named Wighard as the most suitable to follow Deusdedit. Bede says that this choice was made with 'the consent of the holy Church of the English nation', but, unfortunately, he does not tell us how this approval was gained. The two kings sent Wighard to Rome to be consecrated, but, unhappily, he and his companions died of the plague. Pope Vitalian (657–72) wrote to King Oswy to assure him that a new archbishop would be sent to England, 'one apt for learning and adorned with all the qualities to be a bishop.' This proved a difficult task. The Pope's first choice was Hadrian (or Adrian) of African origin and abbot of a monastery near Naples, but he urged his unfitness for such a position; whereupon the Pope asked him to suggest someone else. Abbot Hadrian's choice was Theodore of Tarsus (St. Paul's birthplace), a monk who had studied at Athens and was of high repute. The advance of Islam had driven him to Rome. The pope accepted the suggestion on the condition that Hadrian accompanied the new archbishop to England to ensure that he 'introduced no Greek customs contrary to the true Faith.' The Western and Eastern Churches had not yet separated, but their relations were uneasy. The Greek emperor visited Rome in 663, and the Pope went to Constantinople in 710 but from then onwards the divergences between the Churches became more disruptive.

Theodore was not a priest and some months had to pass before he was ordained; he was consecrated by the Pope on 26th March 668, and two months later set off for England. Hadrian went with him, and another companion was Benedict Biscop who had left the court of King Oswy to become a monk. He had studied at Rome and had spent several years at Lérins where he took the monastic vows. It was on his return from Rome that the Pope asked him to join Theodore's party. This was a happy decision for it meant that, from the outset, Theodore would learn much about the state of the Church in England. The journey from Rome to Marseilles and through France took a whole year. Permission had to be obtained from the various rulers of the states and some of them suspected political implications. So it was not until May 669 that the new archbishop reached Canterbury five years after the death of his predecessor. Theodore was at the advanced age for those days of sixty-six and no one would have dared predict that he would rule for twenty-one years, a period that was to prove formative for the English Church. He must have been a man of tough constitution for he ruled vigorously and endured many long and wearisome journeys. His distinction was, as

Bede wrote, to be 'the first archbishop unto whom the whole Church of the English did consent and submit themselves.'

Theodore was certainly autocratic, but that was the quality needed at that stage in the development of the Church. For seventy-two years St. Augustine and his successors had held their ground; that, in the constantly changing political conditions of the times, was a considerable achievement, and but for their persistence the mission might have foundered. As we have seen, at the death of Ethelbert there was a danger of the bishops throwing up the sponge, and two of the three did leave the country, but the archbishop himself recovered his nerve, and won the king's support. Theodore took a more dynamic view of his function; he was not going to stay at Canterbury and wait for the Church to evolve. He saw that the immediate need was to organise control according to Roman practice. The Celtic bishop was attached to a monastery and was under the rule of the abbot; he went afield wherever he saw the need for evangelisation. The Roman bishop ruled a diocese with defined boundaries. It was this system that Theodore now sought to institute. Within a few months of arrival he set out on a visitation. This in itself was a notable innovation. St. Augustine had journeyed to two conferences on the borders of Wales, but his successors did not attempt to exert their authority outside Kent; they had even abandoned London for some years. This was not, it is true, a matter of choice but in keeping with the political facts. Here we can see how crucial was the reign of Oswy as king of all Northumbria from 655 to 671. His policy of 'one Church' opened the way for Theodore; had Oswy restricted his interest to Northumbrian Christianity, the history of the English Church would have followed a different course. Oswy working with Theodore was the determining factor in the seventh century.

When Theodore arrived in England there were only three bishops; both bishops and priests had fallen victims to the plague that swept the country. Wini had been Bishop of Winchester but, when he quarrelled with the king of Wessex, he had, by simony, become Bishop of London. Chad

(Ceadda) was Bishop of Northumbria at York, a position he had been given by the king during the absence of Wilfrid who had gone to Gaul to be consecrated. It is not known why Oswy acted in this peremptory fashion; it may be that he could not be sure when Wilfrid would return (his journeys were always prolonged), and there was need for immediate episcopal control. Naturally Wilfrid was angry when he did return to find that he had been replaced; he retired to Ripon. Theodore considered that Chad's consecration had been irregular; this may have been because it was according to the Celtic rite. When Theodore removed him from York, Chad, a humble man, accepted the archbishop's ruling and Wilfrid returned to York. Theodore was so impressed by Chad's humility that he consecrated him according to Roman custom, and made him bishop of the Mercians with his seat at Lichfield.

Theodore saw the need for smaller dioceses where the bishops could exert more influence than when they dissipated their energies over enormous areas. Here he met with some opposition; he had therefore to take such opportunities as chanced, such as the death of a bishop, to effect his purpose. He met the strongest resistance from Wilfrid of York.

Wilfrid was the most colourful bishop of his time. His deep devotion to the Church and to Rome cannot be doubted and he accomplished a great work, but his was a prickly personality and he was a stickler for what he believed were his rights; his life was, in effect, a progress from quarrel to quarrel. It is not possible to give here a detailed account of his stormy career, but a brief survey is necessary as it has a bearing on the history of the Church in England. In 669 Theodore had restored Wilfrid as Bishop of Northumbria; it is surprising that Wilfrid did not realise that his vast see, stretching from the Forth to the Humber east of the Pennines, was far too large for one bishop, even himself, to rule effectively. Perhaps Theodore was a bit high-handed in his treatment of Wilfrid, but he was fully justified in dividing Northumbria into more manageable dioceses; three were formed — Lindisfarne, Hexham, and York. Theodore had the support of King Ecgfrith (Oswy's son), and, as Wilfrid proved stubborn, he was banished. He went to Rome in 678 to put his case before the Pope and was away for two years. On his return he was put in prison for nine months; afterwards he spent five years in Wessex, Mercia and Sussex. It was he who effected the conversion of the South Saxons; their territory was the last part of the mainland to be Christianised; it became the diocese of Selsey. Wilfrid was called back to Northumbria on the death of Ecgfrith in 685. For a time the new king, Aldfrith the Learned, and Wilfrid were able to work together but the inevitable quarrel led to Wilfrid again leaving Northumbria in 691; for eleven years he laboured in Mercia. Theobald had died in 690 and his successor, Berhtwald, decided to clear up the Wilfrid imbroglio once and for all. A synod of 703, influenced by King Aldfrith, decreed that Wilfrid should resign as bishop and return to his abbey at Ripon. The irrepressible old man of seventy set off for Rome for the third time to vindicate himself and win the ear of the Pope; this he did. The death of King Aldfrith eased the situation and a compromise was reached; Wilfrid became Bishop of Hexham but spent most of his time at Ripon where he died in 709 at the age of seventy-five.

High among Theodore's achievements must be rated the synods of bishops that he was able to hold. The first and most important was at Hertford in 672 only three years after his landing in England. Four of his suffragans were there; Wilfrid sent a deputy, and Wini of London stayed away; perhaps a guilty conscience about his act of simony made him shy. With the bishops were priests who were learned on canonical questions. This was the first provincial synod according to Roman customs to be held in England, and was indeed more than an ecclesiastical occasion; it was the first legislative gathering of the Anglo-Saxon people, bringing together, as it did, bishops and priests from several kingdoms. Ten articles were agreed on. The Whitby decision on Easter was reaffirmed; a bishop was to restrict himself to his own diocese nor intervene in the affairs of the monasteries; monks were not to roam at will, nor could any cleric leave his diocese without commendatory letters from his bishop; foreign bishops had no authority in England but should be received as guests; the synod was to meet twice in the year; additional dioceses were needed; only lawful marriage should be recognised. Such were the main provisions agreed at the synod of Hertford.

The intention of having regular synods was frustrated by the disturbed state of the country with clashes between the kingdoms, but, in spite of practical difficulties, there were a number of synods in later years. An important one was held at Hatfield in 680 when the assembled bishops re-affirmed their belief 'in the right orthodox faith' and accepted the acts of the five recognised Councils and of the recent Lateran Council. A signed statement to this effect was then entrusted to John the Chanter or Precentor who had come to England from Rome with Benedict Biscop to teach the Roman method of chanting. He had brought with him from Pope Martin an inquiry about the faith being taught in England as there were some heretical opinions that were troubling the Church at that time. This was probably the reason for the Hatfield synod. John died on his way to Rome; the document, however, eventually reached the Pope who expressed his joy at such an expression of orthodoxy.

After his death, a collection of answers on problems of discipline was written down and became known as Theodore's Penitential though it was not entirely a record of the great archbishop's advice to his clergy on how to deal with certain sins and what penances should be imposed. Its main interest is that it foreshadows the function of a parish priest though the parish had not yet become the unit of administration.

Theodore was also responsible for establishing a school and library at Canterbury. He saw the need for the training of priests; this included a thorough knowledge of Latin and other subjects that would fit them for their future duties. Benedict Biscop was put in charge of the school for a short time until Hadrian was ready to take permanent control. The school quickly gained a high reputation and attracted even Irish students thus helping to break down still further the barrier between Celt and Saxon. Bede paid his tribute to this part of the work of Theodore and Hadrian. 'And because both he and Hadrian were fully learned in profane as well as in holy literature, they gathered a company of scholars unto them, and streams of wholesome knowledge did daily flow forth to water their hearts... and even to this day (c. 730) some of their scholars yet living have as good knowledge of the Latin and Greek tongues as if their own.' One of these scholars was St. Aldhelm. About 683 he became Abbot of Malmesbury and he did an important work in promoting religion and education in Wessex under King Ine (688–725) whose law was directed towards the advancement of Christianity. He established the diocese of Sherborne with Aldhelm as bishop from 704 until his death in 709.

From Canterbury Benedict Biscop went to Rome for the fourth time and returned, as he did from each of his six visits, with books, manuscripts and pictures, and other aids to learning and piety. Most precious in the eyes of many would be the relics of the saints he brought. He went back to his native Northumbria and at Wearmouth in 674, on land given by King Ecgfrith, he built a monastery. Once more he set off on his travels, this time to France to bring back stone-masons and glaziers for the building of the monastery church. Eleven years later he founded another monastery at Jarrow only six miles distant from Wearmouth; they became almost one monastery both under the Benedictine Rule. St. Benedict Biscop made two more journeys to Rome and brought back more treasures for his monasteries and especially for their libraries. In this way his monks were encouraged in learning and they established a tradition of sound scholarship.

Of the learned monks trained by Benedict Biscop the first place must be given to Bede. He was born in Northumbria and as a boy entered Wearmouth and later moved to

Jarrow where he spent the rest of his life; he died there in 735. His extensive works cover most of the learning of his times; many of his writings were on scripture or theology, but his greatest book the *Ecclesiastical History* was written in his last years. But for Bede's carefully compiled record our knowledge of the Church in the Anglo-Saxon period would be fragmentary. It would not be an exaggeration to claim him as the pioneer of research historians for he sought information far and wide from those who had first-hand knowledge of events and persons or who had known such authorities. He documented his history from original sources. From an early period he was known as 'the Venerable'; it was not until 1899 that he was recognised authoritatively as Saint and Doctor of the Church. He is the only Englishman to be termed 'Doctor of the Church'; it may be also noted that he is the only one of his race to be mentioned in Dante's *Paradiso*.

> 'And yonder see the fervent spirits flame
> of Isidore, of Bede . . .'
>
> *Par.* x. 130

A hundred miles north of Wearmouth-Jarrow was Lindisfarne which will always be associated with St. Cuthbert. The story of his life as told by Bede was approved by monks who had known the saint.[1] Cuthbert (a Saxon name) was a Northumbrian shepherd boy who felt the call to the monastic life. He entered Melrose (then in Northumbria) about 651; he became prior in 661 but a few years later moved to Lindisfarne where too he became prior. He longed for a more ascetic life and retired to one of the Farne islands where he lived as a hermit. His fame soon spread and many came to seek his spiritual guidance. It was with reluctance that, in 685, he became Bishop of the new diocese of Lindisfarne at the request of Archbishop Theodore. St. Cuthbert died two years later and was buried at Lindisfarne. His influence lay not in church administration but

---

[1] A translation by J. F. Webb of the prose biography is given in *Lives of the Saints* (Penguin Classics, 1965), which also contains a life of St. Wilfrid.

in the holiness of his life. Nearly two hundred years later, in face of the threat of the Viking invasions, his remains were taken to Durham and the bones of St. Bede were placed in the same casket. The shrine was plundered in 1541 but the monks had buried the relics in secrecy. The bones of St. Bede were lost, but St. Cuthbert's body was rediscovered in 1827. In the casket was a copy of the Gospel of St. John written in the seventh century.[1] At the first burial an illuminated manuscript known as the Lindisfarne Gospels was laid on the tomb. This was taken by monks to Ireland but is now one of the great treasures of the British Museum.

Bede's Works (12 vols. 8vo.) and the Lindisfarne Gospels are evidence of the high standard of learning and culture reached in the eighth century. The Gospels were the work of Eadfrith who became Bishop of Lindisfarne. He must have spent many, many years in producing this wonderful manuscript. It has been well said that 'the labour of these artist-monks was prayer — a form of worship. They expressed in colour and pattern, with plait and interwoven bird, the mysteries of this tangled world and the wonder of the universe.'[2]

More must be said later of other aspects of Anglo-Saxon culture.

The story of what has been called the Golden Age of the Saxon Church would be incomplete without a notice of the work of evangelisation done by Anglo-Saxons in Germany (to use the present-day term for what was not yet a unified country). The way was pioneered by St. Wilfrid when he was diverted to Frisia on his way to Rome in 678. The Frisians occupied the coastal lands between the River Ems to the lower Rhine. Wilfrid was not there long enough to effect any permanent conversion. He was followed by St. Willibrord, a Northumbrian, who was to become the first Bishop of Utrecht. He laboured for many years until his death in 739 in Frisia and accomplished a remarkable

[1] Now at Stonyhurst College.
[2] R. H. Hodgkin, *A History of the Anglo-Saxons* (1935), Vol. I., p. 360; four plates of reproductions are there given.

work. He was followed by St. Boniface who must be numbered among the great Englishmen; he came to exert an
important influence not only in his chosen field of evangelisation but in the land of the Franks. He was born at
Crediton in Devon about 680, and, as a youth, entered the
monastery of Nursling in Hampshire. It was there that he
felt the call to the mission among the pagans. For a few years
he assisted St. Willibrord and this gave him a valuable
experience on which to build up his own work. He wanted
to go farther afield. He went to Rome to put his intention
before the pope, who gave him every encouragement and
consecrated him as bishop to Germany. It was the pope who
changed his name to Boniface. It is not possible here to
follow him and his fellow priests in their dangerous mission.
For over twenty years he laboured to Christianise the
German tribes and to establish the Church among them.
He was martyred in 754 on the north coast of present-day
Holland. He had returned to Frisia because, since the death
of St. Willibrord, the people were in danger of relapsing into
paganism.

CHAPTER 5

The Eighth Century

BEDE finished his *Ecclesiastical History* in 731. We lack any similar record of Church affairs for the succeeding years and we have to piece the history together from a number of sources; this makes it difficult to tell a connected story as there are gaps in our knowledge. Four years after writing his great book Bede, not long before his own death, sent a letter of exhortation to Egbert who had just been consecrated Bishop of York. The state of the Church according to Bede was far from satisfactory. He complained that some bishops were lacking in holiness, that many priests were wanting in learning, that dues to the Church were not being paid, that some monasteries were monastic only in name and were occupied by laymen who had no sacred vocation, and that there were too many monks roaming the country. He was shocked at the conduct of some clerics, even those in bishops' households: 'men which are given up to laughter, jesting, tales, revellings, drunkenness and the allurements of dissolute living; which daily rather feed their bellies with feasts than their minds with heavenly sacrifices.' To him it was a dreadful thing that priests could come from celebrating Mass and at once resume their depraved ways. This is a serious indictment that can be supported from the

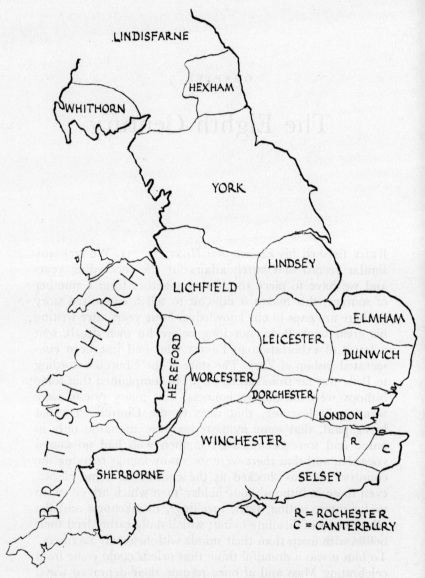

Dioceses c.750. The boundaries are, in some places, conjectural.

letters of St. Boniface; while it is true that he had for some years been out of England, he had kept in correspondence with his old friends and so had learned of their troubles.

This decline was not peculiar to England; it was even more marked in France. Political events such as internecine wars hampered the progress of the Church. The actual state of society must also be taken into account. The country was thinly populated; people lived in small communities which gathered round some leading family, a fact that many a place-name perpetuates. They were often isolated; communications were difficult and, during winter, often impossible; the great forests and marshes were barriers. It was not an urban but a rural society. Agricultural methods were primitive and adverse weather might bring famine. It was also a hot-blooded society; the laws of Ine (King of Wessex, 688–725) laying down a scale of wergelds (compensation payments for manslaughter or murder) are an indication of the hazards of life. The surprising fact is that, in such conditions, the Church had been able to maintain some authority which, although it was to some extent impaired, was not destroyed.

The eighth century lacked the outstanding leaders that had made the previous one so notable in Church history. St. Cuthbert, the pattern of holiness, died in 687; St. Theodore, the architect of the Church, followed him three years later. St. Wilfrid, who in his tempestuous career had achieved so much, died in 709. Their influence was permanent but they had no immediate successors of the same eminence.

Theodore's policy had resulted in fourteen bishoprics being established by the beginning of the eighth century. These were — Canterbury, Rochester, London (including Essex), Dunwich (Suffolk), Elmham (Norfolk), Stow (Lincolnshire), Winchester (Wessex), Worcester, Hereford, Leicester (Midlands), Lichfield, York, Hexham (Durham) and Lindisfarne (East Lowlands).

Of the new leaders, Egbert of Northumbria was prominent in the middle years of the century. He had the advantage of being of the royal family and this had importance in the then state of society. He had been a pupil of Bede and that is why, when Egbert became Bishop of York, Bede wrote to him a letter of advice. Egbert went to Rome in 735 and received the pallium from Pope Gregory III and thus became the first Archbishop of York. Some scholars hold that the English insistence on an archbishop receiving the pallium before exercising his authority as metropolitan was the beginning of a practice that later became universal in the Church. The setting-up of a second archbishop, although in keeping with Gregory the Great's intention, was a step backwards; it tended to separate the Church in the north from that in the south and thus hindered the development of a united English Church under Canterbury. One sign of this was the bickering in later centuries as to the relative authorities of the two archbishops; the problem was not solved quickly or easily. To-day the Archbishop of Canterbury is Primate of All England, and the Archbishop of York, Primate of England, a difference too fine for most of us to appreciate.

When Egbert was consecrated, his cousin Ceolwulf was King of Northumbria; he had an uneasy reign, and in 737 gave up the throne and became a monk at Lindisfarne. Egbert's brother, Eadberht, then became king, but, in his turn, he abdicated and became a clerk in the archbishop's household. It is evident that their religion meant much to this family of kings. For thirty-two years Egbert ruled as archbishop to the great benefit of the Church. His *Penitential* supplemented that of Theodore. Among its provisions for guiding the lives of Christians it was laid down that all should go to confession before Christmas; private confession was followed by private penance and this custom gradually became normal. The *Penitential* covers a multitude of subjects. Its spirit is shown in this formula for the blessing of a cross. 'Let the splendour of the divinity of thine only-begotten Son shine forth in the gold, the glory of his passion in the wood, our redemption from death glow in the crimson, and the purification of our life in the brightness of the crystal.'

Egbert founded a school at York that soon gained a high reputation; a fine library was also established. The most famous pupil was Alcuin who became master of the school and then, for over twenty years, served Charlemagne as master of his Palace School; he had a leading part in the reform of the liturgy, and his revision of the Gregorian Sacramentary had its influence on the *Missale Romanum*. His letters to friends in England contain criticisms similar to those made by Bede and St. Boniface. York Minster, a secular not a monastic foundation, owed much to Egbert and to his kinsman Ethelbert who succeeded him as Archbishop of York in 767.

A council was held at Clovesho (perhaps near London) in 742 for the purpose of correcting some of the abuses that had crept into the pseudo-monasteries against which Bede had inveighed. King Ethelbald of Mercia approved the decrees of this council at which he and his witan were present; indeed, at that stage in the evolution of the Church the approval of a king was essential not only for the calling of an assembly but to give it authority. Ethelbald had been driven from Mercia by Coenred, grandson of Penda. During his exile he consulted St. Guthlac (also of the royal Mercian line) who had become a hermit on the island of Crowland in south Lincolnshire. After Coenred's death, Ethelbald returned to his own country and during the forty years of his reign extended his power so that he could claim to be 'King of the Southern English' (i.e. south of the Humber). He was a generous benefactor of the Church in giving lands and building churches; as a tribute to St. Guthlac he founded the monastery at Croyland. His private life was far from virtuous and for this he was rebuked by St. Boniface. Ethelbald was murdered in 757 and was succeeded by Offa.

Clovesho was also the place of a synod called in September 747 by Archbishop Cuthbert of Canterbury; eleven bishops attended as well as other clergy. This synod had been called at the suggestion of Pope Zacharias (741–52); after it was over Cuthbert sent an account of it to St. Boniface who, in return, described his own experience of synods. The decrees of 747 concerned the functions of bishops and priests and further attempted to regulate monastic life. All priests were enjoined to teach the Lord's Prayer and the Creed and the meaning of the sacraments; such teaching was to be in the language of the people. The litanies and other formularies of Rome were to be observed. Two new feasts were instituted — that of St. Gregory the Great (12th March) and of St. Augustine of Canterbury (28th May). Bishops undertook to make annual visitations of their dioceses; every monastery was to have at least one priest; monks and nuns must observe the seven canonical hours; they had to dress soberly and live soberly; nor were monasteries to become lodgings for poets, musicians and buffoons. These last injunctions are evidence that previous efforts to reform the monasteries had been ineffective. The root of the difficulty and of other problems was that churches and monasteries belonged to the owner of the land who had himself often provided the funds for the buildings. Such property was in the same category as any other personal property and could be bequeathed or sold at will. The priest or abbot would be appointed by the owner often without any reference to the bishop, and such positions were reserved for members of the owner's family. This is the origin of the advowson — the right of presentation to a benefice. This private patronage led to many abuses and even scandals, and it was not until the nineteenth century that any restrictions on buying and selling were imposed by law.

The second half of the eighth century was dominated by King Offa of Mercia; he illustrates once again the influential connection in Anglo-Saxon times between King and Church. Fortunately Offa was a pious Christian, though we should not read into the word 'pious' too high a standard of public and private morality. During the first half of his long reign of almost forty years, he was engaged in subduing the other kingdoms. At the time of his death in 796 he was ruler of the country with absolute authority south of the Humber between Wales (whose boundary he marked with his Dyke) and the east coast, and to the south coast with the exclusion of Wessex over which he exercised lordship. Even Northumbria, up to the Forth, became his ally. He styled himself *rex Anglorum* and this title was used of him by Pope Adrian I (772–95). Indeed it can be claimed that Offa was the first 'King of the English' (not of the country but of the people). Moreover, he looked beyond this country and established friendly relations (not quite undisturbed) with his great contemporary Charlemagne (Charles the Great, 742–814). Offa's relations with the papacy were also close.

From the time of Augustine of Canterbury the connection with Rome was firmly maintained. We have seen how Wilfrid and Benedict Biscop and others made the long and dangerous journey to Rome. It was not only ecclesiastics and a host of ordinary folk who visited the tomb of St. Peter. Caedwalla, King of the West Saxons (685–88) after a career that called for much repentance, went to Rome to be baptised by the pope; the king died there and was buried in St. Peter's. His successor, Ine (688–725), abdicated and, with his queen, went to Rome where both died. Coenred, King of Mercia (704–9), also gave up his throne, and, at Rome, entered religion. There was a large enough number of Anglo-Saxons living in Rome to establish during the eighth century the Schola Saxonum, a military guild for the defence of Rome.

In 786 Pope Adrian sent two legates to England, the Cardinals George and Theophylact. The former was resident at the court of Charlemagne and when the two legates crossed to England, they had with them a Frankish abbot named Wigbod. Although this visit was an opportunity to survey the state of the Church and make sure that its teaching was orthodox, its true purpose was in answer to a proposal from Offa that a third archbishopric should be created in England; he had evidently worked through Charlemagne to get the pope's ear. From the time he had subjugated Kent, Offa had regarded with suspicion the influence of Jaenbert, Archbishop of Canterbury (766–90); as a countercheck the king wanted to have an archbishop under his thumb; it was a derogation of his authority to have to accept the ecclesiastical rule of someone in a client kingdom.

The legates first visited Canterbury to confer with Jaenbert; then they went on to Offa who received them with open arms. Cardinal George with Abbot Wigbod toured Northumbria where they met Eanbald I, Archbishop of York, and King Alfwald. Meanwhile Cardinal Theophylact visited the southern parts of England. A synod was called in the north at Finchale near Durham. This was attended not only by the bishops but by the king and his witan; Alcuin (another link with Charlemagne) happened to be visiting York at the time and he was invited to attend the synod. Cardinal George read his papal brief and then proposed a series of decrees which were accepted. He then took the signed record south, and, accompanied by Alcuin, summoned a national synod at Celchyth (Chelsea). Archbishop Jaenbert and his suffragans were present as well as King Offa and his witan. The decrees agreed on in Northumbria were accepted. These differed little from those made at Clovesho forty years earlier — an indication that, for instance, those affecting monasteries had not rooted out old abuses. An attempt was also made to regulate the dress of clerics; it was declared that 'no minister at the altar shall wear short tunics showing bare legs.' A new provision was made that the secular clergy, in particular those in bishops' households, should lead a common life; those who lived under this rule were known as canons, but the system which had spread in other countries did not then take hold in England. The regular payment of tithes was enjoined. Archbishop Theodore in his time had urged this as a Christian duty, but the method of payment and the application of the results were not yet regularised. The synod also accepted, with some reluctance, Offa's demand for a third archbishopric. Lichfield was chosen as his see. This was a setback to the unity of the Church in England even more than the previous institution of the archbishopric of York which could be justified on the grounds that Northumbria was, under the conditions of the time, remote from Canterbury.

At this synod Offa had his son Ecgfrith hallowed as his successor; this was an innovation, but its purpose was defeated by the son's death within a few months of his father's.

A second unusual outcome of this synod was that Offa, in gratitude to the pope, promised an annual gift to Rome of a mancus (thirty pence) for each day of the year. He had gold coins specially minted for this purpose; one of these has been found in Rome. This seems to have been the beginning of Peter's Pence, or Romescot. When this was regularised anyone who had property of the annual value of thirty pence or more had to pay one penny a year; to this sum, collected by the bishops, the king would add his personal gift and the whole would be sent to Rome. This practice spread from England to other countries.

Under the year 793 (three years before Offa's death), the Anglo-Saxon Chronicle has this entry:

'In this year terrible portents appeared over Northumbria and miserably frightened the inhabitants. . . . A great famine soon followed these signs and a little after that in the same year on 8 January the harrying of the heathen miserably destroyed God's church in Lindisfarne by rapine and slaughter.'

This was the prelude to the greatest trial the Church in England had to undergo.

CHAPTER 6

Alfred the Great

THE raid on Lindisfarne in 793 was the first of many; Jarrow was sacked in the following year and, for a generation, these sporadic attacks became part of the life of the times. There was, as yet, no concerted plan for invasion and conquest; the purpose was plunder, but the raids presaged greater misfortunes for England.

The few months of the reign of Offa's son in Mercia were followed by the twenty-five years of the reign of Coenwulf, a kinsman of Offa. His church policy was a reversal of Offa's since he was willing to see the restoration of the old system of subordination to Canterbury. He wanted the metropolitan see transferred to London and claimed, with some justification, that this had been St. Gregory's intention. There was, however, a revolt in Kent where the loss of its former independence and prestige was resented. Archbishop Ethelheard of Canterbury remained loyal and for two years was a fugitive. In 801 he went to Rome; Leo III did not favour the transfer of the metropolitan see to London. On his return the archbishop called a provincial council at Clovesho and there it was decreed that at his consecration a bishop must reaffirm his orthodoxy and pledge his obedience to Canterbury. The archbishopric of Lichfield was allowed to fade out.

48

With the death of Coenwulf in 821 came another shake of the kaleidoscope. The power of Mercia declined and, under Egbert, came the rise of Wessex which was to affect permanently the history of England. He was a member of the royal Cerdic line of Wessex, but he was driven out of the country in 789 by Offa of Mercia and Beorhtric of Wessex who had married Offa's daughter. Egbert spent his three years of exile at the court of Charlemagne; this close contact with Christian culture undoubtedly had a decisive effect on Egbert's church policy. On Beorhtric's death in 802, Egbert returned to England and assumed the throne of Wessex. Little is known of the first twenty years of his reign save that during this period he consolidated and extended his power and thus became the founder of the Greater Wessex. With Coenwulf's death, Egbert moved to the front of the stage and by his conquests became over-king of the country. Not too much should be read into the term 'over-king'; least of all would it be correct to call him King of England.

The last years of Egbert's reign were disturbed by re-newed and more persistent attacks by the Danes. The period of raiding was over; what the invaders now wanted was land and among them were farmers as well as sea-rovers. The Norwegian assault, the Viking invasion, had so far by-passed England. The Orkneys and the Shetlands and the western shores of Scotland were first occupied; then came the seizure of Ireland and the founding of Dublin as a Viking centre. The first serious invasion of England was in Cornwall in 838 when Egbert defeated the Danes at Hinxton Down. A second invading army came up the estuary of the Thames and sacked London in 842. A third even more threatening; this was in 850–1 when the Danes occupied the Isle of Thanet and settled there.

Egbert was succeeded by his son Ethelwulf whose brother Athelstan ruled under him as King of Kent. The latter defeated a Danish force off Sandwich in 851 and in the same year his brother won a victory at Aclea (perhaps in Surrey).

These were little better than delaying actions; the invaders continued to arrive in increasing numbers, and one of the factors to be taken into account was that the country was still sparsely inhabited. Ethelwulf was an able leader but he was disheartened by this seemingly unrelenting threat to his kingdom. It was in keeping with the thought of the time that he wondered if all this was a judgment of God on a people that had failed to observe the divine commands. As a sincere son of the Church he sought its blessing. It was for this purpose that he sent his youngest son Alfred, a boy of four, to Rome with rich offerings. The pope, Leo III, invested the child with the insignia of a consul. Two years later, as the invaders were still active, Ethelwulf himself, taking Alfred with him, went to Rome with more gifts. Before leaving England he made a donation of a tenth of his own land to the Church. From Rome he went to the court of Charles the Bald who had succeeded to the western part of the dominions of his grandfather Charlemagne. There Ethelwulf and Alfred remained for some months and Ethelwulf married Charles' thirteen-year-old daughter Judith. This sharpened the opposition to him in Wessex that had been growing during his long absence. While his father was away, his eldest son Ethelbald, with the connivance of the Bishop of Sherborne, had plotted to seize the throne; when, however, Ethelwulf at last landed in 856 there was considerable support for him and, had he been of an agressive disposition, civil war might have broken out, and that, with the threat of more Danish incursions, would have meant the end of Wessex. Fortunately Ethelwulf shrank from fighting against his own son and they came to an agreement; Ethelwulf should rule over the eastern half and Ethelbald over the western half of the kingdom. This compromise was observed until Ethelwulf's death in 858. Ethelbald, having married his step-mother Judith, died in 860, and as he had no son, was succeeded by his brother Ethelbert who reigned over Wessex for six years. He too was sonless and his brother Ethelred came to the throne in 866. He had to face the coming of the Great Army of the Danes to East Anglia; this was a full-scale invasion only comparable with that of William the Conqueror two hundred years later.

The events of these critical years must be briefly summarised. Ethelred and his seventeen-year-old brother Alfred worked closely together in the campaigns that filled the five years of Ethelred's reign. The invaders first moved northwards to York and within a short time were masters of Northumbria. Then part of the army moved southwards into Mercia, where King Burhred begged help from his brother-in-law Ethelred who, with Alfred and a strong army, went to his support. However King Burhred decided to buy off the Danes and Ethelred and Alfred returned to Wessex no doubt fully aware that their turn would soon come. Meanwhile the Danes again swept through East Anglia destroying monasteries and churches so that the Church in those parts was for half a century driven underground. It was during this campaign of 870 that Edmund, the last king of East Anglia, after a heroic resistance, was slain in such a barbarous fashion that he was soon known as St. Edmund the Martyr.

Northumbria — Mercia — East Anglia; Wessex remained a tempting prey with its rich farm lands. So the Danes advanced to Reading in 870 and there they beat off an attack by Ethelred and Alfred who quickly assembled fresh forces and at Ashdown won a victory. It was not a decisive battle; the Danes withdrew and consolidated their army. Ethelred died in April 871 and, as his two sons were children, Alfred became king of Wessex.

When he had returned to England with his father in 856, the prospect of kingship was probably not in his mind, nor indeed in the mind of anyone. He had three older brothers but they reigned for only brief periods, and under them Alfred learned the business of fighting. It was indeed a fortunate dispensation that brought this highly endowed young man of twenty-two to the throne of Wessex, for it was by his exertions that the English were put on the road to nationhood and the Church survived the onslaughts of the pagan enemy. His history is our history.

His military campaigns must be passed over; the story in outline is well known. The first months of his reign proved disastrous and he retreated to the marshes of Somerset and from Athelney carried on what we should call guerilla warfare, until he could build up his army again. Then in 878 he confronted and defeated the Danes under their leader Guthrum at Ethandun (Edington), south of Chippenham where peace was negotiated. The Danes were to leave Wessex and Guthrum was to be baptised. This took place at Wedmore. It is natural to be sceptical of such baptisms, but Guthrum seems to have remained faithful to his new religion. This was by no means the end of Alfred's wars; other Danish armies, particularly near London, had to be forced back. A treaty made about 886 drew a diagonal line across the map following roughly the Watling street, leaving the northern part of the country to the Danes (the Danelaw) and the southern to Alfred and Wessex.

When Alfred came to the throne the Church was in some confusion owing to the Danish raids and campaigns. Alfred's grandfather, Egbert, had conquered Kent and had enlisted the support of Archbishop Wulfred of Canterbury. Egbert and his successors were loyal to the Church; we have seen how his son Ethelwulf maintained relations with Rome, and his youngest son, Alfred, was equally devoted to the Church. The fact that the kings of Wessex were not just political churchmen but personally devout Christians was an important factor in the progress of the Church in Southern England.

Archbishop Wulfred, appointed to Canterbury in 805, was a wealthy Kentish landowner; when the Mercian King Coenwulf became overlord of Kent the two clashed. The exact nature of the dispute is not known but it seems to have been about land belonging to the see of Canterbury. An appeal was made to Pope Paschal I, and, apparently for several years, the archbishop was unable to carry out his functions. A settlement imposed by the king was made in 821 at a council at London; by it the archbishop had to give up some of his land and to pay a fine. This episode, unique in our Church history, did much harm for it further loosened discipline which had been weakened by the wars with the Danes. Coenwulf died in 821 and his son Coenhelm was killed that same year at the age of seven. This child is known as St. Kenelm in popular hagiology, but there seems to be little, if any, historical basis for the legends woven round his name. He was succeeded by his uncle Ceolwulf who was deposed in 823 by Beornwulf, King of Mercia. He wished to end the discord with the Church; he held councils in 824 and 825 at Clovesho in which a number of disputes were settled, but in the year of the second council he was defeated by Egbert; in the following year Beornwulf invaded East Anglia and was slain in battle. So Egbert of Wessex became overlord of Kent.

Archbishop Wulfred died in 832; an abbot named Feologild seems to have been chosen to succeed him but he died within a year. Ceolnoth, of whose origins nothing certain is known, then became archbishop and received the pallium in 834. At a council at Kingston in Surrey in 838 he made a perpetual peace with Egbert and his son Ethelwulf; this safeguarded the possessions of the Church. Ceolnoth was also able, in the presence of Ethelwulf at an assembly at Canterbury in 844, to settle outstanding disputes. The Danes attacked Kent and sacked Canterbury in 851. Our knowledge of this period is very scanty and it is impossible to get a clear picture of events. The crucial fact was that the Danes wintered in Sheppey; they had come to stay. It seems that Ceolnoth and the Kentish leaders (Ethelwulf was heavily engaged outside Kent) managed to come to terms with the Danes. Coins that have been found in large numbers struck by Ceolnoth may represent the church treasure that had to be turned into money to meet the Danish demands. Ceolnoth died in 870 and was buried at Canterbury.

Here we may note that the Danes were not attacking Christians as such; the primary object was loot until that gave way to the decision to stay and settle. Their own beliefs in their gods and goddesses did not amount to a religious faith. It was this looseness to their own pagan mythology that made them more susceptible to Christian teaching, and they became Christians within a generation or so, though carrying with them traces of their older beliefs and superstitions. It was to be a very long time before such pagan elements were eliminated.

During the first half of Alfred's reign (871–900) he was fully occupied with the task of saving Wessex from the Danes and it was not until they had been checked that he was able to give his mind to reconstruction. He was as deeply religious as his father Ethelwulf. It will be recalled that as a boy he had twice been to Rome and throughout his life he maintained and valued that connection but without any suggestion that Rome could interfere with the affairs of Wessex except in Church matters. The months he spent with his father at the court of Charles the Bald brought him, boy as he was, into contact with a culture that was lacking in England, but many years were to pass before this experience bore fruit. The Danish raids and the passage of armies meant that the normal life of Wessex was disrupted and the authority of the Church was at a low ebb. The moral tone of the clergy was poor and there were few priests of any learning; many could not read Latin. Alfred recognised that little improvement could come until a more educated clergy could be trained. It was for this reason that he put so much emphasis on learning. He made good use of the few bishops and priests who were sufficiently learned, but he found it necessary to call in help from other countries.

When Alfred came to the throne, Ethelred was Archbishop of Canterbury. They seem to have clashed and Ethelred appealed to Rome, but the nature of their dispute is uncertain. Little is known of Ethelred. He died in 889 and Alfred called Plegmund, a learned Mercian priest, to Canterbury. He went to Rome to receive the pallium from Pope Formosus (891–6). The new archbishop, however, could not have given much time to his episcopal duties as he resided at Alfred's court at Winchester where he did valuable work in the school the king had established on the model of Charlemagne's famous school. Plegmund's first pupil and the most eager was Alfred himself. Another scholar brought to Winchester was Bishop Werferth of Worcester. Others were Gimbald from Flanders. and Asser from St. David's who became Alfred's devoted biographer.

In his desire to promote learning, Alfred had translations made into English of devotional and informative books. As soon as he knew enough Latin, he translated a number of books himself though doubtless his tutors helped him. These books included St. Gregory's *Cura Pastorales*, the *Consolation of Philosophy* of Boethius, the *Soliloquies* of St. Augustine, a shortened version of Bede's *Ecclesiastical History*, and the world history of Orosius which he augmented with geographical information he had gathered from travellers. He set on foot the compiling of the *Anglo-Saxon Chronicle*, an invaluable source-book for our history. In all these labours he was carrying out his main purpose — the promotion of religion and sound learning, but at the same time he was laying the foundations of English prose. His own piety is symbolised by the little book in which he copied some of the Psalms; this he always kept by him.

The collapse of monasticism, of which more must be said, was another problem that Alfred tried to solve. Here he was not successful, mainly because the right leaders were not available. He founded a monastery at Athelney and called John the Old Saxon to be abbot with some foreign monks as a nucleus of a community, but they were soon at loggerheads and came near to murdering their abbot. The monastery had to be abandoned. Alfred's foundation at Shaftesbury for a convent of nuns proved more lasting; his daughter Ethelgifu was the abbess. He planned to found a monastery at Winchester, but he died before being able to do so; his son and successor Edward the Elder carried out his father's intention.

Alfred regularly sent alms to Rome made up of personal gifts and contributions from the people. His successor established these contributions as a regular tax. An entry for the year 882 in the Anglo-Saxon Chronicle reads:

'Pope Marinus sent the *lignum Domini* [a fragment of the Cross] to King Alfred; and the same year Sigehelm and Athelstan took to Rome and also to India to St. Thomas and St. Bartholomew, the alms which King Alfred had vowed to send thither when they besieged the [Danish] host in London.'

It is unlikely that Sigehelm and Athelstan went to India; the entry probably means that part of the alms they took to Rome was earmarked for the support of the Christian community in India that claimed to have been established by St. Thomas the Apostle.

When Alfred did not send alms to Rome, the chronicler thought it worth recording.

'889. In this year no pilgrimage was made to Rome, except for two couriers whom King Alfred sent with letters.
890. In this year abbot Beornhelm took the alms of the West Saxons and of King Alfred to Rome.'

Alfred's code of laws again expressed his concern for religion. The introductory portion was based on the Mosaic law in chapters 20–23 of Exodus, but with modifications that made them less harsh. He referred also to the apostolic letter on the relations with the Gentiles (Acts XV) and to the 'golden rule' followed by his comment, 'From this one law a man may learn how we ought to judge aright. He needs no other law-books; let him bethink himself that he do not to another what he would not have done to himself.' The actual laws were based on those of Ine but with an eye to the laws of Offa of Mercia and Ethelbert of Kent; the decrees of the church councils were also taken into account. All these elements gave the laws a wider basis than if Alfred had limited himself to West Saxon customs and laws. It was another step forward in the development of a national community.

The English colony in Rome was well established with its priests who were enjoined by the Pope to wear the long Roman tunic in place of the short Saxon one. The deposed

THE HOUSE OF WESSEX

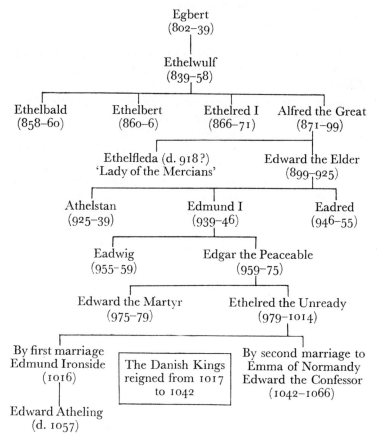

Egbert
(802–39)

Ethelwulf
(839–58)

Ethelbald (858–60) Ethelbert (860–6) Ethelred I (866–71) Alfred the Great (871–99)

Ethelfleda (d. 918?) 'Lady of the Mercians' Edward the Elder (899–925)

Athelstan (925–39) Edmund I (939–46) Eadred (946–55)

Eadwig (955–59) Edgar the Peaceable (959–75)

Edward the Martyr (975–79) Ethelred the Unready (979–1014)

By first marriage
Edmund Ironside (1016)

The Danish Kings reigned from 1017 to 1042

By second marriage to Emma of Normandy
Edward the Confessor (1042–1066)

Edward Atheling (d. 1057)

Note. Some historians prefer Æthel- to Ethel-, but this is not of serious significance.

king of Mercia, Burhred, went to Rome where he died in 874, and fourteen years later his widow, Alfred's sister Ethelswith died at Pavia on her way to Rome. At Alfred's request, according to the Chronicle, Pope Marinus freed the Schola Saxonum from paying certain taxes. Not that Rome at that period was a model Christian community. The papacy of Formosus was lax and there were grave scandals. This, however, did not then, nor in later centuries, lower the pre-eminence of the Pope as head of the universal Church.

Apart from Alfred's own activities, we know little about the conduct of Church affairs in Wessex; the indications are that its general organisation had fallen into decay; even Alfred could not effect much improvement for want of the educated clergy he did his best to produce. There must have been pious and devoted bishops and priests who, almost in isolation, preserved the faith, otherwise the revival that ultimately came would have been delayed even longer.

If our knowledge of the Church in Wessex is scanty, it is almost non-existent for England north of the Humber. The sacking of York in 867 sent Archbishop Wulfhere into hiding for several years, but he was at length allowed to return and exercise his ministry. He died in 900 a year after the death of King Alfred.

CHAPTER 7

Dunstan and after

WE have noted how the prosperity of the Church depended
to a large extent on the authority of the kings. A strong king,
if given some years of rule, could advance the work of the
Church under his protection and patronage. If a weak king
followed, the work would suffer a set-back. It was indeed
fortunate for our country that, beginning with Egbert in
the year 802, until the death of Edgar the Peaceable in 975,
Wessex, and, in the later period, much of England, was
ruled by Christian kings who were men of ability. This
applies particularly to Alfred, his son Edward the Elder,
who reigned for thirty years, and, in turn, to Edward's
two sons, Athelstan and Edmund I and to Edmund's son
Edgar. Thus during a period of nearly a hundred years a
firm alliance between State and Church was maintained and
strengthened. During that period there were only two weak
kings, Eadred and Eadwig, but, fortunately, they did not
reign for long.

The history of the tenth century must be briefly summarised. Edward the Elder (899–925) with his brother-in-law
Ethelred, ealdorman of Mercia, had to force back the Danes
who were again menacing the country outside the old
Danelaw. They were defeated at Tettenhall in Staffordshire

in 910. After Ethelred's death, his widow, Edward's sister Ethelfleda, the 'Lady of Mercia', proved as resolute a leader as her husband and her brother. As a result, England up to the Humber came under Edward's rule; the Welsh also acknowledged him as over-lord. Edward was followed by his no less able son Athelstan who extended his power northwards to the Forth; the decisive battle was at Brunanburgh in 937. The site has not been identified, but it may have been north of Solway Firth. Athelstan did much by his laws to enforce order and justice. He died in 939 and was succeeded by his brother Edmund who had to contend with the Vikings in Northumbria. One of the leaders of the disturbances was Wulfstan, Archbishop of York.[1] He was taken prisoner in 952 and, after two years in prison, was released but was not allowed to return to York; he ended his days as Bishop of Dorchester. His successor as archbishop was Osketel who was of Danish extraction; he did much to restore the Church in Northumbria.

Eventually Eadred subdued the north. He died in 955 and was succeeded by his nephew Eadwig (Edmund's son), a boy of fifteen who alienated many by his uncertain temper, so much so that the Mercians and Northumbrians made his younger brother Edgar their king leaving Wessex to Eadwig. This splitting of the country could have been permanent had not Eadwig died after four years of ineffective rule. Edgar then reunited the country and for sixteen years proved a worthy descendant of Egbert and Alfred. He was, in fact, the last of that line of great kings to rule England with real authority. He died in 975.

While we can narrate the political and military events of the period in fair detail, it is more difficult to give a connected account of Church affairs particularly in the north during the first half of the century. Alfred had had time to do little more than lay the foundations for a renewal of religion; it needed some years to provide an effective clergy.

---

[1] This was the first Wulfstan to be Archbishop of York (931–954). The second Wulfstan was archbishop from 1003 to 1023. Neither should be confused with St. Wulfstan, Bishop of Worcester (1062–1095).

One encouraging factor was that the Danes were steadily becoming Christianised; it was no longer a Christian against a pagan community. Warfare became a question of the distribution of power; paganism, of course, did not suddenly disappear, but it was slowly but perseveringly being eroded.

King Edward in Wessex and his sister Ethelfleda in Mercia continued and reinforced the religious policy of their father Alfred. The work on the New Minster at Winchester was pushed forward; it was dedicated in 903 by Archbishop Plegmund of Canterbury with whom the king was in complete accord. The body of King Alfred was reburied in the New Minster. Ethelfleda and her husband Ethelred were fortunate in having Werferth, one of Alfred's scholar-collaborators, as Bishop of Worcester until 915. They were benefactors of Worcester and of the minster of Gloucester which they richly endowed. To it they transferred the remains of St. Oswald, King of Northumbria, and there they were both buried.

Edward and Plegmund decided that it was necessary to increase the number of dioceses in Wessex. The sees of Winchester and Sherborne were vacant in 909 and to the new bishops for these were added three more — Crediton in Devon, Wells in Somerset and Ramsbury in Wiltshire. In this way Wessex was brought under closer episcopal guidance. Archbishop Plegmund went to Rome to gain the pope's approval for this extension. When he died in 914 he was succeeded by Athelm who had been the first Bishop of Wells; we know hardly anything of his nine years as archbishop. He was followed by Wulfhelm who had also been Bishop of Wells. Apart from the fact that he crowned Athelstan in 925 and later went to Rome to receive the pallium, his nineteen years at Canterbury are a blank. Like his predecessor he remains a shadowy figure. Our ignorance of the work of these two archbishops from 914 to 942 is symptomatic of how little we know of the Church in England during the first half of the tenth century. Perhaps the absence of information may be taken as meaning that

Church affairs were going along peacefully but unspectacularly.

The mists clear as we reach the times of St. Dunstan (c. 909–988), one of the great makers of the Church in England. He was born near Glastonbury and was related to the royal family and also to Archbishop Athelm and to the bishops of Winchester and Lichfield. He was educated at Glastonbury which was no longer a monastery but a clerical community; it had the benefit of a good library of which the youthful Dunstan took full advantage and thereby laid the foundations of his wide culture. He received the tonsure but had, as yet, no vocation for the monastic life. This was not surprising for monasticism had all but died out in southern England owing to the depredations of the Danes and the collapse of ecclesiastical discipline. Dunstan joined his uncle Athelm at Canterbury and was by him introduced to the court of Athelstan. It was another relative, perhaps uncle, Aelfheah, Bishop of Winchester, who persuaded Dunstan to become a monk. He was ordained priest with his friend Ethelwold. He then returned to Glastonbury where he led a strictly regulated life of prayer, study and manual work. He worked in metal, making bells and other church utensils and he composed sacred music.

On the death of Athelstan in 939 his successor Edmund called Dunstan to court as one of his counsellors; he was not well received by some of his colleagues and they persuaded the king to dismiss him, but the reason for this opposition is not known. Shortly afterwards the king was hunting near Cheddar Gorge; in pursuit of a stag he was separated from his companions and in his furious riding he all but plunged into the Gorge. In thankfulness for this escape, he vowed to make amends to Dunstan whom he made abbot of Glastonbury. That year, 943, marks the beginning of the revival of monasticism in England. The Rule of St. Benedict was followed strictly at Glastonbury under Dunstan, and soon others were attracted there who felt the call of the monastic life. Among them was Dunstan's friend Ethelwold, but they seem to have found it difficult to work together, so Ethelwold left Glastonbury with three others to re-establish the monastery at Abingdon.

King Edmund was murdered in 946 and was succeeded by his brother Eadred who welcomed Dunstan as one of his most trusted counsellors. His fortunes again changed on the death of Eadred in 955. Eadwig, who succeeded him, was persuaded to banish Dunstan by, probably, some of the old counsellors of King Edward who nourished their former grudges. This exile from England proved of benefit to Dunstan and to English monasticism for he found refuge in the reformed monastery of Blandinium in Flanders; there he was able to experience the full application of the Rule of St. Benedict.

Things had not been going well in England. During Eadwig's reign of four years the few monasteries began to fall back into their old lax ways. The general discontent that led Eadwig's brother Edgar to become king of Mercia and East Anglia meant the end of Dunstan's exile, for Edgar called him home and made him Bishop of Worcester and later of London.

Archbishop Odo (Oda) died in 959 the year in which Edgar became king of the reunited kingdom. Odo was of Danish extraction and he became Bishop of Ramsbury (Wiltshire) in Athelstan's time. He was sent on an embassy to France and was at the battle of Brunanburgh. It was under Athelstan's brother King Edmund that Odo became Archbishop of Canterbury in succession to Wulfhelm. It may not have been entirely his fault that, in such disturbed times, his cathedral and other church buildings became dilapidated. Odo made it one of his first tasks to restore and enlarge the cathedral, and he reclaimed for Canterbury its former prestige. There had been a decline in its status owing to its out-of-the-way situation in the far east of the kingdom and to the growing importance of Winchester as the royal capital. Odo was the trusted counsellor of Edmund, Eadred and Eadwig though he found the last somewhat refractory due more to his youth than to actual ill-will. In Edmund's time, Odo had been a steady supporter of the king's desire to reform the clergy especially in trying to enforce the rule of celibacy; they also laid down laws on marriage and inheritance. Odo revived the practice of addressing all the clergy in pastoral letters, but he does not seem to have called any synods. Not the least of his good works was his recognition of the merits of Dunstan, who succeeded him as archbishop in 959.

King Edgar relied much on Dunstan's advice and they worked well together. Former monasteries were restored and the Rule of St. Benedict was prescribed in place of the rather easy ways of the past years. Dunstan had two powerful supporters of his church policy; one was his old friend Ethelwold who became Bishop of Winchester, and the other was a younger man, Oswald, who was of Danish extraction like his relatives Archbishops Odo and Osketel. After serving the latter in York, Oswald was made Bishop of Worcester at the suggestion of Dunstan. He became Archbishop of York in 972, but he preferred Worcester and kept that see; this began what was an unfortunate practice of combining York with Worcester; in those days of slow travel this resulted in the Church in the north not getting the attention it badly needed after all the upheavals of the period. Even a bishop as fervent and devoted as Oswald could not effectively compass such a range of labour.

Ethelwold acted vigorously in restoring monastic discipline. At his appointment the cathedral and New Minster at Winchester were served by clerks and Ethelwold decided that both should become regularly constituted monasteries. This was not done without friction. The clerks at the cathedral were reluctant to become monks and vacate their positions. Ethelwold brought some monks from Abingdon which he had reformed in earlier days; they waited outside the cathedral until the end of Mass, and they were encouraged by hearing the words of the Communion: 'Serve the Lord with fear, and rejoice unto him with trembling, get you discipline, lest you perish from the right way' (Psalm 2,11–12). Thereupon they entered; all the clerks left but three returned later and joined the community. It would seem that

Ethelwold was of a more ascetic temper than Dunstan; they did not always work in harmony but Dunstan's rather more benign policy had a greater influence than the somewhat rigid rule of Ethelwold.

There was a steady increase in the foundations of monasteries and convents, and then about the year 970 there was a gathering at Winchester of the bishops, abbots and abbesses with two monks from Fleury (where Oswald had been for some years) and Blandinium (where Dunstan had spent his exile). It is probable that King Edgar and some of his nobles were also present. There was as yet no clear division between clerical and secular government such as eventually was established between the Convocations and Parliament. The King's Council, the witan shared in these decisions. This assembly drew up the *Regularis Concordia Angliae nationis monachorum sanctimonialque* for the regulation of monastic life. It summarised what was best in English tradition and in monasticism in other countries. Two unusual features may be noted. The king and queen were recognised as guardians of the Church and prayers were said for them in the Office, and the Matin Mass was offered for them. Secondly, freedom to elect their abbot, subject to the king's approval, was given to the monks, and, over and above that, where a monastic community served a cathedral, it had the right to elect the bishop, if possible from among themselves. These provisions distinguish English from continental practice, and the last, the election of a bishop, was to have permanent effect in the Church of England though it became a nominal and not an actual rule. Most of the bishops at the end of the tenth century were monks.

The examples of Dunstan, Ethelwold and Oswald in making their monasteries centres of learning brought about what may be termed a renaissance of culture. The monasteries were for some centuries to be the sources of scholarship and of ecclesiastical art. Much has perished either through the lapse of time or through the destructiveness of man but what has survived witnesses to the high level of achievement that had been reached.

It would need a long list to name all the monastic foundations that were established as a result of the work of Dunstan, Ethelwold and Oswald. A few must be taken as typical of many. In the south there were Malmesbury, Bath, Exeter, Cerne, Tavistock, Horton, Cranborne and Buckfast. In the Midlands there were Peterborough, Ely, Thorney, Croyland, St. Neots, St. Albans, Eynsham and Pershore. The number in the north was far fewer but there were Ripon and Deerhurst. Some of these were revivals but so thorough was the reformation that all can be regarded as new foundations.

This reinvigorated monasticism had its influence on the Church at large, not only by exemplifying a more devout religious life dedicated to the *Opus Dei* and by the exact carrying out of the liturgy, but by providing the means by which young men with vocations for the priesthood but not for the monastic order could be trained in letters and learning and in ritual. We must not paint too rosy a picture; considerable as these advances were, they did not immediately eradicate long established weaknesses. Nor should it be forgotten that there must have been many isolated settlements or villages that were cut off from the few main centres of church life. Time and steady guidance were needed, but, as we shall see, these were not given. Once more political events broke into the life of the Church.

With the accession of Ethelred in 979, Dunstan, then an ageing man, withdrew from public life and passed his last years at Canterbury where he devoted himself to the instruction of the young scholars.

Ethelwold died in 984, Dunstan in 988 and Oswald in 992. Their going marked the end of the great revival; they had no successors of equal stature. There were, however, a number of scholars whose work matured after the deaths of these leaders to whom they owed the learning that shone like a light in the dark days that soon came over England. The most important of these scholars was Aelfric. He was born about 955 and died about 1020. He entered the monastery of the Old Minster of Winchester under Ethelwold whose successor, Aelfheah, later Archbishop of Canterbury, sent him to the newly founded monastery at Cerne, Dorset, to take charge of the school there. Aelfric was a prolific writer, producing text-books, homilies, translations and commentaries. His use of Anglo-Saxon is an important contribution to the development of our language. He was not an original thinker nor was he a leader like his master Ethelwold, but his influence was widely spread. A second scholar was Byrhtferth of Ramsey; he wrote in Latin works on language and mathematics. A third scholar was Wulfstan of Worcester whose homilies have survived; one of these describes in impassioned prose the state of England under the renewed attacks of the Danes. Other names could be added to these three to show how the re-establishment of monastic life affected not only the religious but the cultural life of the country. Parallel with this spread of learning should be noted the rise of a school of illumination that produced work of remarkable quality showing originality in design and colouring; to this may be added fine work in precious metals and, for women, beautiful needlework and embroidery. All these talents were devoted to the service of the Church. The troubled times did not seriously interrupt the production of these works of advanced culture.

At the period of the deaths of the three great leaders, Ethelred the Unready (or Redeless or Counsel-less) was still king; as his cognomen implies he lacked the steadiness of purpose and vigour of his father Edgar; the Egbert-Alfredian line was in decline. As his second queen he married a daughter of Duke Richard of Normandy; their eldest son is known as Edward the Confessor. For the involved reign of Ethelred the reader must turn to the history books, but a brief summary is needed to give the background Church affairs. The renewed incursions of the Danes were not met with the determination and military skill shown by the former kings of Wessex. Ethelred preferred to pay Danegeld; as with all kinds of blackmail, the price he had to pay was raised with each demand. Driven desperate, Ethelred had the criminal foolishness in 1002 to order the murder of all

Danes in his service. This brought down on him the anger of King Swein of Denmark who resolved to conquer England and add it to his dominions.

The raids were intensified. In the year 1011 Canterbury was sacked and Archbishop Aelfheah (St. Elphege) was taken prisoner. The Anglo-Saxon Chronicle refers to this event in these lines:

> Then was he a captive, he who had been
> The head of England and Christendom.
> There might be seen wretchedness
> Where often bliss was seen before
> In that unhappy city, whence came first to us
> Christendom, and both spiritual and earthly bliss.

It adds, 'And they kept the archbishop as a prisoner until the time when they martyred him.' This sacking of Canterbury seems to have been exceptional in its savagery. Many of the Danes were at least nominal Christians, and though some churches and monasteries were looted, there was no widespread destruction as in the earlier raids. There were many Danes in the country who had settled after those first incursions and the newcomers would spare their countrymen and their offspring, as well as their settlements.

Ethelred was forced to find refuge in Normandy until Swein's death in 1014. The dead king's second son Canute took up his father's campaign. Ethelred's son, Edmund Ironside showed that he had inherited some of the courage and determination of his ancestors; his cognomen was a recognition of this spirit and of his great physical strength. For a time he ruled the old Wessex while Canute reigned in the Danelaw, but the death of Edmund in 1016 with only two infant sons as his heirs opened the whole country to Canute. The two boys were sent to Hungary for safety. Canute married as his second wife the widow of Ethelred, but his two step-sons, Edward and Alfred were brought up in Normandy.

Canute was King of England from 1016 to his death in 1035; he was also King of Denmark from 1019 and of Norway from 1028. This combination of three kingships was a notable achievement and it is not surprising that he was called 'the Great.' The measure of his greatness was that, although he had to be absent from each of his kingdoms in turn for varying periods, he maintained a firm and, on the whole, just rule in each. He was a Christian by conviction, and, from the outset of his reign in England, he gave the Church his full support. The laws he issued were based on Anglo-Saxon precedents and, among other provisions, fully safeguarded the Church.

There were two innovations in his administration in England that were to have serious consequences. He divided the kingdom into four districts each under an earl (as the ealdorman now became); this gave rise to the over-mighty lord and was to have disastrous results under Edward the Confessor. The second development was that Canute made more and more use of clerics in his government; the fact that they formed the majority of the literate pop-ulation inevitably led to such employment; the mischievous practice of rewarding them with benefices was an unfortunate accompaniment. In the past the bishops had always been members of the king's council or witan, sometimes influen-tial ones such as Dunstan, but they were churchmen first and had little to do with civil administration. Now we see the rise of the political cleric who was primarily a state official and who looked to advancement in the Church as his due.

Canute was fortunate in having Ethelnoth as Archbishop of Canterbury for the greater part of his reign. Ethelnoth was a scion of the Wessex royal house and that meant much at a period when Anglo-Saxons and this new influx of Danes had to learn to live together. His cognomen of 'the Good' indicates his pastoral reputation, and his advice was valued by the king. Wulfstan, the second of that name to be Arch-bishop of York, was, like his immediate predecessors, also Bishop of Worcester but he seems to have given more atten-tion to the north than they had done. He too was esteemed by Canute. Wulfstan died in 1023 and was succeeded by

Aelfric, who, as the other archbishops had done, went to Rome to receive the pallium from the pope. Aelfric had the cognomen of 'Putta', meaning a hawk, an indication of his character. He refused to separate York from Worcester.

Canute enriched many churches and was a founder of monasteries, the most notable being Bury St. Edmund's. An old rhyme gives us a glimpse of how he was remembered.

> Merry sang the monks in Ely
> When Canute the king rowed thereby
> 'Row, knights, near the land
> And hear we these monks sing.'

In 1027 he made a pilgrimage to Rome for the coronation of the Emperor Conrad II whose son married Canute's daughter. As many rulers of other countries were also there, England was once more brought into contact with the mainland of Europe. At Rome he gained from the pope some relaxations of episcopal fees. Even more significant was the intercourse between the Church in England and the Churches in Scandinavia where Christianity had only as yet a tenuous hold; bishops and priests went from England to foster the progress in conversion of Canute's other realms.

Canute died in 1035 and his kingdoms fell apart. His son by Emma of Normandy, Harthacanute, was delayed in Denmark owing to a revolt in Norway. Meanwhile Canute's son by his first marriage, Harold Harefoot, assumed the English throne during the years 1035–40; he died soon after Harthacanute's arrival, thus, for the present, solving the succession problem, but Harthacanute himself died two years later and the witan elected Edward, the forty-year old surviving son of Ethelred, as king. This was a return to the ancient line of Wessex but with a difference. Edward had lived from boyhood in Normandy; England was almost an alien land to him; this in itself would not have greatly affected the government of the country, but the character of the new king brought a new element into national affairs. He lacked the virility and grit of his great ancestors and he was too ready to give way to assertive advisers. He was by nature a celibate and his deep piety gained for him the name of the 'Confessor', and later canonisation. It would however have taken someone with the combined powers of an Egbert and an Alfred to have resolved the problems that faced Edward. The greatest of these, a legacy from Canute, was that the country was divided between three powerful earls — Leofric in Mercia, Siward in Northumbria, and, above all, Godwin in Wessex and East Anglia. We cannot here give an account of the tangled history of the reign; it was remarkable that Edward managed to keep the throne for twenty-four years and to die in his bed. There is some truth in the saying that it was the rivalries among the earls that enabled him to remain king and not his own ability as a ruler.

Edward married Edith the daughter of Earl Godwin, but it became clear that no heir could be expected from their union, so the problem of succession became once more acute. Godwin, to the king's relief, died in 1053; he had been unscrupulous in seeking power for himself and his sons, the eldest of whom, Harold, was a man of different character from his father. He was not only a great war-leader but he was a statesman who could look beyond the claims of the Godwin clan. It was he who brought Edward the Atheling (the royal heir) from Hungary as the legitimate successor to the throne, but the Atheling died in 1057 soon after reaching England leaving only a child, Edgar, as his heir.

Under the two sons of Canute, Harold and Harthacanute, the appointments of bishops and abbots became a question of intrigue and even simony. Eadsige, Archbishop of Canterbury, who crowned both Harthacanute and Edward, had been one of Canute's chaplains. He went to Rome in 1040 to receive the pallium. He worked closely with Godwin, but with declining health his influence also declined, and he died in 1050. Edward thereupon appointed a friend of his Norman days, Robert, abbot of Jumièges, to Canterbury; he had previously been Bishop of London. It was a bad choice, for the new archbishop was an intriguer by nature and it was under his influence that Edward began calling

Normans to his court and appointing them as leading counsellors and some as bishops. A more creditable aspect of Edward's church policy was that the ties with Rome were drawn closer. A bishop and two abbots from England attended a papal council at Reims in 1049, and two bishops were also sent to Rome for another council in 1050. A further indication of these close relations was that two papal legates came to England in 1062, the first since the days of Offa.

When Earl Godwin returned from exile in 1052, Archbishop Robert fled the country; he was outlawed; he went to Rome to plead his cause with the pope, but, in spite of the pope's support, Robert was not able to return to England and he died at Jumièges soon after. Stigand, Bishop of Worcester, then became archbishop, but he continued to hold this see as well as various abbacies. It was his pluralism that counted against him, and his appointment to Canterbury was regarded as uncanonical; there were hints of simony. In consequence of doubts as to his position, newly appointed bishops sought to be consecrated by Archbishop Kinsige of York, a man of exemplary life. On his death in 1060, Ealdred of Worcester became Archbishop of York. He had travelled widely on embassies and had made the pilgrimage to Jerusalem. He went to Rome for the pallium, which the pope refused to grant unless he resigned the see of Worcester. So at last York and Worcester were separated.

Wulfstan became Bishop of Worcester. He was a pious monk who had been elected prior of the monastery there. Earl Harold and others sought his advice for he was a man of wisdom and stood apart from the power-politics of the times. A younger contemporary of Wulfstan should be mentioned. Ethelwig of Evesham brought that monastery to a high standard of order and learning. Leofric of Peterborough was of a different type. His own wealth was lavished on the monastery and cathedral, but he was an example of the bad practice that King Edward condoned of holding several other benefices at the same time. Edward also began the granting of lands in England to Norman monasteries.

It might be expected that under such a king as Edward the Confessor, the general state of the Church would have been enhanced, but he did less than Canute had done. The wealth of some of the monasteries and greater found-ations was considerably increased not so much by the king's bounty as by the munificence of lay benefactors. Herein lay the seeds of future trouble. Edward seems to have had no thought-out church policy, any more than he had a state policy; he was content to let things drift. He is chiefly remembered to-day as the founder of Westminster Abbey; he planned a church on a scale greater than any that had been previously conceived in this country. The building was begun in 1045 and was consecrated twenty years later on Holy Innocent's Day. Edward died a few days later. He was buried in front of the high altar, and in 1269 his body was transferred to the present shrine.

CHAPTER 8

Lanfranc

When Duke William of Normandy landed at Pevensey on the 28th September 1066, he had with him a banner consecrated by Pope Alexander II; this was granted, presumably, for no documentary record exists, on the grounds that Earl Harold had broken the oath he had given that he would aid William to become King of England. The oath was taken in the most solemn manner over a reliquary; defenders of Harold said that he had been ignorant of the presence of these relics of saints. Be this as it may, such an oath was regarded as absolutely binding and the breaking of it was a mortal sin. This fact no doubt influenced some of the English bishops and nobles when they were faced with the choice between accepting William and resistance.

The Normans present a paradox. They could be ruthless and merciless and cruel but they were devoted to the Church. A succession of masterful dukes, of whom William was the most masterful, had built up a state that for military prowess, combined with strong governance, had no rival in Europe. So it was that the coming of the Normans effected a revolution in England. The somewhat loose territorial government of the Old English or Anglo-Saxons was replaced by a closely knit feudal sovereignty and all church lands were brought under feudal tenure. This is not the place for an account of the political changes that came about during the twenty years of William's reign. Our concern is with the determinative effect he had on the Church, for, what happened was willed by him. He was, according to his lights a religious man, though here he was simply the outstanding example of the Norman paradox, and we may find it difficult to reconcile his almost savage iron rule with the spirit of Christianity as we interpret it. As in the State, so in the Church, he demanded good order and discipline. Fortunately his instinct led him to choose the right men for carrying out his policy, and once he was satisfied that his choice was well made, he was content to watch and support rather than interfere; in the political field he sometimes made mistakes which he rectified without mercy, but in Church affairs he was well served. It should be noted that the king was primarily responsible for the appointment of bishops. No doubt he consulted the archbishops and others who knew the men, but the decisions were his, and they were made on merit. There is no hint of simony which was a prevailing sin in the Western Church.

It was typical of William's political awareness that, at his coronation, in Westminster Abbey on Christmas Day 1066, the crown was placed on his head, not by Stigand the doubtful Archbishop of Canterbury, but by Archbishop Ealdred of York. Stigand was removed when papal legates investigated his claims in 1070. As we have seen, Edward the Confessor had brought priests in from Normandy and Lotharingia to serve his court; five of these became bishops and their intrusion was not always welcomed by the native clergy nor were their pastoral duties always uppermost in their thoughts. By the time William became king, there were only two (a third is of doubtful origin) English bishops of whom Wulfstan of Worcester was the outstanding one. He remained bishop until his death at an advanced age in 1095; he was canonised eight years later. In spite of the fact that he had been Harold's close adviser, William, after some hesitation, left him undisturbed. The papal legates who deposed Stigand had also deprived three of the bishops for irregularities in their appointments, probably for simony. This is an indication of the malaise that had settled on the Church under Edward's flaccid rule; in spite of his personal saintliness he allowed his predilection for foreign priests to influence his appointments in the Church; it is difficult to believe that there were no priests who would have made good bishops; indeed one is tempted to think that Edward did not like the English. Harold's reign was too brief to reverse this policy. When William took control, he was not faced with a predominantly English hierarchy, and it is a mistake to say that he immediately swept aside the established bishops and abbots; it was not until 1070, for instance, that the Stigand problem was resolved. Those who were loyal were retained; those who were disloyal were inevitably got rid of. Gradually, as opportunity occurred, Normans were appointed as bishops and abbots so that, by the end of the reign replacement was almost complete.

William had probably already made up his mind who should be Archbishop of Canterbury once Stigand was out of the way; his choice was Lanfranc, the abbot of St. Étienne, Caen, the king's own foundation. When he arrived in England in the summer of 1070, Lanfranc was in his fifties, and he was to rule the Church for nearly twenty years. He was a native of Lombardy; details of his early life are lacking, but he was trained in civil law before deciding that he had a call to the Church. He went to Tours to study theology and then on to Avranches as a teacher in the school, but he was still uncertain as to the right course to pursue. Was the monastic life his true vocation? Instead of going to one of the great foundations, he went to Bec, between Caen and Rouen, where Herluin, a former soldier of noble birth, had settled with two companions in apostolic poverty. Lanfranc presented himself at Bec about the year 1040, three or four years after Herluin had founded the monastery, though as yet it hardly deserved that name. It was not attached to any order; it was as if Herluin was feeling his way and he refused to regard himself as prior. For two or three years Lanfranc followed the simple, almost primitive life of this tiny community which was beginning to attract subjects. Herluin decided that here at last was the man to take authority over them and Lanfranc became the first prior. He established a school which soon gained a high reputation. Among the pupils was the future Alexander II, the pope who gave his blessing to Duke William's English Enterprise. There is no record of how the Duke and Lanfranc came together. They clashed when William wished to marry Matilda, daughter of Baldwin of Flanders and a descendant of King Alfred. Pope Leo IX forbade the marriage, presumably because of affinity. In spite of this the marriage took place; Lanfranc changed his attitude and he was partly responsible for persuading Pope Nicholas II to grant a dispensation. In return the Duke had to found a monastery and the Duchess a convent; these were both at Caen; St. Étienne was the monastery and La Sainte Trinité was the convent. Both survived the battle round Caen in 1944. William appointed Lanfranc as abbot in 1066. Four years later King William decided that Lanfranc should go to Canterbury; it needed the pope's command before Lanfranc would agree.

He was consecrated Archbishop on the 29th August 1070 by nine of the bishops of his province, only two of whom were English. A year later he went to Rome to receive the pallium from his former pupil Alexander II. Ealdred, Archbishop of York had died in 1069 and William appointed Thomas of Bayeux who had come to England as a royal chaplain; he was a scholar of ability and the choice was fully justified. When he went to Lanfranc to arrange for his consecration, Lanfranc refused unless Thomas made a profession of obedience, that is that the province of York was subordinate to Canterbury; he did so at the king's command but stipulated that he was not thereby committing his successors to accepting the primacy of Canterbury. He went with Lanfranc to Rome and there they submitted the question to the Pope who remitted it to a council of the bishops and abbots of England. This synod or council was held at Windsor at Whitsuntide 1072 and it was there decided that the Archbishop of York must make submission to the Archbishop of Canterbury. Thomas complied with this decision but it did not hold good after their deaths; the documentary evidence used by Lanfranc was of doubtful authenticity.

The synod at Windsor was one of a series that Lanfranc called. It was through these assemblies that he brought greater discipline into the Church; the ordinances made were not revolutionary; they followed the precedents of synods held during the period of the flourishing of the old English Church. The fact that the king himself might be present served to emphasise their authoritative character; moreover he ruled that no ordinances could be promulgated without his consent. William and Lanfranc worked closely together; it is surprising that there was no serious friction between them for both were strong-willed men and of autocratic temperament. The Church in England gained by this harmonious co-operation. One consequence is that we cannot always be sure which of them was responsible for a particular policy.

As one who had been dedicated to the monastic life, Lanfranc was resolved to restore full monastic life at Canterbury; the cathedral itself was dilapidated and the monastic buildings partly in ruins; he at once began rebuilding and Christ Church was, in effect, refounded by him. The *Consuetudines* he drew up for the monks were his own compilation based upon customs followed at Bec with some additions drawn from what he had seen in other monasteries outside England. Here he was not so much an innovator as a director; he wished to see a stricter rule in monastic life in accordance with the best practices and traditions. These recommendations for better order were not imposed on monasteries throughout the country. Lanfranc had no authority for doing so, but gradually they were adopted, sometimes in modified form, by many monasteries under their Norman abbots, and this led to a general raising of standards and no doubt had a beneficial effect on the secular clergy and especially on those who went through the monastery schools.

Only two notable new monastic foundations were made during William's reign. The first was Battle Abbey which the king had vowed to build in thanksgiving for his victory. The high altar stood on the place where Harold and his thanes had fallen. William brought in monks from Marmoutier (Loire) to form the first community. It was thus a Benedictine foundation. The second monastery of note was Lewes. This was founded by William de Warenne, one of the Conqueror's companions-in-arms. In reward he was given the rape[1] of Lewes in Sussex. Monks from Cluny were established there. Many of the Conqueror's knights wished to gain merit by making monastic foundations; for this purpose they granted part of their lands to Norman monasteries. Edward the Confessor, as we have seen, had done so on a small scale. It meant that the rents from these lands went abroad to support the parent community, and priories would be established in England with the responsibility of collecting the rents from estates which might be scattered over several counties. These alien priories were more economic than religious institutions and in later times they contributed to the decline in monastic fervour.

We have seen how in old English days a benefactor who built a church on his land became its proprietor. This system was greatly extended under the Normans. The great English landowners had been dispossessed and many of the lesser families had lost their lands by forfeiture or by plain confiscation. The Normans who replaced them built churches for their families, households and retainers as well as providing village churches or rebuilding existing ones. One example must serve in illustration. William de Braose was awarded the rape of Bramber in Sussex with forty-one manors. A mile to the south-east of the castle he was building was the Saxon built church of St. Botolph's. As he wanted

---

[1] In Old English times Sussex was divided into six 'rapes' for administrative purposes. The term is peculiar to Sussex; its origin is unknown.

his own church, he built a new one up against his castle. To serve this he brought monks from the Benedictine monastery of St. Florent in Saumer (Anjou). For some reason not recorded, they did not settle, perhaps because they had little liking for serving a local church; so de Braose built for them a priory a mile to the north-east at Upper Beeding. De Braose probably also rebuilt St. Botolph's; this small Norman building incorporates some of the older Saxon church.

As we go about the country we are often surprised at seeing churches of some size where, to-day, there is only a small community; sometimes the presence of two churches almost within sight of one another is a matter for bewilderment. There may have been a shift or decline of population; whole villages have disappeared and during recent years the sites of many have been traced, but where the village has gone, the church has usually also gone. When, however, we consider that the population of England in Norman times was not more than a million and a half, with perhaps less than a third living in towns, it is clear that many of these churches must have been larger than was really necessary. The churches were not always tailored according to the population; they were built to the glory of God and the prestige of the proprietor. This is not a cynical observation; motives were, as ever, mixed, but the building of a fine church was held to be a meritorious act. There was also another inducement. At a council in Normandy under the direction of a papal envoy, a code of penances was imposed on the Conqueror's army; we need not concern ourselves with the details, but one stipulation was that those who had killed an unknown number of the enemy at Hastings or elsewhere could commute the penance by building a church or endowing a monastery. The Normans were almost fanatical in observing the ordinances of the Church, so we may regard many a manor or village church as an act of penance for having overcome the English.

Masons and craftsmen from Normandy were brought over to build the churches with the aid of native labour. Lanfranc had stone imported from Caen and others followed his example. This must have been an expensive operation with all the hazards of the Channel crossing. One wonders how many cargoes were lost at sea. We have noted that a fair number of Saxon churches had been built, and substantial parts of some survive to this day. These churches would either be used as quarries for the stone, or parts would be incorporated in the Norman rebuilding. The typical Saxon church had a rectangular nave with an almost square chancel; a porch might be added. The Normans often followed the same simple plan but it was not long before the aisled church became more common. There are so many of these churches that we are all familiar with the Norman style — the massive walling and pillars and the rounded arches with their dog-tooth or similar mouldings.

The number of churches in England was considerably increased as a result of all this new building and the religious needs of the people were met more adequately than before. There was one region where this did not happen — the north from York to Durham. The northern rising of 1069, which had Danish support, was suppressed by the Conqueror with ruthless ferocity. The whole region was devastated and all but depopulated and it did not show signs of recovery for many years. One Norman knight, Reinfrid, was deeply affected by this scene of desolation. With two monks from Winchcombe he got permission from Bishop Walcher of Durham (who was murdered in a riot in 1080) to use the ruined church at Jarrow, the church of Benedict Biscop and Bede. This was the modest beginning of the northern revival of religion.

Bishops and abbots began building or rebuilding their cathedrals or monasteries. The Norman-Romanesque style was adopted. Previously only Westminster Abbey had been built in this manner. As part of this development the seats of some bishops were moved from country places to cities; the most drastic was the removal from Dorchester-on-Thames over a hundred miles north to Lincoln. Other changes were: Elmham to Thetford and later to Norwich,

Lichfield to Chester, Sherborne to Salisbury, and Selsey to Chichester.

One defect of Lanfranc was his disdain of the Anglo-Saxon clergy. Their lack of learning was in part the cause of his attitude, but he regarded them as hardly worthy of their calling. The Norman bishops and abbots were equally contemptuous of the native priests and they even ridiculed the Anglo-Saxon saints and their relics. It was not therefore surprising that disputes and even brawls marred their relations. Not until a new generation grew up did a better understanding develop.

The English had to learn by bitter experience what it was to be a conquered people. There was, for instance, the barrier of language. The higher clergy could converse in Latin; how far the parish priests could do so is not known; there is no record of their condition. Norman-French predominated. It was to take many years for it to be assimilated with English; indeed Norman-French, much debased, remained the language of the law until the seventeenth century.

The social system of the country was revolutionised with the development of feudalism. The Conqueror needed a dependable military force at his command. All land was therefore held on feudal tenure, that is, on condition that the landowners provided a stipulated number of knights and men-of-arms according to the extent of their possessions; this may be regarded as the rent they paid. This requirement, which was rigidly enforced, was applied to all church lands, so that abbots, for instance, were under the obligation to provide their quotas of fighting men fully armed. This meant a readjustment of ideas for any English bishop or abbot. The Normans were accustomed to the system and worked it; here we can see one reason, though not the determinative one, for replacing English by Norman clerics.

William also brought about a momentous change in the relations between church and state; it would be more exact to say church and king for the idea of a national state had not yet developed. In old English times, church and the

king's government had been intertwined; thus the ecclesiastical and civil authorities sat side by side in the shire and
hundred courts and together enforced justice, though, in
matters affecting the church the bishop would no doubt
carry most weight. It was about 1072 that William published
an ordinance separating spiritual pleas for determination by
the bishops according to canon law. This ordinance was
reinforced at a council held at Winchester in 1076. This
was the beginning in this country of a situation that was to
lead to serious disputes in later reigns. It seems probable
that William himself was responsible for this change, though
Lanfranc no doubt concurred since it was in keeping with
papal policy. He had copies of the most important canons
distributed to the leading churches. At the same time he
began the reorganisation of the dioceses with archdeaconaries
so that administration could be more effective and discipline
enforced more easily.

The Conqueror's relations with Rome call for special
attention. The fact that the pope had blessed the Norman
invasion did not, in William's view, put him under any
special obligation. Both Alexander II and his redoubtable
successor Gregory VII (Hildebrand) claimed that England
was a papal fief. To this William replied, 'Fealty I have
never willed to do, nor do I will to do it now. I have never
promised it, nor do I find that my predecessors did it to
yours.' When they raised the question of Peter's Pence,
he promised to resume payment. He also laid down that
no papal briefs or other communications could be received
in England without his consent. He firmly controlled the
relations between England and Rome.

The Conquest brought England into closer contact with
Europe than ever it had been before or indeed since. It
is true that in old English times there had always been a
close relationship with Rome, but the claims of the popes
at that period had been more modest than they were soon
to become especially under Hildebrand. William defined that
relationship and his successors did not reverse his rulings.
There was at the same time a constant going to and fro

between England and Normandy. The new Norman barons and landowners regarded England as a conquered country; their first loyalty was to Normandy and the king and his military leaders frequently crossed the Channel to look after their interests or to fight their enemies. So the two countries became mixed up in each other's affairs. England gave the prestige of kingship but it also had to find the money for wars.

So the old English kingdom came to an end. Many who could not bear to live under the Conqueror left the country; some joined the Byzantine Emperor's Varangian Guard.[1] Others fought against the Normans wherever a chance arose, as, for instance, against the Norman kingdom in southern Italy. Their native land had become foreign to them. The church was the one constant element of continuity and although only two English bishops (Wulfstan of Worcester and Giso of Wells) were alive when William died in 1087, that continuity was not broken. It was not until the end of the next century that Norman and English were no longer markedly distinguishable in society. They had the faith in common.

[1] By the end of the century the Varangian Guard was predominantly Anglo-Saxon.

CHAPTER 9

Anselm

THE Conquest brought England into closer contact with the Continent at a time when three developments were in progress:

1. the increasing authority of the papacy,
2. the revival of monasticism, and
3. the Crusades.

Each of these had its effect on the Church in England. Their nature must be briefly described.

1. *The Papacy*

From the time of Charlemagne (742–814) the popes had been, in effect, the nominees of the secular power — the German kings and emperors. This had replaced the primitive custom of popes being elected by the clergy and laity of Rome, just as bishops had been chosen locally, sometimes by simple acclamation. At the Lateran Council of 1059 under Pope Nicholas II (1059–61) it was decreed that in future the popes were to be elected by the cardinals alone and not by the decision of the emperor nor by pressure from the turbulent Roman nobility. The fact that Henry IV, the future emperor, was then a boy of nine eased the situation, but a papal decree of itself could not determine such a vexatious question and it took several centuries before papal elections could be freed from all outside influence.

Nicholas II had been able to take a firmer line because his predecessors had raised the prestige of the papacy. Some of them were little better than the puppets of the emperor or of the Roman nobles; many were old when they were appointed and their reigns were too short for anything radical to be achieved; thus during the tenth century there were twenty-three popes. Then there was the disruption resulting from the setting-up of rival or anti-popes when, for instance, the emperor objected to the policy of the reigning pope. In spite of these handicaps one or two resolute popes did effect some reforms. Leo XI (1049–54), a Lotharingian, was notable for what he achieved. He spent only six months of his five-year reign in Rome. He tirelessly travelled to hold local councils and synods, and archbishops and bishops had reason to be apprehensive when he was in their neighbourhoods. The synods he held issued canons and ordinances which were designed to improve the standards of the clergy and to remove glaring faults. Simony has already been mentioned as a prevalent sin; it was ubiquitous and was corrosive of moral influence; it took many forms, from the direct purchase of a benefice to promises of mutual benefits. All too often the first consideration was not religious fitness but material advantage, or family connexion. Clerical marriage was another blemish. Celibacy had been enjoined from the fourth century if not earlier but the rule was widely ignored and we have seen how this problem had come up again in synods under the Archbishops of Canterbury. Concubinage was condoned as a concession to human frailty, but actual marriage was a scandal and it became flagrant when, for instance, a son succeeded a father as an abbot. Council after council, synod after synod, inveighed against these evils, but to little effect.

It was under Pope Gregory VII (Hildebrand), who

reigned for twelve years (1073–85), that the most determined efforts were made to purge the Church of its most serious defects and to assert the independence of the papacy. His running fight with Henry IV cannot be followed here. The pope excommunicated[1] and deposed the king in February 1076; a year later Henry submitted at Canossa and was absolved. That part of the story is well known; the sequel is often overlooked. Gregory died in 1085 as a fugitive from Rome which had been occupied by Henry and where he had himself crowned emperor by his anti-pope Clement III. Gregory had also taken a firm stand on two other matters. He forbade the laity to attend masses celebrated by married priests. His second action was to promulgate an Investiture decree which forbade the investiture to ecclesiastical office by a layman. The struggle over this problem was to be waged for a long time. The root of the conflict was the impact of the feudal system on the Church. Bishops and abbots as tenants of lands owed military and other obligations to the king just as lay landowners did. As a sign of this the newly appointed bishop or abbot took the oath of fealty for his temporalities; the king then invested him with the ring and staff (crozier). Consecration followed with profession of ecclesiastical obedience to the archbishop. The pope's consent was rarely asked, but, following the early English example, it became the practice for archbishops to receive the pallium from the hands of the pope himself, thus being confirmed in their office and authority. All this was anathema to Hildebrand and his successors since they demanded complete independence from the ruling lay authority. Feudal homage, they claimed, should come after consecration and should not include the bestowal of the ring and staff by the temporal prince; otherwise it might seem as though it was he who made the bishop. We shall see how this problem was to raise critical issues in England.

---

[1] The greater excommunication excluded the sinner completely from Christian fellowship so that all were forbidden to have any association with him. The lesser excommunication excluded only from the sacraments.

2. *Monasticism*

Mention has already been made of some notable Norman and French monasteries such as Marmoutier, St. Florent, Bec and Caen. These were pioneering the way to a full revival of the full monastic life — strict observance of the rule and of the liturgy and the encouragement of learning. It would be wrong to give the impression that monasticism had decline generally in England by the tenth century. Worcester and Evesham, for instance, maintained their high ideals. It is, however, true that many monks had lost their religious fervour, and some monasteries had become comfortable residences for a few clerics who undertook no duties and followed no rule. The development of monasticism in Normandy was fostered by the dukes and it had some of the characteristics of the feudal system whereas in Anglo-Saxon monasteries there had been a less rigid and looser-knit association with the court and with one another. A great impulse towards a revival of monasticism came from the Burgundian abbey of Cluny under St. Hugh the Great (1049–1109). It was not long before there was a desire that the Cluniac observance should be followed in other countries. The foundation of Lewes in Sussex in 1077 by Cluniac monks has been already mentioned. Cluny did not establish a new order but set new standards of observance within the rule of St. Benedict. The revival of monasticism meant so much in England that we must return to consider it in greater detail later in this chapter.

3. *The Crusades*

Pope Urban II preached the First Crusade at the Council of Clermont in Novemeber 1095. The response to this appeal to Christendom to march to the East to stop the Turkish advance and to free Jerusalem was immediate and enthusiastic. The idea appealed strongly to the Norman warlike temperamant, and younger sons could find a new outlet for their combativeness in a campaign, blessed by the Church, that might give them lands of their own. This is not to suggest that the religious impulse was insincere; it was indeed strong; here again we have the Norman paradox demonstrated — devotion to the Church combined with an aggressive military spirit. The later Crusades lost the original religious fervour and became contests for power between rival princes. The first Crusaders came mostly from France and Normandy. Here it may be noted that the rise of chivalry in France was further promoted by the early Crusades. Two military religious orders were established: the Hospitallers, or Knights of St. John of Jerusalem (1113) cared for poor and sick pilgrims, and the Knights Templar (1118) protected the pilgrim roads. Both were established in England in the twelfth century. Before the Conquest England had been untouched by the code of the knights-errant; thus there were no tournaments — the training ground for knighthood — and those few who wanted to share in these contests had to cross the Channel. Tournaments were frowned upon by the Church. After the Conquest, the idea of chivalry gradually spread in this country, and it was fostered by the Arthurian legends in the *History of the Kings of Britain* by Geoffrey of Monmouth in the twelfth century.

William the Conqueror left Normandy to his eldest son Robert, called 'Curthose' as he was short and fat, and England to his second son William, known as 'Rufus' for his ruddy complexion. Lanfranc crowned William II at Westminster on the 26th September 1087, and, for the two years of life left him, the archbishop had a restraining influence on the new king. William Rufus was one of our 'bad' kings; popular verdicts of this kind may call for qualifications but they are usually well-founded. This was certainly so for William Rufus. He had abilities that could have made him an efficient successor to his father, but he was cruel, tyrannous and dead to honour. He showed no sign of religious feeling and his high-handed treatment of the Church was in striking contrast with the way in which its welfare had been safeguarded by the Conqueror. No sooner was Lanfranc dead (1089) than Rufus set out to achieve his great ambition — to wrest Normandy from his brother Robert, a man of different temperament, easy-going and generous. For several years there was war between them, but when in 1096 Robert took the Cross he pledged Normandy to his brother for ten thousand marks. In the Holy Land he gained a high reputation for his bravery and good comradeship. He returned to Normandy in 1100 a month after his brother's death who had been killed while hunting by an arrow perhaps shot accidentally but possibly intentionally. Such was the reputation of Rufus he was buried in Winchester Cathedral without a mass being said for the repose of his soul. He was unmarried and had not designated his successor.

William Rufus had revealed his mind and intention when he refused to let the see of Canterbury be filled for four years. As feudal overlord, the king could appropriate the revenues of a vacant see or abbacy and, less legitimately, annex some of the lands. Thus the longer the appointment of a bishop or an abbot could be delayed, the more profitable it was for the king. Canterbury was only the most conspicuous example of this unscrupulous treatment. At the end of the reign eleven of the wealthiest abbeys and three bishoprics were unfilled. When, however, Rufus was stricken with what seemed a mortal illness in 1093, he thought to expiate his sins by allowing an election to go forward. The name of Anselm, abbot of Bec and the leading theologian of his day, was at once proposed. He was a native of Lombardy and had gone to Bec because of the reputation of his countryman Lanfranc, whose disciple and successor he became. Bec was given lands in England and this brought Anselm here to deal with business affairs. It so happened that he was in England when Rufus was so seriously ill. Anselm tried to avoid the appointment to Canterbury, but was led to accept by the entreaties of the bishops. He was consecrated on the 4th December 1093 by the Archbishop of York after he had done homage to the king for his temporalities. He was well aware that a clash with the king was inevitable for, as soon as Rufus was on his feet again, he showed that he had forgotten his anxiety for his soul's welfare. William wanted all the money he could get for his designs on Normandy and he had no concern for England; it was his milch-cow. In this business of finding new ways of extracting money, his chief adviser and instrument was Rannulf Flambard, a Norman clerk of great ability but utterly unscrupulous; he was eventually to become Bishop of Durham in addition to holding many other rich benefices. Against two such unprincipled manipulators, it must have seemed that an unassuming monk would not have a chance, but Anselm proved as firm in his adherence to moral principles as they were indifferent.

The king agreed to restore the lands of Canterbury to what they had been in Lanfranc's day; when Anselm stipulated that his advice must be paramount in spiritual affairs, the king was evasive; he postponed a decision on a third matter — the recognition of Urban II as pope. Christendom was divided on this question. France and the West stood by Urban but the German states supported the Emperor's anti-pope Clement III. As abbot of Bec, Anselm had already given his allegiance to Urban, but William had not made his choice, though it is difficult to believe he cared one way or the other. Anselm also wished to go to Rome to receive the pallium but the king forbade him to leave the country. He himself crossed to Normandy.

When he returned, Anselm demanded that the Great Council should be called to decide whether his obedience to Urban was consistent with his allegiance to the king. The Council met at the castle of Rockingham in Northamptonshire in February 1095. The king with his personal council was in one room and the clerics in another with messengers passing between them, rather like employers and employees discussing a wage claim to-day. Anselm put it to the bishops that as they had persuaded him to accept the archbishopric, they should now support him in his dispute with the king. The bishops, with the exception of Anselm's aged friend Gundulf of Rochester, urged Anselm to submit to the king's wishes. Anselm refused to give way. Support came for him from the barons and laity, who, even in face of the king's wishes, declared that, though the bishops could withdraw their obedience from Anselm, they could not do so as they owed him no fealty. 'He is our archbishop and is our guide in religion, and he has committed no offence.' William dared not resist this opposition, so he decided to adjourn the discussion.

William sent two clerics to Rome to find out if Urban was really in authority, and, if they were satisfied, to ask Urban to send the archbishop's pallium to the king who would give it to an unnamed priest; in this way he hoped to get rid of Anselm. William was no match for a skilled diplomatist such as Urban (this was a few months before he preached the First Crusade); he sent Cardinal Walter of Albano as his legate to England, but Anselm was not told of what was going on. Once William had agreed to recognise Urban, the Cardinal became less co-operative; he refused to depose Anselm; he handed over the pallium to the king who recognised that he had been outmanoeuvred. He agreed to be reconciled to Anselm, who, however, had the last word; he refused to accept the pallium from the hands of the king; the legate, with great ceremony, laid it on the altar of Canterbury Cathedral for Anselm to assume. The truce, as it may be termed, between king and archbishop did not last. In 1097 William summoned Anselm to his court to answer a complaint that the military contingent he had sent for the war in Wales was inadequate. Anselm refused to attend this secular court and asked licence to go to Rome to consult with the pope. This the king refused to grant, so Anselm left without permission. The king at once treated the see of Canterbury as vacant and annexed the revenues. Anselm was received in Rome with marked honour in tribute to his great reputation as a theologian.

His book on the Incarnation, *Cur Deus Homo*, was among the influential treatises of the day and long remained so. The pope supported Anselm against Rufus and would have excommunicated the king for simony and as an oppressor of the Church had it not been for Anselm's more moderate counsel. It was clearly impossible for him to return to England so he went to Lyons where he stayed with an old friend, Archbishop Hugh. On the death of Rufus, Anselm was able to return to England after an exile of nearly three years.

William's younger brother Henry was hunting with him at the time of his death; without waiting to see that due respect was shown to the dead king, he rode at once to Winchester to secure the royal treasure. He was crowned at Westminster three days after William's death. When Duke Robert returned from Palestine soon afterwards, he claimed the English throne. The two brothers were at war off and on for six years until Robert was defeated and captured at Tinchebrai in 1106; for twenty-eight years he remained his brother's prisoner in England but with honourable treatment. Henry was as ruthless as William but he had a more stable disposition and could shape a policy. He had no wish to continue the dispute with Anselm and, although they clashed, the argument was carried on with restraint, and certainly the king had cause to complain. When the temporalities of Canterbury were restored to Anselm, the king required the usual homage due to him for the lands; this was to repeat what Anselm had conceded to William. It so happened that Anselm had just come from a Council in Rome where a decree had been made, with his approval, against lay investiture; he therefore felt obliged to refuse to do homage to the king. Rufus would have flown into a rage, but Henry was willing for the problem to be put to the pope. Three successive embassies failed to win any concession. Anselm himself went with a fourth embassy but he too could not shake the pope's determination. The king intimated that until the pope did yield, Anselm had better remain abroad, so once more he went to stay with Archbishop Hugh at Lyons, and the revenues of Canterbury were again paid into the exchequer. In 1108 the pope threatened to excommunicate the English bishops who had been invested by the king and Anselm threatened to excommunicate the king himself. Henry realised that the situation was critical. He met Anselm in Normandy, and ofter one more appeal to the pope who was less intransigent, a compromise was reached. This was confirmed at a Council in London in 1109. The king agreed to be content with the bishop or abbot elect doing homage; he would no longer give the ring and staff. This may seem to us a storm in a teacup, but it was fundamentally an attempt to define and demarcate the respective spheres of the secular and the spiritual. This was never achieved. Princes were not prepared to leave the appointments of bishops and abbots to the Church authorities since feudal relations were involved and they had to be satisfied that those appointed were loyal. In theory cathedral and monastic chapters elected their bishops and abbots, but in practice they had to conform to the wishes of the king.[1] Popes might object to specific appointments but usually such disputes were settled on a give and take basis. The problem eventually faded out.

Anselm died two years after this settlement had been reached. What had he accomplished during his six years as archbishop? He had been out of the country for more than half that time and there were murmurings that he was neglecting his proper duties. An abbot friend of his put the complaint into verse.

> Why is the shepherd absent from the field?
> The flock is wandering leaderless astray:
> None brings it back.

Anselm fought for what he considered a fundamental principle. The steadily encroaching interference of the king

[1] This system still obtains in the Anglican Church. The *congé d'élire* issued to a chapter is little more than a formality; the appointment is, in fact, made by the Crown on the advice of the Prime Minister.

with spiritual matters was a threat to the life and influence of the Church. He did not win his battle but he warned kings that there was a limit to their powers. Henry had accepted a compromise that may seem to us to have had little subtance. Yet in an age when symbols were important, the fact that a change was made in the investiture of bishops and abbots was important; the emphasis was now placed on consecration as the decisive act in the process, the king's part being limited to the act of homage for temporalities. As we shall see the compromise was not always observed, but it remained as a standard to which kings were expected to conform.

It made little real difference to Henry, nor did he reform his treatment of the Church in other respects in spite of Anselm's protests. He continued to keep bishoprics and abbacies vacant while he pocketed the revenues, even going so far as to confiscate a dead prelate's personal belongings. He discovered a new source of revenue; he levied fines from married priests who were then allowed to keep their wives; they were disobeying Church decrees but it was for the Church to impose penalties not for the secular power. A final example of his contumacy may be given. After Anselm's death, the see of Canterbury was kept vacant for five years. These and other malpractices were in contravention of the king's coronation promise:

'First I make the holy church of God free so that I will neither sell it nor place it to farm, nor, on the death of an archbishop, bishop, or abbot, will I take anything from the domain of the church or from its tenants until a successor has been instituted to it.'

Henry I's only legitimate son William was lost at sea in 1120 (the king had over twenty illegitimate children). His daughter Matilda (or Maud) had married Henry V of Germany in 1114 who died in 1125. Three years later she married Geoffrey Plantagenet of Anjou. Henry had exacted an oath from the barons that they would accept her as heir to the crown, but the idea of a queen-regnant was strange and distasteful. Had she been a more amiable person her succession might have proved practicable, but she displayed to excess some of the less attractive Norman characteristics; her haughtiness and arrogance made enemies wherever she went; in her later years she also carried to excess her religiosity. Two alternative candidates were available; they were the brothers Theobald and Stephen of Blois, Henry I's nephews. Stephen acted more resolutely than he was ever to act again; like his uncle before him, he at once went to Winchester to make sure of the treasury; he was supported by his younger brother, Henry, Bishop of Winchester, by the archbishops and other bishops. He was crowned in December 1135, three weeks after Henry's death. As he had spent his life between Normandy and England, where he had great estates, he was well-known and well-liked for he had not inherited the hard Norman character of his ancestors. His comparative mildness of temperament proved a disadvantage in a tough world. The barons asserted their independence; they strengthened their castles and defied the law. There was the further complication of the attempts of the Empress Matilda to win the throne. The course of events during what is called 'the Anarchy' is not our concern. The upshot was that by the treaty of Wallingford in 1153 it was agreed that Stephen should remain king but that Matilda's son Henry would succeed him. Stephen died a year later and Henry II was crowned on the 19th December 1154; he was already the ruler of Normandy, Anjou and Aquitaine.

Anselm's successor was the Norman Ralph d'Escures. His belated appointment was notable as being a free election by the clergy and Council; in this Henry lived up to his promises, even giving way when his own choice was not accepted. It was a good appointment. Ralph had been a friend of Anselm and also of Gundulph whom he had succeeded as Bishop of Rochester. He was enthroned at Canterbury on the 17th May 1114; he was unable through illness to go to Rome to receive the pallium, so the pope, Paschal II, sent it by Anselm of St. Sabas, a nephew of the great Anselm. The appointment of a new bishop for St. David's raised the problem of the relations between the church in Wales and Canterbury. The king, who spoke of Wales as 'Britain', insisted on the bishop-elect taking an oath of obedience to the Archbishop; so the Church in Wales came under the jurisdiction of Canterbury. A far more contentious matter was re-opened when Thurston (a Norman) was chosen to succeed Archbishop Thomas at York in 1114; he was a good choice, an ascetic and a founder of religious houses. He refused to give obedience to the Archbishop of Canterbury even when ordered by the king to do so. The dispute continued when William de Corbeil succeeded Ralph at Canterbury in 1123. They took the matter to Rome and three successive popes tried in vain to get the disputants to come to an agreement. Legates to England also failed. Eventually Pope Honorius II (1124–30) by-passed the problem by appointing William his *legatus natus*[1] for England and Scotland; this gave him authority over all other bishops. This precedent was followed in later years and it became customary for the Archbishop of Canterbury to be *legatus natus* of the pope. We may feel that this scurrying to and fro Rome by the archbishops was a profitless business, but in feudal times the idea of who was over whom was dominant. The three archbishops concerned were worthy bishops and well aware of their duties to their dioceses.

It has already been noted how, soon after the Conquest, Norman master builders (architects as we should call them) and masons were brought over to England to build cathedrals, abbeys and churches in what is known as the Anglo-Norman Romanesque style. This work rapidly expanded during the twelfth century from Durham in the north to Chichester in the south, from Norwich in the east to Hereford in the

[1] A legate is the pope's personal representative. The *legatus a latere* (from the pontiff's side) was sent for a particular purpose, such as settling a dispute, and had authority to make decisions in the pope's name. His authority ended with his mission. A *legatus natus* gave an archbishop full jurisdiction in his country over all other bishops; he could not make decisions in the pope's name.

west. Clearly there must have been available a host of Anglo-Saxons with the necessary skill in working stone and wood for such vast undertakings to be achieved. There were certainly not enough Normans for the work; the master builders from Normandy and France would be responsible for the plans for the more important buildings and for supervising their erection, and would have some of their own masons and craftsmen under them, but they must have needed local labour and the Anglo-Saxons were receptive of ideas, even if coming from their conquerors, and they quickly learned the new techniques and styles. We can all see what was accomplished, for none of us lives very far from an ancient church. Few are just as they were built in the post-Conquest generations; they have been altered, partly rebuilt, enlarged but much of the old work is still there. This truly astonishing achievement is not always appreciated.

There was also a parallel and vigorous expansion of monasticism. Cardinal Newman once labelled the years before the thirteenth century as the Benedictine Age. Monastic life had hitherto been based on the Rule of St. Benedict; it was not always followed closely but it provided the framework and the ideal. Some monasteries were influenced by the Cluny reforms, but most were content to continue in the old ways, each monastery being an independent community. The twelfth century saw the rise of new Orders. The Cistercians (white monks) were the first to arrive in England. They derived from Cîteaux (in Burgundy, fifty miles north of Cluny) where the Benedictine rule was strictly observed. Its most famous abbot was St. Bernard (*d.* 1153), a Doctor of the Church. A small community was established at Waverley in Surrey in 1128, to be followed by the more famous Rievaulx in 1132, and, in the same year, Fountains was founded by some monks from York. Rievaulx owed its establishment to St. Bernard of Clairvaux which was a daughter house of Cîteaux (hence Cistercian), one of the creators of which was St. Stephen Harding who had been educated at Sherborne.

Some forty houses were founded in England in that century. Their spread north of the Trent helped to strengthen religious life in a region that had not yet fully recovered from the Conqueror's harrying. The Cistercians looked for seclusion from the world and a simpler monastic life; manual labour was an essential part of that life and they attached to them *conversi* or lay brothers for the rougher agricultural work. They transformed the wild country in which they chose to settle into flourishing farmland and sheep-walks. They had a corporate form of constitution that linked their monasteries together with regular chapters and visitations.

A new body of regular canons, the Premonstratensians or Norbertines, the white canons, was established in 1120 at Premonté near Laon; the purpose was to combine monastic with apostolic or missionary work. Their first house was founded in England in 1143 at Newhouse in Lincolnshire; ten years later came Welbeck in Nottinghamshire. By the end of the thirteenth century there were thirty houses.

Only one new Order was of English origin, the Gilbertine canons, established by Gilbert, a secular priest at Sempringham in Lincolnshire about 1130. This began as a community of nuns with canons to direct them; this kind of 'double' monastery was an innovation that proved acceptable; by the end of the thirteenth century there were twenty-three such foundations.

The Augustinian, Austin or black, canons were established first in Italy in the late eleventh century as a movement towards the reform of the secular clergy by substituting communities of priests living under a rule of St. Augustine, a less rigorous one than that of St. Benedict; in later years many communities gave up parochial work and were, in effect, monks. A hundred and seventy houses were in existence in England by 1400.

The Carthusians were derived from the Grande Chartreuse (Charterhouse) near Grenoble; the strictness of their enclosed life, almost eremetical, could attract only those of deep religious conviction. Only two houses were established in England before 1300; they were both in Somerset, one at Hinton and the other at Witham, which was founded by Henry II as part of his penance.[1] The London Charterhouse was not founded until 1371.

There were nine nunneries, mostly in Wessex, at the time of the Conquest; their numbers increased rapidly after that and by 1300 there were about a hundred and fifty houses in England mostly Benedictine or Cistercian.

With such an upsurge of monasticism it was inevitable that sooner or later the relations between bishops and monks would have to be regulated. Some monasteries claimed that they were not subject to episcopal visitations and control and, before the Conquest, some maintained their freedom. There were many appeals to Rome from bishops and abbots and at first the popes were chary of granting complete exemption. Where a monastery was a royal foundation such as Battle, the bishop's authority was restricted. The process of winning exemption was a gradual one. By the end of the thirteenth century there were only seven exempt abbeys; four of these, Battle, St. Alban's, Bury St. Edmund's and Westminster were royal grants. The other three, St. Augustine's (Canterbury), Evesham, and Malmesbury were very old foundations.

It has been estimated that in the thirteenth century there were about 11,000 monks and some 7,000 nuns in a population of up to three millions.

If we keep in mind the vast amount of church building and, at the same time, the numerous new monastic and religious foundations during the two centuries following the Conquest, we cannot but be impressed by the religious fervour that inspired this expansion. The religious map, as we may call it, had been redrawn.

[1] See below p. 114.

CHAPTER 10

Becket

WE have now reached a pivotal period in the history of the Church. We have seen how the popes steadily increased their influence and power. The reign of Innocent III (1198–1216) marked a climax in both. There were many signs of the increasing influence of the papacy. The sending of legates to settle disputes became more and more frequent. Connected with this was the codification of canon law. Gratian, a Bologna monk, completed his *Decretium* about 1140 in which he harmonised the varying texts of the canons and so facilitated systematic study. Bologna became the centre for the teaching of canon law and clerics of many countries found their way there. One may note too the number of ecumenical councils held. Lateran I in 1123 was the first to be held since 870, though the popes called local synods and councils away from Rome. This council was followed by three others at the Lateran (the palace of the popes) in 1139, 1179 and 1215. There were two at Lyons, 1245 and 1274, and one at Vienne in 1311. This increased activity inevitably led to the need for greater financial support for the papacy. This ultimately resulted in many abuses until it became impossible to get anything done except by the payment of large fees and by bribery.

A new and revolutionary factor entered the Christian community with the coming of the friars during the thirteenth century. It is not necessary here to recount the inspiring story of the life of St. Francis of Assisi (1181–1226). He formed a company dedicated to a life of poverty and simplicity, moving freely among men as Christ did, preaching the Gospel wherever they could find hearers. While completely obedient to the Church and accepting its teaching without question, they brought new urgency to the saving of souls. It was inevitable that, as with most human institutions, the first fervour cooled; dissensions arose and there were breaks-away from the original conception. One of the great paradoxes is the contrast between the life and practice of St. Francis and his companions and the vast basilica that commemorates him at Assisi.

The grey friars arrived in England in September 1224, two years before the saint's death. Their leader was Fra Agnello of Pisa who had been chosen by Francis himself; he had eight companions with him of whom three were of English birth. Their first settlements were at Canterbury, London and Oxford. Twelve more houses were founded by 1230 and twenty more in the next decade. The appeal of the friars was to ordinary folk; as preachers and confessors they were welcomed widely for they breathed fresh air into the life of the church. By papal dispensation they were allowed to preach where they would and to hear confessions; this led to many disputes with the bishops and the parish clergy who felt that their authority was being undermined by these mendicant friars.

A second order of friars was founded by St. Dominic (1170–1221); their name 'Order of Preachers' indicates their primary purpose. They originally set out to combat heresy; they lived a quasi-monastic life in which the study of theology and apologetics was basic. Here they were unlike the Franciscans who, in their early years, set little value on learning. The Dominicans, the black friars, came to England in 1221 and within forty years had established as many houses.

The Carmelite friars originated on the slopes of Mount Carmel as eremeticals, but they later developed on lines similar to those of the Dominicans. Their earliest houses in England were established by the middle of the thirteenth century in Norfolk, Kent and Northumberland; eventually there were about forty friaries; they were the white friars.

A fourth order of friars were the hermits of St. Augustine, or Austin Friars (not to be confused with the Austin Canons). Like the Carmelites, they were nearer the Dominicans than the Friars Minor. They too came to England in the middle of the thirteenth century; they had about thirty houses in all.

The above were 'the ordres foure' to which Chaucer referred in the Prologue to *The Canterbury Tales*. In addition to these there were several other orders of friars, among them the Friars of the Cross (Crutched Friars), Friars of the Sack, and the Pied Friars, but none of these made a deep impression on the religious life of the country.

The twelfth–thirteenth centuries were notable not only for the increase in the prestige of the papacy, the resurgance of monasticism, and the coming of the friars, but also for a renaissance of thought and learning comparable with that of the period denominated The Renaissance. We can do little more here than indicate some of the landmarks. Reference has already been made to Bologna as the nursery of the study of canon law; to it flocked men of all countries and the riotous and often scandalous behaviour of these footloose students bears comparison with that of our own days. It was the period of the wandering scholar in search of the master who best suited his needs. Out of this demand for knowledge grew the universities. Paris became the magnet for the student of theology, while Montpellier was famed as a medical school. Oxford was established about 1170 and Cambridge some forty years later. A few outstanding names may be mentioned. It was the period of Peter Abelard (1079–1142), and of Peter the Lombard (1100–60) whose *Sentences* became the accepted text-book for many years. In the thirteenth century the Dominicans were distinguished by two great theologians; Albert the Great and his more famous pupil St. Thomas Aquinas (d. 1276). The Franciscans gave up their distrust of learning and in the Englishman, Alexander of Hales (d. 1245), and in St. Bonaventura (d. 1274), had a leading place in theological studies. Another Franciscan of England, Robert Grosseteste, Bishop of Lincoln (d. 1253) was a scholar of note though the name of his pupil Roger Bacon (d. 1292) is better known. The name of a Scot, John Duns Scotus (d. 1308), must end this catalogue, for it can be little more in our space. He was important as the first to make a breach in scholasticism — that is the system of which Aquinas was the dominant mind which tried to bring human reason and divine revelation into harmony. In its heyday this teaching was a powerful intellectual stimula but it became too formalized.

The free movement of teachers and scholars can be illustrated by noting where English scholars and clerics were to be found. Nicholas Breakspear became Pope Adrian IV in 1154; Robert of Melun, Adam du Petit Pont and Alexander Neckam were teaching in Paris; Robert Pulleyn was papal chancellor; Herbert became Archbishop of Compsa, Richard of Syracuse and Walter of Palermo, while John of Salisbury, the companion of St. Thomas Becket, became Bishop of Chartres. There was no problem of intercourse as they all spoke Latin. This mingling of men from various countries serves to point to the absence of any feeling of nationalism; this was to be a later growth and was to prove inimical to the papacy. During the Middle Ages, the Church was the great unifying factor in western civilisation; under its shelter men of all countries could come together.

It was one of the paradoxes of the times that the expansion of monasticism in England came during the anarchy of Stephen's reign (1135–54), but the Church also strengthened its position owing to the precarious position of the king. He could not risk antagonising the bishops and he did not, in his early years, force his proposals for new appointments. There was, however, an interval of just over two years between the death of Archbishop William of Canterbury and the appointment of his successor. Stephen's brother, Henry, Bishop of Winchester, hoped to be made archbishop. He was a man of greater strength of character than his brother, but he was overbearing, yet at the same time carried out his episcopal duties efficiently. His succession to Canterbury was probably prevented by the papal legate, Alberic of Ostia, who held a legatine synod in England. This would explain the choice of Theobald of Bec who became Archbishop in January 1139. Henry of Winchester was consoled by being appointed *legatus natus* by Innocent II, a position that put him above the archbishops. Theobald's authority was thus much diminished but he took the situation calmly; he knew that with the death of the reigning pope, the appointment would lapse, and that happened in 1143, after which Theobald himself was *lagatus natus*. Negotiations with Rome were hampered by the mortality of the popes; there were five of them during the nineteen years of Stephen's reign. The coming of a new pope meant that any cause before his predecessor had to be opened afresh thus entailing more expense.

The story of St. William of York is typical of how church problems were handled. Archbishop Thurston of York died early in 1140. The king nominated his nephew William Fitzherbert, treasurer of York to the vacant see. The choice was unexceptional but it roused the antagonism of the Cistercians of Rievaulx. Here it should be noted how within a decade this Order had achieved a prominent and influential position in the church especially in the north. They objected to William on the grounds of simony and unchastity and because he had been appointed by the direct action of the king. William was inducted by Henry of Winchester as legate thus putting aside the authority of Theobald. The Cistercians sent a deputation to Rome; one member was Ailred whose name is linked with Rievaulx of which he became abbot in 1147. St. Bernard gave his powerful support to them. The case was postponed for a year for consultations and this time the abbots of Rievaulx and

Fountains both went to Rome. There were further delays as two popes died in quick succession and then Eugenius III (1145–53), himself a Cistercian, deposed William Fitz-herbert, and in 1147, the abbot of Fountains, Henry Murdac, was elected Archbishop of York; he was consecrated by the pope and King Stephen confirmed the appointment. Murdac died in 1153, in the same year as the pope and St. Bernard; by then the storm had blown itself out; William went to Rome and the new pope, Anastasius IV, granted his petition to be restored to York. He died within a few months of his arrival in York; rumour said his archdeacon had poisoned him. Many miracles took place at the tomb of Archbishop William and for this reason he was canonised by Honorius III in 1227. It is a strange story but medieval in its character.

Theobald was the third Archbishop of Canterbury to come from Bec; he and Lanfranc and Anselm were among the greatest of the archbishops. He was a man of deep piety that had been fostered under the Rule of St. Benedict; he was mild-tempered and long-suffering but was firm where the welfare of the Church was in question. As a scholar he gathered round him young men who sought knowledge, and he made Canterbury a school for the study of canon and civil law. His secretary was John of Salisbury who had served in the papal curia; he did much to regulate the working of the ecclesiastical courts. Theobald was a loyal supporter of Stephen but he did not hesitate to oppose him when he doubted the wisdom of the king's policy. The archbishop's work was hampered in his early years by the over-riding authority of Henry of Winchester as legate. When Henry lost his legateship in 1143, he still tried through his influence over his brother to make things difficult for Theobald, and it was probably at his suggestion that Stephen refused the archbishop permission to attend the papal council at Reims in 1148. He, however, evaded the watch on the ports and crossed to Normandy in a fishing-boat; with him was Thomas Becket, a member of his household who had already been his companion to Rome in 1143. The king and the archbishop were reconciled a year later and Theobald returned to Canterbury where he was to have disputes with the monks of both St. Augustine's and Christ Church; with papal support he was able to resolve the differences. In 1152 Stephen held a great council at which he asked the barons to swear fealty to his son Eustace as his successor, but Theobald refused to crown him; he was put under house arrest but escaped and once more went into exile. The death of Eustace in 1153 put an end to Stephen's hopes; once more he was reconciled to Theobald who played an important part in the treaty by which Stephen recognised Henry Plantagenet as his successor.

Theobald crowned Henry II on the 19th December 1154; the new king accepted the archbishop's suggestion that Thomas Becket should be made chancellor of England. Theobald's last years were spent quietly in carrying out his duties as archbishop. He died on the 18th April 1161. One of his last wishes was that Thomas Becket should be his successor at Canterbury.

Thomas Becket, also known as Thomas of London, was born on the 21st December 1118. Both his parents were Norman and came from the Bec region.[1] The father prospered as a merchant and became portreeve (mayor) of London. Thomas was sent to school at Merton, Surrey, a priory of the Austin Canons. Although he had not the instincts of a scholar, he showed a quick intelligence. There was another kind of training that proved important. A friend of the family sometimes took the youth into the country and initiated him into the field sports of the day. He proved a ready pupil and became an expert with horse, hawk and hound. After Merton, Gilbert Becket sent his son to Paris for further studies; he was there for three or four years, but, about the year 1140, his father's affairs declined and the son had to begin a career. He was recommended to Archbishop Theobald who took him into his household. The Bec association probably played its part.

---

[1] Jean Anouilh's play *Becket* makes him out to be a Saxon with a Saracen mother! He was pure Norman.

Theobald soon recognised Thomas's outstanding abilities
and he sent him to Bologna and Auxerre to study canon law.
On his return he was entrusted with several missions, including some to Rome. Thomas became archdeacon of
Canterbury in 1154 when he was ordained deacon. A year
later he became chancellor.

The king was then twenty-one years old and his chancellor
thirty-seven. Together they made a striking contrast. The
king was thick-set, even squat; he was red-headed and
indifferent to how he dressed. Thomas was tall and hand-
some, black-haired and hook-nosed and always richly
dressed. They were a contrast too in temperament. The
king was a man of violent, even terrifying temper, who,
at times lost all control of himself. His chancellor was
always master of himself. They had, however, much in
common. They both had a passion for the chase. Henry was
a statesman with clear objectives; he was determined to
establish law and order in a country that was almost lawless.
He was fully supported by his chancellor whose administrative gifts were what the king needed and appreciated.
In one respect, the two were completely apart. The king
was of loose morals on a royal scale. Thomas, as his contemporaries testified, was a man of irreproachable life.

A year after the death of Theobald, the chancellor became
Archbishop of Canterbury, an office he accepted with
reluctance; indeed, he went so far as to warn the king that
they might clash on church affairs. Henry had it in mind
to have a chancellor-archbishop who would support him.
Thomas, however, abruptly resigned the chancellorship
to concentrate on his new responsibilities. He became the
total churchman; he led a rigorous life of prayer, meditation
and penance. He was ordained priest and consecrated
archbishop on the 3rd June 1162, the Sunday after Whitsun.
He decreed that this Sunday should be observed in England
as the Feast of the Holy Trinity, a feast that did not become
universal until 1334.

His first step was to get back church lands that had been
alienated in the anarchy. His chief opponents were the

brothers Ranulf and Robert de Broc. Thomas demanded the immediate return of lands they had occupied unlawfully. This action annoyed the king; the de Brocs were his vassals and he should have been consulted. A far more serious problem was illustrated by the case of a canon of Bedford who had been acquitted in the church court of homicide. The sheriff was not satisfied and reopened the case in his own court. The king approved of his action, but the archbishop refused to allow a clerk to be tried in a civil court. Herein lies one of the reasons for the clash between Henry and Thomas. A clerk was anyone in orders, even one who had received only the tonsure, and, under canon law, he could be tried only in a church court which could not inflict the death penalty even for murder. This led to considerable abuse. Many a rogue evaded serious penalties on the plea of being a clerk; to be able to read was regarded as sufficient evidence of his status. The king wanted to modify the system but he found a determined opponent in the archbishop, who, it will be recalled, had spent several years studying canon law.

In May 1163, Thomas attended, with the king's consent, the council at Tours called by Pope Alexander III; on his return he was welcomed by the king but within a few months they had their first serious dispute. The king claimed that his courts should pass sentence on criminous clerks who had been found guilty in the church court. Thomas persuaded the bishops to resist this demand, and when the king went further and insisted that they should swear to obey the established customs of the country, they did so with the reservation 'saving our order.' This phrase infuriated the king who turned his wrath on the archbishop, deprived him of lands granted to him as chancellor and removed his eldest son Henry from the archbishop's household where the boy was being brought up.

It was after this council that dissensions began to appear among the bishops. Archbishop Roger of York was a persistent opponent. A more formidable critic was Gilbert Foliot who had been made Bishop of London at Thomas's suggestion. He was convinced that the policy of meeting the king head-on was wrong. Thomas appealed to the pope. Alexander III, one of the better popes, was in a difficult position. He had been driven out of Rome by the Emperor Frederick Barbarossa who had set up his anti-pope. Alexander had found refuge at Sens, south of Paris, and he relied on the support of the kings of France and England, with neither of whom could he afford to quarrel, but he was not subservient and showed skill in safeguarding the rights of the Church. He came to like and respect Thomas and did all he could to curb the archbishop's tendency to carry things to the extreme. In face of the pope's inability to take drastic action, and of the growing opposition of the bishops, Thomas seems to have felt unsure of himself. He met the king at Woodstock and gave his assent to Henry's wishes. Later the king held a council at Clarendon in order to get Thomas to make his agreement public. Some of the bishops were reluctant to assent to Henry's demands, and, for a time, it looked as though Thomas would withdraw his consent, but suddenly he gave way and publicly repeated his promise to observe the ancient customs. The king was still not satisfied; he wanted the agreement in black and white. The Constitutions of Clarendon were the result; these codified the relations between the king and the church; the provisions included one by which clerks who had been convicted in a church court should no longer be protected, but be liable to civil penalties. It is indeed surprising that the archbishop accepted this and other provisions; he declared that he did so but evaded putting his seal to the document. His doubts grew as he rode back to Canterbury, and he came to regret deeply that he had given way; perhaps it was simply some lingering thought of his old friendship with the king. He imposed severe penancies on himself until the pope absolved him though he declared that the provisions were contrary to canon law — a fact of which Thomas was well aware.

The king knew of the archbishop's consultations with the pope and the reason for them; Thomas had some bitter

critics such as Gilbert Foliot and Archbishop Roger who
prejudiced the king against him. Henry showed the worst
side of his character in the sequel. Their next confrontation
was at a council held at Northampton in October 1164.
Thomas was summoned to answer a suit brought against
him about some church lands; it was a small matter in
itself and normally would have been dealt with by negotia-
tion. The case was, in fact, not dealt with, nor did the
question of the Constitutions arise. The conflict between
king and archbishop was part of the larger problem that
was troubling the Catholic world, namely the relations
between Church and State. It is in this context that we
should see this local dispute.

The king's first act was purely vindictive; he demanded
that the archbishop should at once submit a full account
of the financial proceedings as chancellor. Thomas rightly
objected that this was an unreasonable demand at such
short notice. He called the bishops together and forbade
them to pass judgment on him. At the final session he entered
with his archiepiscopal cross before him, and, after a stormy
scene, he strode out amid cries of 'Traitor!' He knew now
that the king was bent on his destruction. So that night,
with three companions, he slipped out of Northampton,
and, by devious routes, made his way down to Sandwich
and crossed the Channel. He found refuge in St. Omer, and
from there he sent messengers to King Louis and to the pope.
Henry had already sent his own envoys to Alexander with
Gilbert Foliot as their spokesman. He was rebuked by the
pope for his intemperate attack on the archbishop. He would
not judge the issue until his legates had been to England.
Later Thomas himself went to see the pope who reassured
him as far as he could. The archbishop withdrew to the
Cistercian Abbey of Pontigny where he led a rigorous life
of self-mortification.

Henry was not content with having driven Thomas out of
the country; he forced his sisters and dependents to follow
him. King Louis attempted to reconcile the two men but
in vain. Meanwhile the pope had been able to return to

Rome and thus had greater freedom of action. He made Thomas his personal legate to strengthen his position. It was not until 1169 that Louis at last got the two antagonists to meet at Montmirail, but nothing came of it. Thomas insisted on qualifying any proposal with the words 'saving the honour of God and my order.' This proviso enraged the king. They met again some months later and it looked as though agreement would be reached, but Henry refused to give the kiss of peace, which, with its sacred association with the Mass, was the most solemn of pledges.

In the summer of 1170, the king complicated matters by deciding to have his eldest son Henry crowned king in order to ensure a smooth succession. It had always been the prerogative of the Archbishop of Canterbury to crown the king, but, as Thomas was in exile, Henry ordered Roger of York to perform the ceremony. He was supported by the Bishops of London (Gilbert Foliot) and of Salisbury. The pope at once suspended Roger as archbishop and Thomas excommunicated the two bishops. It proved impossible to get these decrees published in England, so they were held in obeyance.

Then came a surprising development. Henry and Thomas met again and, to the astonishment of everyone, the two spent several hours together in friendly talk. There is no record of what passed between them except that the king was willing for Thomas to return to England. Henry was beset by many troubles at this time and he may have wished to get this maddening dispute out of the way. Thomas sent off a messenger to deliver to the three prelates, York, London, and Salisbury, the decrees against them; they at once crossed the Channel to protest to the king. The archbishop landed at Sandwich on 1st December. A small group of knights tried to prevent him from landing but the great gathering of ordinary folk made that impossible. All the way to Canterbury, the people greeted with joy the return of their archbishop. His first journey from Canterbury was to Woodstock to do homage to the fifteen-year old king, but Thomas's enemies had convinced the young king that the archbishop would depose him, so he refused an audience, and Thomas returned to Canterbury. There he vigorously set to work to get his diocese in order and on Christmas day in the cathedral he excommunicated the de Brocs and other filchers of church lands.

Meanwhile the three prelates had put their grievances before the king; these lost nothing in the telling; their spokesman, Roger of York went so far as to accuse Thomas of plotting against the crown. At length Henry's terrible temper broke out and he cried, 'What cowards are round me that not one will free me of this low-born priest?'[1] Those who were used to such outbursts wisely waited until the king had calmed down, but, on this occasion four knights took him at his word; they were Reginald FitzUrse, William de Tracy, Hugh de Moreville and Richard le Breton. They rode to the coast and crossed to England. There is no need here to tell once more the tragic outcome of their journey.[2] They arrived at Canterbury Cathedral on the 29th December 1170. With the archbishop were John of Salisbury, Robert Merton, his confessor, William Fitz-Stephen, his chaplain and Edward Grim, a visiting monk. All four wrote accounts of the murder of which they were witnesses. Thomas Becket's last words were, 'For the name of Jesus and the defence of the Church, I am willing to die.'

The murder of an archbishop in his own cathedral sent a shock of horror throughout the Church. The grief shown by Henry II was sincere. He at once sent off an embassy to the pope to disclaim responsibility. The pope was under pressure from King Louis and the French bishops to lay an interdict[3] on Henry's lands; this was done for his continental possessions but not for England. The king's war in

[1] Or, 'This turbulent priest'; or, 'this upstart clerk.' The exact words used by Henry are not known; he spoke in Norman-French. The several accounts are in Latin and vary as not one of the writers was present on this occasion.

[2] The best narrative is still Dean Stanley's in his *Historical Memorial of Canterbury* (1875).

[3] An interdict meant the excommunication of a whole country or province. Churches were closed, but the ban was lifted on the greater feasts, and the last sacraments were allowed to the dying. The difficulties of enforcing an interdict, especially outside the towns, made the incidence variable.

Ireland postponed further action. Eventually he had to renounce customs detrimental to the Church, return all church lands, and send a contingent of knights to the Holy Land. It was not until 1174 that he himself made a pilgrimage to Canterbury and submitted to a scourging. His gifts were the beginning of a flow of offerings during the next three centuries. In 1179 Louis of France with Henry made the pilgrimage and gave a famous jewel, the *Regale*.[1]

Popular pressure was so widespread that the pope canonised Thomas of Canterbury on the 21st February 1173. His cult spread with an astonishing rapidity; churches were dedicated to him; Thomas became a favoured Christian name, and he was represented in sculpture, painted glass and in mosaics. In Syria an Order of St. Thomas was founded at Acre (Acon), and the saint's sister gave them the birthplace as their London home. His body was translated on the 7th July 1220 to a shrine behind the high altar at Canterbury, in the presence of Henry III, the papal legate and other high dignatories. The pilgrimage became a national devotion, though Chaucer's *Canterbury Pilgrims* does not suggest an atmosphere of piety.

> From every shire's end
> Of England, to Canterbury they wend,
> The holy, blissful martyr for to seek.

For a time after Becket's death, Henry was careful not to antagonise the bishops, but after he had been reconciled on the 21st May 1172 at Avranches, he resumed his earlier policy. There were seven sees vacant in 1173 and these were filled by safe men. Henry followed his predecessors' practice of allowing sees to remain vacant for two or three years so as to enjoy the revenues. The pope had not required at Avranches a specific undertaking in the matter of criminous clerks; it may have been assumed that the promise not to follow customs detrimental to the church was sufficient. In practice, various ways round were used and malefactors

---

[1] After the destruction of the shrine in 1538, Henry VIII wore the *Regale* as a ring.

did not find it easy to prove their clergy. On one point the pope was successful; Henry promised not to forbid appeals being made to Rome, and, as a consequence, the number of such appeals increased.

The Thirteenth Century

THE period from the death of Henry II to that of Edward I, 1189–1307, was formative in our political and constitutional history. Richard I (1189–99) had no interest in England where he spent only six months of his reign; to him it was little more than a source of money, first for his wars to maintain the Angevin empire, which covered more than half western France, and secondly for the Third Crusade, and finally for his enormous ransom of over £100,000 in the values of that day. Although Archbishop Baldwin preached the Crusade there was little response in England except from individual knights. The archbishop himself went on the Crusade and died in the Holy Land in 1190. Hubert Walter, Bishop of Salisbury, also followed the king; he returned in 1193 and was one of the commissioners who had the onerous task of collecting the ransom for the imprisoned king. By royal mandate he was elected Archbishop of Canterbury and was enthroned in November 1193. During Richard's absence the country had been governed by William Langchamp, Bishop of Ely and chancellor. His unscrupulous and harsh administration made him widely hated and there was rejoicing at his death in 1197. Hubert Walter was justiciar, but in 1198 Pope Innocent III decreed that clerics must not be secular officials; Hubert

Walter resigned, but, he defied the pope's ruling by becoming King John's chancellor in 1199. For the first decade
of the reign Hubert Walter exercised some restraining
influence over John, a man endowed with the Plantagenet
acuteness of intellect but also with the same instability of
temper and the same ruthlessness both carried to the extreme. Hubert Walter was a responsible statesman and
would have made a better king than John. As Archbishop
of Canterbury he was misplaced. He died in 1205.

Meanwhile the barons and knights were getting restive;
they were war-weary and resented the constant demands
on their services and the extortionate taxes. The unexplained
disappearance in 1203 of John's nephew Arthur of Brittany
and, at that date, John's heir, and the loss of Normandy[1]
in the following year robbed the king of any prestige he
still enjoyed. The severing of the ties between Normandy
and England forced the barons to decide to which country
they would belong; those who had great estates in Normandy
had few hesitations, but most decided that England was their
home. This was another step towards the rapidly developing
idea of Englishry.

When Hubert Walter died, the king went to Canterbury
to ensure that his nominee John de Gray, Bishop of Norwich,
was elected, but the monks of Christ Church were not
compliant and they hastily chose their sub-prior Richard.
Then followed the long process of appeals and counter-
appeals to the pope, the formidable Innocent III. Eventually
he put aside all proposals and himself consecrated his old
friend Cardinal Stephen Langton[2] on the 12th July 1207.
He was an Englishman, a noted scholar and theologian. It
is interesting to note that within a few years of the loss of
Normandy, Canterbury had a native archbishop. John
refused to confirm the appointment and for the next six
years Langton lived for the most part at Pontigny, the

[1] The Channel Islands are all that remain to the British Crown of the Duchy
of Normandy; they are independent of Westminster.
[2] It is probably to him that we owe the 'Golden Sequence', *Veni, sancte
spiritus*.

Cistercian monastery that had sheltered St. Thomas Becket a generation earlier. Meanwhile the king seized the revenues of Canterbury and expelled the monks who went into exile. Not long before this the Archbishop of York, Geoffrey Plantagenet, a natural son of Henry II, had resisted the exhorbitant demands on the clergy and had forbidden them to pay the tax. So he too had to leave the country and his revenues were also seized. This meant that for some years England was without an archbishop.

This outrageous conduct of John which amounted to an attack on the Church, led Pope Innocent to place an interdict on England in March 1208. One immediate result was that four bishops chose to go into exile; at that time there were three vacant sees and two bishops died shortly after the imposition of the interdict. England was thus without an effective hierarchy for six years. The temporalities of all these sees were taken over by the king. Nor did the monasteries escape the royal anger; there had earlier been a dispute with the Cistercians who refused to pay the ruinous tax demanded of them. This quarrel was patched up by Hubert Walter shortly before his death, and John promised to found an abbey in recompense. This he did at Beaulieu in Hampshire and some monks were brought from Cîteaux itself to establish the community. John showed no signs of making further amends when the quarrel over Canterbury broke out. Indeed some of the poorer monasteries were ruined and the great abbeys had to find enormous sums to satisfy the king.

As John remained obdurate and continued to vex the Church, he was excommunicated by Pope Innocent in November 1209. This was a far more serious matter than the interdict for it isolated the king, and those who associated with him were liable to papal penalties. For four years he tried by diplomatic means to circumvent the consequences of his excommunication and the Church had to bear the brunt of his anger. Then he seemed to repent for, at the end of 1214, he suddenly granted the church a charter of liberty, but the dispute had gone too far for that to succeed in separating the bishops from the barons. The pope threatened to announce his deposition. Eventually John had to give in; he agreed to confirm Langton as archbishop, to allow the exiled clergy to return, and to recompense the Church for its losses. The papal legate Pandulf arrived in England and John resigned England and Ireland to the pope and received them back under an oath of fealty and homage to Rome, an act of subservience his predeccessors had refused to make.

This is not the place to record the events that led to the signing of Magna Carta on 15th June 1215 at Runnymede. Stephen Langton, supported by the bishops, played an important part in the settlement between the king and the barons. It is said that the archbishop produced the coronation charter of Henry I as an indication of the policy to be followed. What resulted was not a revolutionary document but a restatement of what were believed to be the customs of the country. The Carta was framed within the feudal system and was not a declaration of rights in the sense in which we think of them; it was not directly concerned with the welfare of ordinary folk. Later generations put interpretations on the Carta that were not valid, but the 'myth of Magna Carta', as it has been called, was more powerful in the struggle for the liberties of the subject than the actual terms to which John was forced to submit.

The first clause of the Carta is important for the history of the Church. It refers to the ecclesiastical charter that had not satisfied the bishops. It undertook,

'that the Church of England be free,[1] and have her rights intact, and her liberties unimpaired; and so we will it to be observed, which appears from the fact that freedom of elections which is considered to be most important and more necessary for the Church of England, we have by our uninfluenced and spontaneous will, before discord had arisen between us and our barons, granted and

[1] St. Thomas More quoted this at his trial (*ut ecclesia Anglicana libera sit*). The fact that he did so and that his Judges could take the point, suggests that Magna Carta was not so forgotten during Tudor Times as some historians have stated.

confirmed by our charter, and have secured its confirmation by the lord Pope Innocent III, which we shall observe and also will that it be observed in good faith by our heirs for ever.'

The last clause of the Carta (No. 63) reaffirms the first clause.

'Wherefore we will and firmly command that the English Church be free.'

These clauses went some way to prevent the intrusion of unsuitable royal nominees, but it never became a reality, less so to-day than ever before.

Then followed an occurrence that is puzzling. John appealed to Pope Innocent as his overlord; he annulled the Carta and suspended Stephen Langton from office; in addition the leaders of the opposition to John were excommunicated and an interdict was placed on London whose Mayor had been active in support of the barons. This exercise of the pope's new relationship with England put the archbishops and bishops in a dilemma — if they obeyed the pope they would betray the Carta and all that it meant. Stephen Langton at once set out for Rome to justify his policy, but the pope refused to allow him to return to England. The death of Innocent in July 1516 and of John three months later entirely changed the situation and the archbishop was able to return to England in May 1218 with his authority fully restored. It is idle to speculate what might have happened had pope and king lived longer.

Henry III was only nine years old when he ascended the throne. In the absence of the archbishop, Peter des Roches, Bishop of Winchester, crowned the boy at Gloucester on the 26th October 1216; as the royal regalia were not available, a circlet belonging to his mother was used. On instructions from Pope Honorius III, Langton, on his return, re-crowned Henry on Whit Sunday 1220 in Westminster Abbey. It may have been then that the boy-king chose St. Edward the Confessor as his patron saint. At the

time of the coronation, the archbishop was able to announce
the canonisation of St. Hugh of Lincoln, and, on the 7th
of July he directed the transfer of the body of St. Thomas
Becket to its new shrine in Canterbury Cathedral.

It is worthwhile retracing our steps to say something of
St. Hugh of Lincoln. He was a Burgundian who, as a youth,
found his way to the Grande Chartreuse. During his seventeen years there his fame for holiness of life spread widely.
Henry II's Carthusian monastery at Witham had not
prospered and the king asked that Hugh should be allowed
to come to England to take charge. Hugh did not welcome
such a call, but under obedience to the chapter he accepted
the invitation. The new prior found that the monastery
had not made an effective beginning; this was partly the
king's fault as he only half-heartedly provided the necessary
money and sometimes seemed to forget that buildings had
to be paid for. Hugh did not shrink from chiding the king
for his shortcomings, an action that called for courage
when the violence of Henry's temper is kept in mind. Thus
Hugh pointed out the scandal of leaving the see of Lincoln
vacant for nearly eighteen years save for one brief period.
One might say that the king got his own back by having
Hugh nominated to be Bishop of Lincoln; he tried to avoid
it but again the chapter of the Grande Chartreuse ordered
him to obey. At Lincoln he proved to be a truly pastoral
bishop particularly by his frequent preaching and by the
instruction he gave to the young. The cathedral was sadly
dilapidated when he went there and it was under his direction that it was practically rebuilt. It was by his efforts too
that many Jews were protected during the savage pogrom
that broke out in England when the Third Crusade was
being preached. He resisted Richard I's demand for sub-
sidies from the clergy towards the cost of his wars in France,
nor did he shrink from rebuking the king himself. It is to
the credit of Richard that, like his father, he recognised the
essential holiness of the bishop. King John sent Hugh to
France on diplomatic business; he was able to visit the
Grande Chartreuse, Cluny and Cîteaux. On his return he

made a pilgrimage to the shrine of St. Thomas Becket; soon after he was taken ill at his house in the Old Temple (the future Lincoln's Inn), and died there on the 16th November 1200. There were present at his burial in Lincoln Cathedral the kings of England and Scotland, a prince from Wales, Stephen Langton and most of the bishops and abbots.

Soon after the translation of the relics of St. Thomas Becket in 1220, Stephen Langton went to Rome and gained from the pope three rulings: the Archbishop of York must not assume metropolitan dignity outside his own province; papal provision[1] should not be exercised twice for the same benefice, and, during his lifetime, there should be no papal legate in England. The first was a problem that proved endemic; we shall have to deal in more detail with the question of papal provisions. The third decision was of more immediate importance. Since 1211 the papal legate, Pandulf, had exercised supreme authority in the pope's name; he had negotiated between the king and the pope and had remained in England after the surrender; he filled up bishoprics and other benefices at his pleasure and made full use of his legatine powers. As a result of Langton's appeal to the pope, Pandulf left the country in 1221; a year later the pope consecrated him Bishop of Norwich; he did not visit his diocese but his body was brought to England and buried in the cathedral there after his death in 1226.

Stephen Langton called a synod in April 1222 and afterwards he issued what are known as his Constitutions which became binding on the ecclesiastical courts. These covered the many problems with which the church had been concerned since Anglo-Saxon times, such as celibacy of the clergy, pluralism, the care of property, the instruction of the people and so on. There was hardly anything that had not been said time and time again; this suggests that not much progress had been made in remedying long established defects.

With the return to normal conditions, Langton was able

[1] That is, the appointment to a benefice by the pope directly.

to devote more time to church affairs. He had always been a scholar as well as a priest and he wrote voluminously — commentaries and theological treatises. During the first twelve years of the new reign, he was a moderating influence in political affairs. He died at his manor of Slindon in Sussex on the 9th July 1228 and was buried in his cathedral.

Henry III reigned for fifty-six years, the longest reign before that of George III; it was a disturbed time of importance for constitutional reasons. The king was pious and devoted to the Church. At the beginning of his reign he had renewed his father's fealty to the pope to whose demands he eagerly submitted. Gregory IX (1227–41) and his successors were locked in conflict with the Emperor Frederick II (*stupor mundi*); more and more money was needed in this struggle and the unceasing demands on the papal vassal states became increasingly onerous on clergy and people. Henry enforced these demands as well as imposing heavy taxation for his own futile foreign entanglements as well as to meet his own extravagances. Here perhaps we can see the first signs of that anti-clerical (not anti-church) feeling in the country that was to prove such a disruptive element. Moreover the popes appointed (provided) more and more of their curial officials to English benefices.

Richard Grant of Wethershed was elected Archbishop of Canterbury and received the pallium in 1229. The election was free though the final decision lay with the pope. The new archbishop opposed the king's demand for an exceptional scutage[1] not only from the barons but from the clergy. Richard went to Rome to seek the direction of the pope and this and other questions, but he died in August 1231 on his way home. There was an interval of three years before a new archbishop was appointed. The first three nominated by the monks of Christ Church were unacceptable to the pope; they were in fact indifferent choices. At last, however, the monks found the right man; he was Edmund Rich, treasurer of Salisbury who had been a leading theologian at Oxford as well as a noted preacher.

[1] A tax paid in lieu of military service (shield-money).

He was consecrated on the 2nd April 1234. The condition of the country under Henry's spineless government gave cause for anxiety and the new archbishop joined with the barons in solemnly warning the king of the need for wiser counsellors than those he favoured. Chief among these was Peter des Roches, a Poitouvan, Bishop of Winchester, who had been justiciar in John's reign. He was more a warrior than a priest and did not hesitate to take an active part in military adventures. He was unscrupulous and amoral in his conduct, yet he built a number of churches including two Premonstratensian abbeys, a Dominican house and an Austin priory; the sources of his wealth were questionable. He died in 1238.

Edmund Rich presided at the king's ratification of the Carta in 1257. This was the high light of Henry's good intentions. His marriage to Eleanor of Provence the previous year was to prove a disaster politically; she gained considerable influence over her weak-willed husband and brought in a swarm of Savoyard relatives for whom she obtained lucrative positions. Thus among the beneficiaries was Peter d'Aigueblanche who became Bishop of Hereford and packed the chapter with his own relations from Savoy. He was a political bishop and was closely involved in the disputes between the king and the barons. This is but one example of how Henry ignored his promise of free elections. A more glaring instance was the favour he showed to his half-brother Aymer de Lusignan. When William Ralegh, Bishop of Winchester, died in 1250, the king ordered the chapter to elect Aymer. They did so reluctantly. Pope Innocent IV confirmed the appointment and gave the bishop-elect permission to receive the revenues before his consecration, which, for various reasons, military and political, did not take place until 1260 when Alexander IV consecrated him at Rome; Aymer died in his way back to England.

King Henry showed small respect for the Archbishop of Canterbury when he asked the pope to send a legate to England. Cardinal Otto arrived in 1237. He issued canons on the discipline of the clergy but also showed favour to the foreign holders of benefices. Edmund Rich's efforts to promote better relations between the king and the barons were hampered by the greater authority of the legate who was ignorant of the situation in England. The archbishop also had his troubles at Canterbury. Archbishop after archbishop had been at loggerheads with the monks of Christ Church; sometimes the dispute was over domestic problems, but that with Edmund Rich was more complicated and there seems to have been a disruptive spirit among some of the monks. He took the matter to Rome in 1237 and, on his return, as the monks remained contumacious, he excommunicated seventeen of them. Both the king and the legate refused to support the archbishop. The next trouble was a demand from the legate of a fifth of the clergy's possessions to support the pope in his quarrel with the emperor. At first Edmund Rich and the bishops withstood this tax but in the end royal and papal pressure forced them to give way. A further demand from the legate was that three hundred English benefices should be made liable to papal provision. These and other impositions made the archbishop's position intolerable; whichever way he turned, the king and the legate were obstructive; so he decided to leave the country. It is not known whether he intended to return for he died on the 16th November 1240 at Pontigny where he was buried. So for a third time that monastery sheltered an Archbishop of Canterbury. In spite of the opposition of Henry III, Edmund Rich was canonized in 1248.

With St. Edmund at the time of his death was a former pupil who became his chancellor at Canterbury; this was Richard de Wyche (now Droitwich). When Ralph Neville, Bishop of Chichester died in 1244, Henry instructed the chapter to elect one of his more unpopular officials, Robert Passelewe; his appointment was opposed and the matter submitted to the pope who chose Richard and consecrated him on the 5th March 1245. The king however refused to grant the temporalities or even to allow Richard to live in the episcopal palace, so for two years he lived in a parsonage and, like the earlier bishops, he became a missionary-preacher in his diocese. On being threatened with excommunication, Henry at last gave way. Richard's simple life and his apostolic zeal and charity won the devotion of priests and people. He died on April 1253 and was canonized in 1262.

To these two saints of the period should be added the name of a great scholar-bishop, Robert Grosseteste. He was a Franciscan and their first rector of studies at Oxford where one of his pupils was Roger Bacon. Grosseteste was elected to Lincoln in 1235; it seems to have been a free election. He was indefatigable in reforming the monasteries and the clergy of a diocese that covered eight counties; he withstood the king and the pope himself when they wanted to intrude their own nominees to benefices in his diocese; he had a combativeness that his friend St. Edmund Rich lacked. At the same time he continued his labours as a scholar, and, it has been said, that no one had a greater influence on English thought in religion and philosophy for the next two centuries. He died in 1253. Appeals were made for his canonization to three popes but were unsuccessful.

St. Edmund Rich was succeeded at Canterbury by Boniface of Savoy, one of the queen's uncles; this was an appointment imposed by the king. The archbishop roused much resentment when he claimed the right to make visitations in all the dioceses of his province and sometimes he met with physical opposition. He did protest at the exactions demanded by the king from the clergy but he was not prepared to carry his objections to extremes so he effected nothing, and his frequent absences from England weakened his influence at Canterbury and in the council. From 1265 to 1268 there was a new legate in England, Cardinal Ottbuono, who preached the Crusade in which Henry's eldest son Edward took part; it was a muddled affair and brought no glory to anyone. The legate also held a council at which he issued constitutions for the clergy; these were on the customary lines.

It seems a contradiction that King Henry could be

intensely pious and yet allow the Church in England to be taxed and despoiled and the authority of archbishops and bishops to be flouted. His piety was sincere but how far it was the expression of a genuine spirituality is not discernible. He liked to be present at two or three Masses every day, but in this he was not unique; other kings and princes did the same in his day and for long afterwards; among the later ones was Henry VIII.[1] Did this verge on a superstitious interpretation of the sacred mysteries? The key to this contradiction lies in the king's total acceptance of his position as a vassal of the pope; he was determined to do whatever the popes wished. Hence his request for a resident legate. A king with a quicker sense of the welfare of his country would have resisted the more onerous of the papal demands for money which were occasioned by the growth of the curia. It was the story so familiar to us of an expanding bureaucracy with its multiplication of jobs and, of course, fees.[2] Moreover Henry himself was by nature a spendthrift and he did not see anything reprehensible in the increasing burden put on the country by this subservient attitude to Rome.

Yet, in spite of his serious weaknesses of character, he was a far better man than his Plantagenet forebears, his private life was irreproachable; his contemporaries spoke of his 'simplicity' meaning by that a lack of wordly wisdom. His most noticeable trait was his appreciation of the fine arts especially architecture. In honour of St. Edward he decided to rebuild the Confessor's church at Westminster. The eastern part of the Norman building was pulled down; during the king's lifetime the choir, the transepts, part of the nave and of the cloisters with the chapter house were completed. The new church was consecrated and the body of St. Edward translated to its new shrine behind the high altar at a solemn ceremony on the 13th October 1269.

Westminster Abbey is but one example of Henry's passion for building; work was also carried out at Winchester, Windsor, Gloucester and other places. He was not alone in

[1] They were probably abbreviated or 'hunting' Masses.
[2] In fact, Parkinson's law in operation.

this architectural revival. We have seen how after the Conquest many parish and manor churches, cathedrals and abbeys were built. There was a halt during John's reign; owing to his exorbitant demands for money, there were no funds left for building, but in Henry's reign there was a renewed activity that did not end until the Reformation. The influence of French styles was apparent in the first stages, but it was not long before an English style began to emerge; it was as if a growing national consciousness wanted to express itself in native terms. So came what is known as the Early English style of which Salisbury Cathedral is the finest example; inevitably this style was developed and elaborated but many regard as unrivalled the simplicity and grace of Early English architecture.

The ninety-one years covered by the reigns of Henry and his son Edward I after much civil turmoil set the country on the way to Parliamentary government. Edward I, a great king, has been called our English Justinian, for more was done in his reign to stabilize the administration of justice and to enact new laws than at any previous period. His Parliament was not of two Houses but one assembly with the king's council. Its main purpose was to vote supplies and deal with petitions. To it he summoned by personal writ the barons, lay and spiritual, and the sheriffs were instructed to send up representative knights and burghers. Edward was not so bound to the popes as his father had been, neither did he interfere in the appointment of bishops. Most of the elections seem to have been free but the final decisions were left to the popes, and even when the king put forward a nominee, he did not press his choice if the chapter put up another name. Nor did he delay appointments in order to profit from the temporalities. On one matter Edward would not budge; he claimed and enforced the right to tax the clergy; here he was in conflict with some of the bishops but they usually had to give way. Not only the king but the barons were getting disturbed at the amount of land that was being bequeathed to monasteries and churches; it was more serious from the king's point of view as such land was freed from the duty of military service. By his Statute of Mortmain (1279) he made a first step towards remedying what had become an abuse; in future no such gifts could escape the feudal obligations. The bishops and abbots objected but had to submit. They were not now dealing with a pliable king like Henry but with one who made firm decisions and knew where he was going.

The archbishops and bishops of the reign were, on the whole, well fitted to their duties. The pope's choices for both Canterbury and York were of a high quality. Robert Kilwardly, a Dominican scholar, was Archbishop of Canterbury from 1273 to 1279; he was made a cardinal in the latter year; unfortunately he took with him when he went to Rome the Canterbury registers as well as some of the treasure. He was followed by a Franciscan scholar, John Pecham, a notable archbishop who did much to correct clerical abuses and monastic irregularities; his weakness was too great an insistence on his prestige and prerogatives which led to a number of disputes with his suffragans. In spite of his ceaseless activity, Pecham wrote many books on theology and science.[1] He died in 1292; his successor was Robert de Winchelsey, a secular priest, who was elected freely by the Canterbury chapter. He had to oppose the king when Pope Benedict issued in 1296 his bull *clericis laicos* in 1296 prohibiting the payment of taxes to the state by the clergy. The archbishop lost his temporalities, but later he and the king were reconciled; at the end of the reign they were again at cross-purposes and Edward deprived him of his see. The archbishop went abroad until after Edward's death. He himself died in May 1313.

The involved story of the disputes between archbishops and bishops and between bishop and bishop makes sad reading. The argument about precedence between Canterbury and York was taken up by each archbishop in turn and was never settled. Then there was a long drawn-out quarrel between the Archbishop of York and the Bishop of Durham

---

[1] He was the author of two Latin hymns, *In majestatis solio*, and *Ave vivens hostia* (See *Oxford Book of Medieval Latin Verse*).

over their respective rights. Most of the disagreements were on jurisdiction. Appeals to Rome were part of the process and these dragged out disputes while the contestants were absent from the country for a year or more at a time. To that must be added the expense not only of the tedious journeys but of the fees and bribes at Rome. There was too a noticeable increase in the use of excommunication by one bishop of another, but this weapon was used so frequently that it became blunted. A whole volume could be filled with an account of these ecclesiastical squabbles. A note on a typical case must suffice here. Its interest is that it involved Archbishop Pecham and the Bishop of Hereford who was later canonised, the only canonised saint of Edward I's reign who himself initiated the cause.

Thomas de Cantipule, of a noble Norman family, studied at Oxford, Paris and Orleans; he returned to Oxford and was elected chancellor in 1262. In the baronial revolt against Henry III he sided with the barons; during the period of their ascendancy Thomas was made chancellor of England but he was deprived of the great seal when Simon de Montfort was defeated and slain at Evesham in 1265. Thomas went to Paris where he lectured on theology until the death of Henry III in 1272 when he returned to Oxford as a regent. In June 1275 he was freely elected by the chapter of Hereford as their bishop. He became one of the most trusted advisers of Edward I. Thomas had a difficult task in his diocese which had been neglected by his predecessors; moreover it bordered on Wales which was at war with England until 1295. The new bishop retrieved church lands that had been overrun and he laboured to raise the standard of the parish clergy. He was particularly anxious to check pluralism. Here we may see an incongruity for he himself, by papal dispensation, was a considerable pluralist, but, the records claim that he took care to appoint worthy vicars to his benefices and he would pay them unheralded visits to see that they were carrying out their duties. He does not seem to have sought a quarrel with Archbishop Pecham; the questions at issue were involved but the root difference was the extent of the archbishop's jurisdiction over the bishop's own courts. Pecham excommunicated Thomas in February 1282, but some of the bishops refused to publish the sentence. Thomas set off for Rome but died at Orvieto that September. Pecham tried to carry his feud beyond the grave by refusing Christian burial to the remains of Thomas when they were brought back to England, but the king and the bishops ignored this vindictive prohibition and the bones were transferred in the presence of the king to the tomb that can be seen in Hereford cathedral. Many miracles were worked at his shrine and in 1305 Edward put before the pope the case for canonisation, but it was not until 1320 that Thomas de Cantipule became St. Thomas of Hereford.

CHAPTER 12

Medieval Church Life

THIS history of the Church in England must seem so far to have been largely a record of its public and official life. We have been concerned with the relations with Rome, the policies of kings, the struggle to ensure that 'the Church of England shall be free', and the disputes between archbishops and bishops. This emphasis is inevitable since it is such matters that get documented. They are all of great importance as part of the development of the Church. The ecclesiastical documents that survive, such as visitations, tend to emphasise what was at fault. As St. Thomas More said, 'For men use if they have an evil turn, to write it in marble, and whoso doth us a good turn, we write it in dust.' Or as Shakespeare put the same thought,

> 'The evil that men do lives after them,
> The good is oft interred with their bones.'

We must, therefore, try to preserve a sense of proportion and remember that had the Church as an institution been as corrupt as its decriers have painted it, it could not have endured. There were pastoral bishops and numerous, nameless priests, who were dedicated and devout servants of God.

The reader must have asked himself, 'What of the real

Medieval dioceses.

life of the Church, and what of the beliefs and practices of ordinary folk — the forgotten people?' The answer has to be pieced together from hints here and hints there; an attempt must now be made to bring these fragments together. There can, however, be no answer to the further question, 'What of the spiritual life of the people?' Of this little can be said with confidence; because of its nature, this inner life lies hidden.

1. *Bishops*

Something of the organisation of the Church must first be said. England was divided into two provinces, Canterbury south of the Humber and York to the north. In medieval times there were seventeen dioceses, only three of which were in the province of York. Four dioceses were added to Canterbury when Wales was subjugated in 1284. The Cistercians had already established six houses in that country; Tintern Abbey, for instance, was founded in 1131.

We may get the impression from our reading of political history that most of the bishops were what we should call ministers of state or civil servants; this was not so. In 1300 out of seventeen bishops only two were engaged in state affairs; in 1400 there were seven. Some positions, such as Chancellor and Keeper of the Privy Seal were usually held by archbishops or bishops. Others were sent from time to time on diplomatic missions, and there must have been rarely a year when an English bishop was not in Rome. The other clerks in the king's service looked for benefices, even for bishoprics, in return for their work, and many of the king's nominees were his clerks. After Henry II's time elections were reasonably free, occasionally completely free, but Edward I and his successors rarely insisted on their nominees being appointed though they carried great weight. As long as England was a fief of Rome, 1213 to 1366, the pope had the last word.

As far as the records show, nearly all the bishops who were

not otherwise closely involved in public duties, carried out their religious obligations diligently. Inevitably there were varying degrees of zeal, and there were two or three who were unworthy of their positions, but the overall picture is creditable. When a bishop had to be absent from his diocese for any length of time, he would appoint a suffragan; this might be a bishop from Ireland or one holding a title *in partibus infidelium* consecrated by the pope for this purpose. Franciscans and Dominicans were often so appointed. The Archbishop of Canterbury had the largest responsibilities for public duties even when he was not chancellor. It is significant that Archbishop Boniface began the building of Lambeth Palace in 1262; from then Lambeth rather than Canterbury became increasingly the usual residence of the archbishop.

Not many accounts of episcopal visitations have survived but the indications are that they were made in spite of the practical difficulties of travel and accommodation. Getting from place to place could be an adventurous business; it was done on horseback and the bishop would have with him a retinue of officials, servants and guards. Although parish priests were liable to entertain their bishops, this was not practicable. The parsonage was often a two-roomed dwelling not much superior, if at all, to those of his neighbours, and the task of lodging and feeding the bishop's retinue was beyond the resources of any village. He would use his own manors, or monastic manors, as convenient stopping places from which he could visit the surrounding country.

There is a good example of such a visitation by Richard Swinfield, Bishop of Hereford in 1290.[1] He had been the chaplain and confidant of St. Thomas of Cantilupe. His party numbered thirty when he left Hereford on the 9th April and he was away until the 31st May. It was a tour of about two hundred miles.

Before such a visitation the bishop would send his archdeacon or another of his officials to places on his route to

[1] There is a good account of this, with map, in J. R. H. Moorman, *Church Life in England in the Thirteenth Century* (1945), pp. 187–191.

warn them of his lordship's coming and to gather information about the state of the parishes. This inquiry was searching; it dealt with the personal life of the priest (celibacy, for instance), the parish finances, the upkeep of the church, the proper provision of vestments, missals and Mass equipment, and so on. Sometimes the archdeacon visited parishes outside the bishop's official tours, and he could impose fines for any offences against canon law. He would also follow-up the bishop's visitation to see that weaknesses had been corrected. It is not surprising that archdeacons were the most unpopular of the bishop's officials; indeed, Duns Scotus once questioned whether an archdeacon's soul could be saved! Such visits were not frequent; the size of most dioceses and the problems of travel made it impracticable to get round more often, so the slack priest could lapse back into his slackness in the hope that it would be some time before he saw the bishop or archdeacon again. On the other hand, infrequent as such visits were, they must have checked many an abuse and have stimulated the priests to better service; outside the towns, priests must have felt cut off from other priests and the arrival of even the archdeacon must have been a relief in his loneliness.

The chief clerks after the bishop were his Official and the Vicar-General, or Commissary-General; these positions became merged into that of the Chancellor of the diocese who had full powers in jurisdiction and administration but could not carry out such episcopal functions as ordinations and confirmations. There does not appear to have been much emphasis put on confirmation; this was probably due to the fact that opportunities for its administration were rare. When it was known that the bishop was on his way, parents would bring their children down to the road to meet him; he would put on his stole and lay his hands on the heads of the children and then continue his journey. There seems to have been little if any preparation for the sacrament.

Rural deans were appointed early in the twelfth century but we have little knowledge of their work or authority.

The incomes of bishops varied considerably ranging from

nearly £3000 a year at Winchester down to £300 at Rochester. This enormous difference lasted well up to the twentieth century. Bishops had great expenses beginning with the initial fees to Rome of a year's income. They had large households to maintain, such as the many legal officials, chaplains and clerks, stewards and bailiffs, servants and guards. A small number of bishops, careerists, did accumulate wealth but most of them inherited debts.

Diocesan synods were held at least once a year but attendance seems to have been poor; this was in part due to the long distances to be travelled and the cost of lodging. The decrees issued dealt with such matters as celibacy, absenteeism, inadequate ordination, and so on. Suggestions were also made for instruction to the people, the correct way of saying Mass, and for the priest's own improvement in knowledge.

The bishops' consistory courts had an extensive jurisdiction; they dealt with matrimonial and testamentary (probate) cases, with the morals of the clergy and with the conduct of the laity. These courts were unpopular, an unpopularity that increased with the years; their protracted proceedings and the large fees extracted were constant grievances and the laity resented the snooping and bribery involved.

The cathedrals and collegiate churches stood outside the diocesan administration as did some of the monasteries. Some were wealthy with canonries and prebends at their disposal. A small group of resident canons would carry out the minimum duties while most were absentees, and it was here that lay much of the patronage bestowed on royal clerks and officials.

2. The Priests

We have to distinguish several kinds of priests.

(i) *Rectors*. Some lived in their parishes and received the whole of the tithes while acting as parish priests. Others arranged for a vicar or chaplain to carry out their duties. This second group were more intent on the proceeds of their property and paid their deputies a stipend. Many rectors were lords of manors and laymen; monasteries also were, by gift, proprietors of churches and so responsible for appointing vicars.

(ii) *Vicars*. They were acting for rectors or were delegated by a monastery or chapter.

(iii) *Assistants or curates*. Every parish priest (the parson) was supposed to have at least one assistant who might be in deacon's orders; he was paid by the incumbent. A parish clerk, who would be a layman and perhaps local schoolmaster, was also desirable.

(iv) *Chaplains*. Some lords of manors had their private chaplains. Chantries were built on to churches, or part of a church would be set aside, for Masses to be said for the repose of the donor's soul and the souls of his relatives. Chantry priests might do some teaching but had little else to do and they became something of a scandal as their numbers increased as more and more chantries were established.

The rector received all the tithes (greater on corn; lesser on other produce) which were given in kind. If he had a vicar he would usually allow him the lesser tithes. In addition the vicar would have his glebe (often of farm size). Then too there were offerings at the four great feasts; these would be shared usually between the rector and the vicar. Mass-pennies and offerings at the annual confession as well as various offerings (they were not yet fixed fees) at baptisms, weddings and funerals went usually to the vicar. The values of livings varied considerably and there were some vicars who had little more than an adequate income out of which they had to provide for a curate. The curates were poorly paid; the clerk would have some secular employment. In assessing these values, it should be remembered that the Middle Ages, especially outside the few big towns (London was always exceptional), were not under the kind of money-economy to which we are accustomed. It suggests poverty to say that a vicar might have £10 a year and his curate £5, but the produce of the land was an important addition to a cash payment and there was much barter between neighbours. To this must be added the offerings and small tithes. It is probably true to say that the curate of the eighteenth and early nineteenth centuries was worse off than his medieval predecessor.

The clergy came from all stations in society from country labourers to the nobility. Bishop Grosseteste, for instance, came of a poor Suffolk family. The scales, however, were weighed in favour of influential families when preferment was considered; thus among the bishops we find such names as Courtenay, Beaufort, Arundel and Neville. By the fourteenth century, with the increasing influence of the universities, the scholar was making his way into the higher ranks of the clergy; several instances of this have already been noted.

It seems strange to us that there was no systematic training for the priesthood; that did not come until the Council of Trent (1545–63), and the Universities of Oxford and Cambridge were not founded until the end of the twelfth century. Exact statistics of graduates among the clergy are not available, but, as far as can be judged, an average of ten per cent in the later thirteenth century would seem a fair estimate; it should be remembered that theology was a post-graduate study and did not come in the normal course. The bulk of the clergy had their education in the grammar schools or in those attached to cathedrals and monasteries. This gave them a grounding in Latin. Undoubtedly there were some whom we should consider uneducated, though they could still be good parish priests. There was no thorough system of examination before ordination. The bishops were well aware of this weakness and did what they could to remedy it by encouraging priests to improve themselves. Occasionally priests would be sent to a grammar school for a year to get more learning. Many manuals were issued dealing with such subjects as moral theology, the hearing of confessions, the administration of the sacraments and ways of instructing the laity on the ten commandments, the seven works of mercy, the seven virtues, the seven vices and the seven sacraments. The manuals were usually written in English and often in verse for ease of memorising. The many copies that have survived for more than five hundred years indicate how widely these booklets circulated. As printing had not yet reached England, the parish priest would copy the text lent him and then pass it on to another priest. There is no way of knowing how far this was effective. Nor were the needs of the laity forgotten; for them there were *The Lay Folks' Catechism* and *The Lay Folks' Mass Book*. These provided simple instruction for those who could read for themselves or could read aloud to others. Again the number of copies surviving suggests a wide usage.

The parochial clergy and the friars were often on bad terms. They disputed over the friars' liberty to preach where they would, their licence to hear confessions, and, in later years, on their right to bury the dead in their own churches. Many of the bishops welcomed the ministrations of the friars. It has already been noted that Archbishop Pecham and Bishop Grosseteste were Franciscans and Archbishop Kilwardly a Dominican. The friars could fill out some of the deficiencies of the parish clergy, particularly as preachers; they were famed for their racy sermons and they were better trained for the confessional. People were still obliged to make their Easter confession to their parish priest. No doubt the friars attracted many from the parish church when they came on a preaching mission, and for the people there was the lure of novelty to draw them to listen to a friar and to go to him for confession. Where the friars had their own churches, many forsook their parish churches. Those laymen who belonged to a Third Order would naturally wish to be buried in the habit in a Franciscan or Dominican church. The parish clergy were not entirely disinterested in their complaints; the activities of the friars meant a loss of offerings. Then there were disputes between Franciscans and Dominicans that were far from edifying. Both orders lost their first fervour, one might say their innocence. They gradually acquired property and built fine churches. Grey Friars in London for instance was one of the largest churches in the country. Just as ownership of land with all the business it brought led to a decline in the quality of monasticism, so well-built friaries and great churches drew the friars farther and farther away from their early simplicity and poverty; they begged not as originally for bread to keep them alive but for bricks and stone. The time came when a friar was regarded as little better than a rascal.

Two of our poets, exact contemporaries, Geoffrey Chaucer and William Langland, help us to know something of the fourteenth century clergy as they knew them. Chaucer's character sketch of the 'poor parson' is well known. 'Parson' meant a rector who was a parish priest. At the opening of the *Parson's Tale*, the host asked him:

> 'Sir priest,' quoth he, 'art thou a vicar?
> Or art a parson?'

There is no answer to this question, and the parson, instead of telling a tale preaches a sermon which is well worth reading as an example of contemporary religious thought. Parts of the passage (modernised) read as follows:

> A good man there was of religion,
> And was a poor Parson of a town;
> But rich he was of holy thought and work.
> He was also a learned man, a clerk,
> That Christ's gospel truly would preach . . .
> Full loath were him to curse for his tithes,
> But rather would he give, out of doubt,
> Unto his poor parishioners about
> Of his offering, and also of his substance . . .
> He set not his benefice to hire,
> And left his sheep encumbered in the mire,
> And run to London unto St. Paul's,
> To seek him a chantry for souls . . .
> A better priest, I trow that nowhere none is.
> He waited after no pomp and reverence,

> Nor maked him a nice conscience,
> But Christ's lore, and his apostles twelve,
> He taught, and first he followed it himself.

He came of a labouring family, for the poet adds,

> With him there was a Ploughman, was his brother . . .
> His tithes paid he full fair and well,
> Both of his proper work and his cattle.

Commentators warn us that this an idealised portrait but they advance no evidence for saying so, nor does there seem to be any reason why Chaucer should have drawn a less convincing portrait of the poor parson than he did of the sorry group of other clerics who were also on the pilgrimage. There was the fastidious prioress with her chaplain and three priests; the monk who loved the chase; the begging friar 'a wanton and a merry', and a pardoner[1] with his wallet stuffed with 'pardons come from Rome all hot' as well as with a sack of spurious relics.

Langland in the Prologue to *Piers Plowman* also had something to say about the pardoner with his trade in indulgences.

> There preached a pardoner / as if he priest were:
> He brought forth a brief / with bishops' seals thereon,
> And said that himself might / absolve them all
> From falseness in fasting / and of broken vows.
> Laymen believed him / welcomed his words,
> And came up on their knees / to kiss his seals,
> He cozened them with his brevet[2] / dimmed their eyes,
> With his parchment / got his rings and brooches:
> Thus they gave their gold / gluttons to keep.

The poet was equally critical of bishops and priests who neglected their proper duties.

> Bishops and bachelors / both masters and doctors,
> That have charge under Christ / and the tonsure as token
> And sign that they should / shrive their parishioners,

---

[1] He was licensed to sell papal pardons or indulgences.   [2] Indulgence.

Preach and pray for them / and feed the poor,
These lodge in London in Lent / and at other times too,
Some serve the king / and his silver count
In Chequer and Chancery courts.

Long Will (as he was nicknamed) took a jaundiced view of the clergy and especially of the friars. The passage just quoted does tell us what he held to be the right functions of bishops and priests, but he does not give us, as Chaucer did, a sketch of the good priest. We must not let his very one-sided opinion lead us to think that there was little that was praiseworthy in the Church. Bishops and priests varied, as always, in their fervour and selflessness. These pages have recorded the work of bishops who were devout Christians and eager to promote true religion in clergy and laity alike. There must have been numerous priests, monks and friars who were devoted to the Church and served it faithfully. It is in the nature of surviving records that little is said of these unassuming and unnamed labourers in the vineyard. The effects of their work was shown in the religious life of the ordinary folk they served.

3. *The People*

When we go into one of our old churches, our first impression is of greyness, of stone walls broken only by memorial tablets. Had we entered the same church five hundred years ago, our impression would be of colour. No doubt we should find much that, by our present-day tastes, seems crude and even vulgar, but we should also find ourselves caught up in a vigorous community life utterly different from our going-to-church-on-Sundays-only custom.

The walls were often covered with paintings[1]; they were artless and the colours were bold reds and blues and yellows

---

[1] While many wall-paintings have been uncovered and restored, no Rood has survived; it was the first thing the iconoclasts destroyed.

and greens — no pastel shades. The most elaborate painting was over the chancel arch; this was the Doom, a picture of the Last Judgement with souls being welcomed into heaven or thrust down into hell. Across that arch would be the Rood beam; on this stood the great carved crucifix with, at the foot, figures of Our Lady and St. John and five candles as tokens of the five wounds of Christ. It was from the rood beam that the priest read the Passion on Good Friday and the Gospel on the greater feasts. Many churches had a screen below the rood beam separating the nave from the chancel. All woodwork was coloured. More colour was provided by the stained or painted windows.

The high altar, of stone, was lower than is now usual; it was covered with a hair cloth; the frontals were not changed in accordance with a liturgical sequence but the richest would be used on greater feasts. The reredos might be of carved wood or stone but often of painted cloth; the crucifixion was the subject, the cross being in the centre. There was no crucifix on the altar. Two candles were the only ornaments. Hanging from the roof or cross beam was the pyx or tabernacle for the reserved sacrament; this might take the form of a dove or a crescent moon or even of a ship in metal and adorned with jewels. It was kept veiled. During Lent a veil was hung in front of the altar; the hooks for this can still be seen in some churches. The altar was flanked by two curtains called riddels.

On the Gospel side against the wall was a statue of Our Lady with five candles for the five Joyful Mysteries of the Rosary (Beads); these candles were known as the gaudies. On the Epistle side would be a statue of the Patron Saint. These, and any other statues, were coloured and often clothed in contemporary style; thus Our Lady would look like a great lady of the period; the redressing of these statues from time to time was a happy occasion.

At Mass the priest vested before the altar, the vestments and altar vessels being kept in a chest. The people knelt during Mass, except for the Gospel when they stood; they sat on the floor during the sermon or instruction. Benches or pews did not come into use until the fifteenth century; there might be one or two or a stone bench for the elderly. There was no heating system save, perhaps, a few braziers. During the summer the floor, often of beaten earth, was covered with rushes, and with straw in winter. At the end of Mass the pax (a painted board of the crucifixion rather like a hand mirror) was first kissed by the priest and then passed round the congregation in order of social precedence, a matter that sometimes caused unseemly squabbles. The people made oblations of bread to the priest, who, after Mass, blessed the loaves and cut them into pieces for distribution, some to the donors and some to the poor; any bread left over was the priest's perquisite; this was the holy bread and not to be confused with the sacramental unleavened bread, the wafers of which were made in an oven at the church. This holy bread was sometimes given a superstitious value to ward off evil spirits and cure diseases. The gift of candles was another normal offering.

The order of Mass was traditional but, before the Council of Trent, there were a number of local usages just as the Dominicans to-day retain their special customs. The one commonly followed in England was the Sarum rite[1] drawn up by St. Osmund, Bishop of Salisbury (Old Sarum) in the eleventh century. The Bidding of the Bedes (the praying of prayers) was part of the Mass; this practice has now been revived. Here are two medieval specimens.

'For the Parson of this parish and others that have the cure of men's souls, that God give them grace well to teach their subjects [i.e. their parishioners] and their subjects well to work after wholesome teaching, that both teachers and subjects may come to eternal bliss.'

'And for all them that would be here and may not for sickness or travail or any other lawful occupation, that they may have part in all the good deeds that shall be done here in this place or in any other place.'

[1] The Sarum rite was used in England until the end of Mary Tudor's reign. The Roman rite was introduced at Douay in 1577. Many of the Collects in the Anglican Book of Common Prayer are from the Sarum rite.

Mention has already been made of *The Lay Folk's Mass Book*. The way in which verse was used as an aid to the memory may be illustrated by two quotations.

At the Sanctus

'Sweet Jesu, grant me now this
That I may come unto thy bliss,
There unto angels for to sing
This sweet song of Thy loving,
Sanctus, Sanctus, Sanctus
Jesus grant that it be thus.'

At the Elevation

'Jesu, all my joying,
That for me spilt Thy Blood,
And died upon the Rood;
Thou give me grace to sing
The song of thy praising.'

There were three services on Sundays. As Langland wrote,

'Upon Sundays / God's service to hear
Both Matins and Mass / and, after meat, in churches
To hear evensong / every man ought.'

Everyone was expected to go to Mass but the records show that there were always some who shirked the duty; their numbers were probably few, and, in a small community like a village, absence would soon be noted. In a town where there might be several parishes (there were ninety in London) it would be more easy. We have no indication of how far the people attended Matins and Evensong. There was also a daily Mass, but there is no record of how many used to go; more would probably attend on holy-days,[1] and would be expected to go on the greater feasts. There were complaints of irreverent behaviour at Mass, particularly of gossiping, but the visitor to Italy to-day, for instance, can be equally

[1] There were about fifty of these; the Church courts could summons anyone who made his men work especially at times of Mass. The Reformation did away with holy-days; three or four bank holidays are a poor substitute.

shocked. Perhaps the explanation is not irreverence but familiarity.

The fourth Lateran Council had decreed that everyone should make his communion and go to confession at least once a year, at Easter. Communion was, of course, taken at any time to the sick and the dying. The manuals giving guidance to priests on confession show that this was a thorough examination. Not only was the penitent's conduct probed but his knowledge of the faith was tested. Questions ranged from, 'Have you taught your children the Lord's Prayer and the Creed?' to 'Have you left the churchyard gate open so that cattle have got in?' There were no confession boxes; the priest sat in the chancel in his stall, or in a special confession pew; the penitent stood to make his confession and knelt for absolution. This long process must have meant many hours over several weeks for the priest.

One form of penance was the pilgrimage, though this might be self-imposed. The most distant places were Rome, Compostella in Spain for St. James, and the Holy Land. Even the poorest folk might set out for one of these long journeys, and the pilgrim was an accepted figure in the medieval scene and he would be charitably treated. There were many centres in England, the most famous being Canterbury, with Our Lady of Walsingham as the next-favoured one; there are many records of kings and queens going to both.

Something should be said of the marriage ceremony of those days. The first stage was the troth-plight or hand-fasting. The couple, before witnesses, declared their intention of marrying and the man gave the woman a ring. The priest might be there as a friend but he had no official part to play. This civic ceremony, as it may be called, was often followed by a long enough period to ensure that the woman could have a child. The next stage was the church ceremony. The priest met the couple at the church door and made sure that there had been a hand-fasting and that there was no impediment. Then he led them into the church for the nuptial Mass. It will be recalled of Chaucer's Wife of Bath, 'husbands at church-door she had five.'

The people loved processions on feast days and some old churchyards have retained the processional paths. The church would be decorated for the occasion: holly and ivy for Christmas, palm and box for Palm Sunday, roses for Ascension Day, flags (iris) and woodruff for Corpus Christi, and boughs of birch to mark Midsummer. The Blessed Sacrament would be carried under a canopy and the parishioners would follow with the banners they had made. Sometimes the procession would go beyond the churchyard, for instance at rogationtide for the blessing of the crops and for the beating of the bounds. The parishioners would process from boundary stone to boundary stone and at each the boys would beat the stones, or other landmark such as a tree, with wands; in some places the boys themselves were beaten to help them to remember where the boundary lay. Sometimes there were violent clashes if the processions of two neighbouring parishes happened to meet and they began disputing about the position of the boundary marks.

How was all this paid for? The lord of the manor or a landed lay-rector would often be generous in support of his church; he was expected to look after the chancel under which he might have his family vault. Then there were bequests; a parishioner might leave a few sheep or a cow which could be hired out to a farmer; it would have been thought shocking if a parishioner with any property failed to leave something to the church and the poor. On one farm to-day, for instance, there is a field known as Lamp-Acre Piece; no doubt this was left to endow a light in the church. The upkeep of the main fabric was the responsibility of the parishioners and the fact that this was taken seriously is evidenced by the survival of so many medieval churches, for any building that is neglected will become dilapidated within a generation. Some churches were neglected but this may have meant a shifting of population.

The key men were the churchwardens. They were elected by the people and it was their business to organise the raising of funds. They also served as watch-dogs for the priest and even for the bishop in reporting frequent absentees or any other serious matter affecting the parish. Some part of the free-will offerings was ear-marked for maintenance, another part went to the poor and a third to the priest. The methods used were of the same kind as we use ourselves. A market, sometimes held in the church itself, was one way. Another was the church-ale or scot-ale.[1] The churchwardens begged malt and then brewed it. Everyone made his own ale in those days and the church had its means for doing the same. Bishops frowned on church-ales as they led to unseemly revelry; indeed it may be doubted if many villagers got to bed sober, if they got there at all. The day would be spent in all kinds of athletic competitions including archery. Our bazaars and bring-and-buy sales are like the markets; we no longer have church-ales; perhaps the coffee morning is the degenerate descendant.

The church was the real centre, indeed, the only centre, of the community life of the parishioners; it was *their* church and they used it for all kinds of purposes. Religious plays were performed in them; meetings for organising their affairs took place in them, even dances — to the scandal of the bishops — were held in them. The church, in fact, was as much a part of their lives as their own homes. They worked for it, took a pride in it and looked after it as well as worshipped in it. Perhaps sometimes they went too far; perhaps we do not go far enough.

[1] Beer became more common with the greater use of hops in the fifteenth century.

CHAPTER 13

The Later Middle Ages

THE fourteenth century in England was a period of ferment and turbulence.

1. Two kings, Edward II (*d.* 1327) and Richard II (*d.* 1399) were deposed; the first was murdered and his great grandson was probably murdered.

2. The Hundred Years' War began in 1338.

3. The Black Death, a bubonic and pneumonic plague, destroyed perhaps a third of the population between 1348 and 1369.

4. The Peasants' Revolt of 1381 was a threat to the social order; it had no religious significance although its prophet was John Ball, a priest.

5. John Wycliffe's teachings on the government and doctrines of the Church during the last quarter of the century unsettled men's thoughts on established religion.

6. The papal court left Rome for Avignon in 1309 and remained there until 1377; this was followed by the Great Schism of the next forty years.

Edward II's conflict with the barons inevitably involved the bishops and some of the abbots as, by their temporalities, they were barons and sat in the thirty Parliaments of the reign. Most of them supported the movement to get rid of the king's favourite, Peter de Gaveston, and the twenty-one Ordainers included the Archbishop of Canterbury and six bishops. The first of the Ordinances of 1311 read,

'First, it is ordained that Holy Church shall have all her liberties, as formerly, as she ought to have.'

The opposition of the Church led the king to interfere more decisively in the elections of bishops; he naturally wanted to have his own supporters in such key positions. When Archbishop Winchelsey died in 1313, the Canterbury chapter wanted Thomas Cobham, known as 'the good clerk.' It was a wise choice but Edward persuaded Pope Clement V to prefer Walter Reynolds, the chancellor and an intimate of the king. The appointment was certainly simoniacal and, morally and intellectually, the new archbishop was not worthy of his high position. The archbishopric of York fell vacant in 1315; here again the king insisted on one of his close supporters, William Melton, being elected. In March 1318 Melton was involved in an affair that illustrates the disorder of the times. The king with the army was at Berwick preparing to advance against the Scots who sent a marauding force southwards towards York. There were no regulars to oppose them so the archbishop took the initiative and hastily formed an irregular militia. They were routed at Myton in Swaledale. Among the dead were so many priests that the battle was called 'The Chapter of Myton', and as there were Cistercians (white) monks among them it was also known as 'The White Battle of Myton.' Melton was not the last Archbishop of York to appear in arms. This is but one example of the problems that faced the bishops and the clergy during the bitter struggle between the king and his barons. The execution of their leader, Thomas, Earl of Lancaster, in March 1322, brought a brief respite. There was very little to be said in his favour; he was an unloved and unloving man, yet, after his burial at Pontefract, miracles were said to have been worked at his tomb, and his canonisation was seriously considered.

In 1321 Edward wrote to Pope John XXII asking that

Henry Burghersh, Bishop of Lincoln, Adam Orleton, Bishop of Hereford, and John Droxford, Bishop of Bath and Wells, should be removed as they were obnoxious to him. The pope refused and urged the other bishops to mediate between them and the king. An even more subversive situation arose when Edward's queen, Isabella, and her paramour, Roger Mortimer, landed near Harwich in 1326 and declared war on the king. The bishops had again to make difficult decisions. Archbishop Melton remained loyal to the king to the end; he and the Bishops of London, Carlisle and Rochester spoke against Edward's deposition. Archbishop Reynolds sent considerable funds to the queen and then shut himself up at Canterbury; he did not oppose the deposition. Bishops Burghersh, Orelton and Droxford, three careerists, supported the queen and Mortimer. When the Londoners rose in their support they murdered Bishop Stapledon of Exeter and captured Robert Baldock, the chancellor, and put him in Newgate where he died. The first article of the deposition of Edward II stated that he was guilty of 'the destruction of Holy Church.' Edward III was crowned on 29th January 1327 by Archbishop Reynolds; Archbishop Melton refused to be present. The deposed king was imprisoned in Berkeley Castle. A Dominican friar, Thomas Dumhead, plotted with some friends to rescue him. Edward had founded the Dominican house at Langley (now King's Langley) his favourite manor. The conspirators succeeded in getting Edward as far as Corfe Castle, but they were captured. Edward was taken back to Berkeley where he was murdered on the 21st September 1327.

The transfer of the papal court from Rome to Avignon, 'the Babylonish Captivity' as Petrarch called it, was justifiable as the warring factions of nobles at Rome threatened the security of the pope. Avignon was chosen as the Venaissin was a papal county. The move meant that the popes came under the influence of the French kings and the College of Cardinals became predominantly French. The most noticeable feature of the Avignon Papacy was its vast bureaucratic expansion. This was partly the result of the increasing number of appeals bringing with it an inevitable increase in the numbers of legal officials and clerks with the demand for more fees and bribes. The expenses at Avignon were constantly mounting, and anyone who visits that city must wonder where all the money came from for the papal palace, the cardinals' palaces, the churches and the massive walls. Hence the unending search for new sources of wealth. John XXII (1316–34) made the payment of annates (the first year's income of a benefice) obligatory; tenths were demanded for crusades that came to nothing; visits by legates and papal collectors had to be paid for by the clergy, and so on. Not all the money extracted from England reached Avignon; by unspoken custom, the king retained a portion and the ecclesiastics who handled the money had their pickings. It has been said with some exaggeration that 'the pope incurred the odium, the king got the money.'

Langland had his say about Avignon.

'I knew never cardinal / that came not from the pope,
And we clerks, when they come / for their provisions pay,
For their fur and their palfreys' meat / and pillagers that
   them follow.
The commons *clamat cotidie* / each man to other,
"The country is the curseder / that cardinals come in;
And where they lie and linger most / lechery there
   reigneth."
Therefore, quoth this vicar, by very God, I would
That no cardinal come / among the common people,
But in their holiness / hold them still
At Avignon, among the Jews.'

Another field of contention was that of provision — that is, the right of the popes to provide incumbents for vacant benefices which were not elective or otherwise provided for. Gregory XI (1370–8) claimed total authority in making provisions. The results were increasingly irksome; absentee foreigners or unfit clerks were sometimes appointed; benefice-hunters took the road to Avignon and by bribery got what they wanted, or, by dispensation, were allowed to evade the canon law on pluralism. The system, put thus baldly, sounds wholly objectionable, but it had its good side; the pope often put deserving priests, especially scholars, into benefices they could not otherwise have had.

Dissatisfaction with the system of provisions mounted and at length the first Statute of Provisors (1351) was enacted. Its purpose was to protect ecclesiastics, and at the same time preserve the powers of the king in the appointment of bishops and abbots and other clerics. No bulls of provision could be received; the king would have authority to expel anyone intruded by the pope and could then himself nominate someone to fill the benefice. No appeal to Avignon was permissible. Two years later the first Statute of Praemunire (1353) was passed. Cases cognisable in the king's courts were not to be taken abroad, that is to Avignon; this was to stop the pope adjudicating in cases the king regarded as more properly dealt with in his own courts. These statutes were later renewed in strengthened forms. Had they been strictly enforced the influence of the pope in England would have been considerably limited, but there was much give and take between king and pope; each, in turn, could be helpful to the other. The main effect was that the volume of appeals to the pope was reduced and the number of foreigners provided to English benefices decreased. The limited purpose of the Statutes of Praemunire should be noted; the wider interpretation put on them by Henry VIII had no justification.

The popes tried to get the tribute paid which King John had promised when he made England a fief of Rome. The answer took the form of passive resistance. By 1310 the tribute was twenty years in arrears. Token payments were occasionally made but nothing was paid during the thirty years after 1333. When Urban V demanded payment with all arrears, Edward III referred the matter to Parliament in 1365; the reply was a denial of any obligation on the grounds that King John had acted in violation of his coronation oath. Nothing more was heard of England being a vassal of Rome.

The Great Schism which began in 1378 and lasted until 1417 did much to lower the prestige of the papacy. It was not a religious division but political and kings and princes supported whichever pope suited their own interests. Thus England recognised the Roman pope, Urban VI, while France favoured Clement VII who had established himself at Avignon; this was a typical division as England and France were at war. Ordinary folk were not concerned with clerical taxes and provisions, and the disputes between king and pope passed over their heads; after all, popes and kings had always been at variance, but the schism must have shaken their loyalty to the Holy See. What could they make of a situation in which there were two, and for a time, even three claimants to represent St. Peter?

Neither Edward III nor his grandson Richard II can be considered a man of religious convictions; they did what was expected of a king in founding monasteries or providing funds for building, but both interfered with the elections of bishops; in this they were rarely thwarted as the pope they supported needed their support. These royal nominees were mostly from the king's administrative staff; some of the bishops proved diligent in the care of their dioceses, but others were too absorbed in state affairs to have time for pastoral duties. On the whole, however, diocesan needs were met by the work of local ecclesiastics in the absence of their bishops. One or two, such as William Wykeham, amassed wealth, which, in his case was used for the foundation of Winchester College and of New College, Oxford. The bishops were good administrators when they gave their minds to their dioceses; this was to be expected from their training and experience in the royal service. Too often the trouble of the times forced on them the need for taking sides in political disputes. A convenient visit to Avignon was one way of avoiding committment, but too often it meant trying to find a safe course between Scylla and Charybdis. The risks were considerable; the murder of Bishop Stapledon by the London mob in 1326 has been noted. During the Peasants' Revolt of 1381 Archbishop Sudbury met the same fate. These murders were not outbursts of anticlericalism; both bishops died because they were royal officials.

In spite of the disturbed times the religious houses prospered. The Black Death reduced the number of monks, friars and canons by about half though the incidence was uneven. There was some recovery but the total number by the fifteenth century had declined to less than 1,700. Some of the smaller and poorer houses had closed owing to financial difficulties, and, as an inevitable result of the French war, the alien priories were gradually reduced in numbers until their suppression about 1414; some became colleges of secular canons. The Knights Templars were also suppressed in 1308 but without the foul measures taken in France.

The most notable advance in monasticism was the foundation of six more Carthusian houses after 1350 including the famous London Charterhouse. One of these was established at Shene in Surrey by Henry V. In the following year he was also responsible for the only Bridgettine house at Syon in Middlesex. In Shakespeare's play, the king refers to these two foundations as being reparation for

> 'the fault
> My father made in compassing the crown . . .
> . . . . and I have built
> Two chantries, where the sad and solemn priests
> Sing still for Richard's soul'

The strictly ascetic life of the Carthusians was attractive only to those with deep religious convictions; the total number of houses was nine but their reputation for complete obedience to their Rule surpassed that of other Orders, so that it could be said of them, 'Never reformed, because never deformed.'

These two centuries saw an astonishing efflorescence of church building. The Early English style, so attractive in its simplicity, gave way to what is termed Decorative which in its turn led to the Perpendicular style. Sometimes all stages of this architectural development are to be seen in one great abbey or cathedral since they incorporate the work of long years. We see the completed buildings, or its ruins, but contemporaries must have been familiar with it in the process of being enlarged. A very long list could be made of these masterpieces — Ely, Peterborough, Winchester, Durham, Sherborne, St. George's, Windsor, to name only a few, culminating in King's College, Cambridge and Henry VII's Chapel at Westminster.

Some of our cathedrals were originally monastic and the fact that they have been in continuous use has preserved them. Other abbeys have fallen into ruins since the Reformation, thus robbing us of a glorious heritage. These abbeys were not intended for lay worship. We make a mistake if we picture these vast naves crowded with worshippers in medieval times. Sometimes there were comparatively few lay folk living in the neighbourhood but there would be the people working on the monastery lands. The naves provided space for the many altars needed for the priest-monks to say their daily Masses; they also gave room for the liturgical processions such as the one at High Mass on Sundays and the Great Feasts. Some of the abbeys and priories allowed the nave to be used for lay-worship with a special altar, but as this interfered with the monastic office, a separate church was often built nearby for parish use. A good example of this is St. Margaret's, Westminster, built close to the Abbey. There were not only these magnificent abbeys and cathedrals. Up and down the country can be seen churches built by the wealthy wool-merchants and by others of the rising new land-owning class. They believed that a right use for their wealth was to build a church to the glory of God, though more self-regarding considerations may have been present. We have seen how the village and town churches were cared for by the parishioners; extensions to old buildings were made as well as other improvements. All this work went on until the Reformation.

Then, too, there were a number of colleges being built at Oxford and Cambridge; both universities were rapidly expanding during these centuries. One impressive aspect is that there must have been an army of sound builders and craftsmen spread over the country. It has sometimes been said that the men who designed these buildings have remained anonymous, but in recent years the names of many of the master-masons, such as Henry Yevele (1320–1400), have been recovered. These wonderful buildings not only display a genius for construction in the overcoming of structural problems, but they reveal also the widespread talent there was in wood and stone-carving. Each craftsman followed his own ingenuity in inventing decoration, whether on stone capitals or wooden bench-ends. There must have been a lot of fun in all this, for often grotesque carvings are hidden away where no one could see them; the same artistry was shown in small statues high up out of the public gaze. Tombs and effigies are among the finest works of the period; the alabaster figure of Edward II at Gloucester with its splendid canopy comes to mind. Another form of memorial was the brass, the earliest surviving one being that of Sir John Daubernon at Stoke d'Abernon in Surrey dated 1277. English painted glass achieved a new standard of design and execution as can be seen, for instance, at York Minster and Malvern. Mural paintings, where they have been uncovered, give only a ghostly indication of their original colouring. The Wilton Diptych in the National Gallery and the portrait of Richard II at Westminster are examples of panel painting of which little else survives. Nor must we forget the illuminated manuscripts; the British Museum has a great Bible dating from Richard II's reign and there is also the Sherborne Missal at Alnwick. The Syon cope in the Victoria and Albert Museum reminds us that embroidery was one of the notable English decorative arts; *opus Anglicanum* was greatly admired and copied in Europe. All these arts and skills were used in the service of the church. Had we need any proof of what religion meant in those days, we could find it in this pervasive influence in what men built and designed. It is as if there were two Englands; the one of wrangling kings and barons, and the other the land where men delighted in the work of their hands. This aspect of the Middle Ages has been wildly romanticised, but there was a substratum of fact in a world where there was much that was lovely but also much that was unlovely.

In trying to assess the meaning of religion in the fourteen and on into the fifteenth century we must take into account the unique group of English mystics. Four are notable: Richard Rolle (1290–1349), the unknown author of *The Cloud of Unknowing* (1360), Walter Hilton (1330–96), and Dame Juliana of Norwich (1340–1420).[1] Their purpose was to lead the individual seeker through prayer and meditation to an intense experience of the presence of God. These writers were not thinking of the generality of men, but of the individual soul; they knew that this mystical experience could be reached only by a rare believer who could give his whole being to its pursuit.

Richard Rolle was born in Yorkshire, and, after Oxford, he returned to his native country, determined to live as a hermit. He formed a friendship with an ancress, Margaret Kirkby, for whom he wrote some of his works. His best known is his *Form of Perfect Living*. His deepest devotion was to the Holy Name of Jesus and to the Passion. The great number of manuscript copies of his writings that have survived show how widely he was read. The author of *The Cloud of Unknowing* remains anonymous; this and other writings reveal a depth of spiritual experience unique in our religious history. Walter Hilton, author of *The Scale of Perfection* (*Scala Perfectionis*), was also, for a period, a hermit before he entered the Augustinian priory of Thurgarton in Nottinghamshire. He too wrote for the guidance of a friend or disciple. Dame Juliana of Norwich was also a recluse whose *Revelations of Divine Love* had a wide influence. Though she was not a mystic in the full meaning of the term, mention should be made of Margery Kempe (1373–1438) who wrote an account of her spiritual trials and of her journey to the Holy Land and Rome. If one book evokes the later Middle Ages more than another it is *The Book of Margery Kempe*.

[1] All these dates are approximate.

It is interesting to note that St. Thomas More, writing in 1532, advised his readers not to trouble their heads with controversial books such as his own but to read 'Bonaventure of the life of Christ, Gerson of the following of Christ, and the devout contemplative book *Scala Perfectionis.*' The first two may not be recognised by the titles More used. The book by St. Bonaventure was a translation of his *Meditationes* under the title *The Mirrour of the blessed lyf of Jesus Christ.* Thomas à Kempis' *Imitatio Christi*, one of the most influential of spiritual writings, was long believed to have been written by Jean Gerson (1363–1429), Chancellor of the University of Paris.

Although copies of some of these mystical writings had a wide circulation, they could not have affected the people as a whole; their influence was restricted to those who longed for a deeper spiritual experience — a number that is always severely limited among believers. It is not therefore surprising that copies were possessed by the Charterhouses and Syon Abbey, and no doubt by other monasteries. Hilton's *Scale of Perfection* was first printed by Wynkyn de Worde in 1494 and several times reprinted; this brought it to many who could not have had access to a manuscript copy.

Rolle, Hilton and Dame Juliana were recluses. This brings us to consider a kind of religious life that seems as strange to us as that of the Desert Fathers. The hermit, recluse or anchorite (ancress) was not independent of all authority; the bishop's or abbot's licence was granted on the taking of appropriate vows. Not all lived in desolate places. Many had cells assigned to them at abbeys and an ancress would have a servant. We must not think of them as being walled-up. There was a famous recluse at Westminster who was consulted by Richard II and Henry V. Recluses were regarded with special reverence and people sought their advice.

England had been singularly free from heresy but in the last quarter of the fourteenth century the teaching of John Wycliffe brought about the rise of the Lollards. He was a distinguished Oxford theologian and first came into public life when he was sent with a delegation in 1374 to discuss with Gregory XI's representatives the payment to Avignon of tribute the pope claimed was due from England. We have seen how Parliament later on refused to make any such payments. The direct experience of papal rapacity and of his emissaries may have set Wycliffe thinking out the whole problem of church authority and administration. All that can be given here is to indicate a few of his more explosive tenets. His basic test was — 'Does present practice agree with that of the early church as recorded in the Gospels and Acts?' If the existing system was contrary to primitive usage, then it should be abolished. So he advocated doing away with the papacy, the rejection of canon law, the exclusion of bishops from state administration, the abolition of the religious orders and of many of the devotions that the Church fostered. His demand was for a clean sweep; he did not make it clear what he would put in the place of existing institutions. This largely negative programme could make a wide appeal since every man could find something in it that he himself disliked. Two concomitant questions arose: why should the Church services be in a language ordinary folk could not understand? And, why should not the Bible be made available in English? We cannot here go into the question of the use of Latin in the Mass, but the Lollard Bible does call for a note. The translation was not made by Wycliffe but by two of his disciples. It is an almost unreadable translation in its first form as it was far too literal. Nor could it be widely disseminated. The cost of a copy, written by hand (some 600,000 words) was prohibitive; even the Latin Bible of which over the centuries there were many copies in more than one version, was too expensive for most parish priests to buy. A further reason for the lack of an English Bible was the problem of language. Parts, such as the Gospels and Epistles, had been translated into Anglo-Saxon, but into what language could a translation be made after the Conquest? There was in fact a Norman-French version but that was of no use to most people. It was not until English speech had settled down and its dialects sorted out about the middle of the twelfth century that a common language was possible.

It has sometimes been said, and indeed is repeated even now, that by a decree of the Council of Oxford in 1407 by Archbishop Arundel, the translation of the Bible into English was forbidden; this was not so; what was prohibited was a translation that had not been approved by the Church. The Wycliffe Bible was condemned because the prologue was tendentious; unorthodox opinions were expressed on the Eucharist and on other matters such as the celibacy of the clergy. When these objectionable opinions were removed, the revised Wycliffe Bible was available for those who could afford it and copies were owned by religious houses and the nobility. Henry VI, for instance, presented a copy to the London Charterhouse. For reasons already given the complete Wycliffe Bible did not circulate among his lowly followers; parts, such as a Gospel, were more easily copied out, or even learned by heart, and there seems to have been a special liking for the Epistle of St. James which Luther later called 'a thing of straw.' All this is not to suggest that the populace was ignorant of the contents of the Bible. Far from it. The Gospel or Epistle read at Mass was the usual topic for the priest's homily or instruction. The painted walls and coloured glass told the Old and New Testament stories, and the religious plays were biblical. Illiteracy, curiously enough, can mean a more retentive memory, and the memorising of passages and texts was encouraged.

Wycliffe did not found a society; to have done so would have been in contradiction of his principles, which, had they been put into practice would have led to chaos. The followers who spread his teaching were known as 'poor men of the treasury of Christ.' The name 'Lollard',[1] of doubtful derivation, was first used as a nickname but became accepted, just as, much later, 'Quaker' was accepted. The message preached by the 'poor men' was not always fully understood and some strange and almost meaningless distortions

[1] On five occasions Margery Kempe was accused of being a 'false Lollard.'

became current. Wycliffe himself escaped any severe penalties as a heretic though his opinions were condemned; he was protected by John of Gaunt for political reasons. Wycliffe died at his Lutterworth parsonage in 1384.

Lollards were persecuted. The heresy statutes of 1401 and 1406, *De heretico comburendo*, were directed against them, but very few went to the stake; most recanted. There was the threat of a rising in London in 1414 but the leader Sir John Oldcastle was captured and later hanged and burnt. There were local risings in other parts of the country which were easily suppressed. After 1414 Lollardry ceased to be an active force, but this did not mean its end. There were groups of Lollards in Buckinghamshire, Berkshire and Essex and in the north; the adherents were nearly all of the craftsman and artisan classes. It would be a mistake to think of this vestigial Lollardry as ushering in the Reformation; it did, however, turn over the soil in preparation for a later sowing.

A brief note is all that can be given here of the one canonised saint of the fourteenth century. After two years at Oxford, John Thwing returned to his native Yorkshire where he became an Austin Canon at Bridlington which he never left. He was prior for the last seventeen years of his life. His brethren and all who came to know him recognised his prudence, his serenity and his holiness. He died on 10th October 1379 and the miracles that were wrought by his intercession led to his canonisation in 1401. St. John of Bridlington is an outstanding instance of how an obscure monk living far from the bustle of life could so impress his contemporaries that they came to think of him as a saint. England had to wait more than five centuries for another native saint to be canonised.

CHAPTER 14

From the Old to the New Monarchy

HENRY IV's accession in 1399 did not bring peace to the realm. Scotland and Wales were constant irritants and there were revolts by the northern earls. People were shocked by the king's treatment of Richard Scrope who had been appointed Archbishop of York at the insistence of Richard II against the wishes of the chapter. The details of the Scrope conspiracy do not concern us. He appeared in the field in armour and among his active supporters were several priests from the Minster, parish priests of York, and members of the four mendicant orders. They were captured at Shipton Moor in May 1405. The king insisted on immediate trial — if trial it could be called. Chief Justice Gascoigne refused to try an ecclesiastic in a secular court. Thomas Arundel, Archbishop of Canterbury, joined his objections to those of the Chief Justice, but Henry ignored their pleas on the grounds that Scrope was being tried as a baron and not as a bishop. So Scrope was condemned and executed.

The main religious problem of the reign was the suppression of Lollardry. Archbishop Arundel was resolute in trying to eradicate the new teaching. A priest, William Sawtrey, was summoned just after the statute *De heretico comburendo* had been passed. Among other opinions he thought money spent on pilgrimages would be better given to the poor, and he denied the doctrine of transubstantiation. Arundel spent many days trying to get Sawtrey to recant but he was obdurate and under the new law he was the first to be hanged in chains and burnt at Smithfield. A second case was that of John Badby, a blacksmith. He denied that the consecrated host was in any sense the body of Christ. Henry, Prince of Wales, was present at Badby's burning in Smithfield and offered him a free pardon if he would recant, and, cruelly as we should think, had the fire put out when the victim was already in agony and again offered pardon, but Badby proved constant and the fire was relit.

Henry V was of a more religious temper than his father. When Archbishop Arundel died in 1414, the king nominated Henry Chichele, Bishop of St. David's, to Canterbury. He was a canon lawyer who had been among the earliest students at William of Wykeham's New College at Oxford. Chichele had successful diplomatic experience under Henry IV and Henry V. He supported the latter's war with France but did not advocate it, as Shakespeare's play represents. He was among the best of the archbishops of Canterbury; he held many synods; he looked to the time when only university graduates would be ordained as priests; the number was on the increase during the fifteenth century but it long remained only a small percentage of those ordained. He also limited the functions of married priests. One odd decree was that barbers were not to work on Sundays; presumably the weekly shave kept the men from church. Chichele was the closest of Henry V's advisers. He was a patron of learning and established the Chichele Chest at Oxford to aid poor students. He was the founder of All Souls College, the endowment for which came in part from lands confiscated from the alien priories.

The Great Schism ended at the Council of Constance (1414–18) while Chichele was archbishop. The purpose of the Council was to remove the scandal of the Schism and, at the same time, to assert that full authority in the Church resided in the ecumenical councils to which, as its decree laid down, 'all men, of every rank and condition, *including the Pope himself*, is bound to obey in matters concerning the faith.' This was the triumph of the conciliar movement which aimed at imposing some kind of control over the popes. The Council had reached a deadlock when Henry Beaufort, Bishop of Winchester, arrived at Constance to represent Henry V. He persuaded the rival parties in the Council to reach an agreement. Cardinal Oddone Colonna was elected pope on the 11th November 1417 and took the name of Martin V. The anti-pope was ignored and soon faded out. The new pope wanted to make Beaufort a cardinal, but Archbishop Chichele objected and Henry vetoed the appointment; four years after the king's death Beaufort accepted the cardinalate but a writ of praemunire was issued against him. The matter was smoothed over by a restriction on his powers in England. Fortunately he was chiefly occupied with foreign affairs especially with the Hussite wars and was often out of the country. He supported the pope who was determined to recover full papal powers and had no intention of being ruled by a council. Beaufort was entirely secular in his outlook and he managed to amass great wealth. Archbishop Chichele was further humiliated when Pope Eugenius IV made John Kemp, Archbishop of York, a cardinal in 1439. Like Beaufort he was primarily a politician; he was a hard-working member of the council and York saw little of him. Chichele died in 1443. He was followed by John Stafford, a careerist who spent most of his life in public administration. When he died he was succeeded by Cardinal John Kemp but he died two years later.

In the Epilogue to Shakespeare's *Henry V* we read,

> 'Henry the Sixth, in infant bands crowned king
> Of France and England, did this king succeed:
> Whose state so many had the managing,
> That they lost France and made England bleed.'

That is not a bad summary of the tragedy of Henry VI. We remember him now as the pious founder of Eton College and of King's College, Cambridge. That is as it should be.

He was utterly unsuited to kingship at a time when only a masterful ruler could have kept control over the magnates who were jockeying for power and over the factious barons. When the Hundred Years' War ended, all that was left of the Angevin empire was Calais, and after that came the so-called Wars of the Roses. Henry was a man of religious conviction, a lover of learning and of sensitive taste. Could anyone have been more inadequate to meet the harsh realities of a ruthless and brutal age? For that was the other side of the coin; on the one side we have seen the wonderful flowering of the creative arts, but on the other its harshness and cruelty.

Thomas Gascoigne, four times chancellor of Oxford University, the last time in 1445, declared that there were three ways of making a bishop: 'the will of the king, the will of the pope or the court of Rome, and, the money paid in great sums to that court.' It will be noted that he said nothing about election by the cathedral chapters. Henry VI seems to have had small personal influence on the appointments since the great lords of the council spoke in his name. Two examples must suffice. Both the king and the pope, Nicholas V, agreed on Thomas (brother of John) Kemp being made Bishop of London in 1448 and the pope had actually made the provision, but the Duke of Suffolk, who was then the dominant person in the council, wanted a supporter of his, Marmaduke Lumley, Bishop of Carlisle, appointed; so the king wrote to the pope to say that he had changed his mind. However, the pope, no doubt sensing the pressure brought to bear on Henry, insisted on Thomas Kemp's appointment; at the same time he provided for the translation of Lumley to the more lucrative see of Lincoln. The second example was in 1457 when the see of Durham was vacant. Henry wanted John Arundel but the pope, Calixtus II, appointed Lawrence Booth who had been urged upon him by the queen and nobles.

The case of Thomas Bourchier is of interest. He was a descendant of Thomas of Woodstock, the youngest son of Edward III. He went to Oxford but does not seem to have made any mark. His birth explains why he was recommended for the see of Worcester in 1433 when he was not of canonical age. The pope had provided Thomas Brouns, dean of Salisbury, but the Commons urged the king to recommend Bourchier. There is no clear explanation of why the Commons took so much interest in promoting Bourchier on this occasion nor on later ones. The pope withdrew his provision of Brouns and Bourchier was appointed. When Ely fell vacant in 1435, the pope, at the request of the chapter, issued a bull for Bourchier's translation, but the council refused ratification as they preferred Cardinal Louis de Luxembourg, Archbishop of Rouen, who was chancellor of the English possessions in France; in spite of Archbishop Chichele's objections, the pope agreed to the Archbishop of Rouen administering the see of Ely. Louis died in 1443, and Bourchier, at the request of the king, the council not objecting, was translated from Worcester. Cardinal John Kemp, Archbishop of Canterbury, died in 1454; the Commons petitioned for the appointment of Bourchier; to this the lords agreed and the pope authorised the translation. Bourchier had no special qualifications either scholatic or pastoral for this series of promotions which culminated in his appointment as cardinal in 1473. He crowned Edward IV, Richard III and Henry VII. His career shows the working of an involved system by which bishops were appointed; it also illustrates that there was a ladder of promotion; Rochester and the Welsh sees were at the bottom of the ladder and Canterbury at the top.

An eccentric prelate was Reginald Pecock, a Welshman and former fellow of Oriel College, Oxford, who was successively Bishop of Bangor (1444) and of Chichester (1450). During a ten years' residence in London he had come into contact with the Lollards and set out to refute them. A sermon he preached at Paul's Cross in 1447 startled all shades of opinion as he defended absentee bishops (like himself), nor did he think bishops should preach; he also defended the use the pope and the Church made of their wealth; in his view the adoration of images was not to be

confused with the worship of God. He wrote many controversial books in which he put emphasis on the use of reason
in the reading of the Bible and of the Early Fathers; 'we
even believe Revelation when we see that it is reasonable.'
All indeed must be harmonised with the law of nature which,
in his view, was above the scriptures and the sacraments.
He even devised a new creed. His original intention of
refuting Lollardy had, in fact, led him to adopt some of their
opinions. His trial and condemnation as a heretic was
inevitable. He resigned his bishopric and was confined to
Thorney Abbey (Benedictine) and was not allowed writing
materials; for such a compulsive writer this last must have
been his greatest deprivation. The curious aspect of this
blatant case of heresy was that two popes, Calixtus III and
Pius II, intervened on Pecock's behalf. They could not have
known the nature of his teaching; probably they were
chiefly concerned with their responsibility for the bishops.
John Foxe included Pecock in his *Acts and Monuments of the
Martyrs*. There is no evidence that he had any substantial
support.

Edward IV was of no discernible religious conviction;
his private life went beyond the licence that custom overlooked in a king. He observed the proprieties due to the
Church and made two pilgrimages to Canterbury. When
bishops had to be appointed, he saw to it that they strengthened his position. Thus George Neville became Bishop of
Exeter at the early age of twenty-six as he was the son of
the Earl of Salisbury and brother of the future Earl of
Warwick. It was presumably to secure the support of the
Church that Edward issued a charter enforcing benefit
of clergy; in future all criminous clerks as well as those
charged with civil offences were to be tried in the ecclesiastical courts. This was putting the clock back, since his
predecessors from the time of Henry II had, in practice,
limited the jurisdiction of these courts.

From our point of time we can see that the most momentous happening in Edward IV's reign was the introduction
in 1476 of printing by William Caxton; this new way of

multiplying copies mechanically had been used on the continent for twenty years before then and it was to spread with astonishing rapidity. It would not be an exaggeration to say that the religious controversies we call the Reformation could not have had so great an influence but for the invention of printing. There must have been a large literate public waiting, as it were, for this development, and the publication of books quickly enlarged that public. It is noticeable that religious books such as missals, primers and devotional writings accounted for about half of the output of the presses for many years. This is another indication of the religious temper of the times.

The character of Richard III will always be an enigma. When he became Protector he imprisoned Thomas Rotherham, Archbishop of York, because he showed too great a loyalty to Elizabeth, the queen-dowager. The archbishop was released after the coronation of Richard III, but he pointedly absented himself from the reception given to the new king at York. Rotherham was a great benefactor to both universities; not the least of his achievements was that he saved Lincoln College, Oxford, when it was in financial difficulties. Archbishop Bourchier had persuaded the queen-dowager to hand over her second son, Richard, to his uncle and had pledged his word for his safety. There is no record of the archbishop's subsequent feelings. In 1484 the king issued a circular to the bishops enjoining them to combat the immorality of the times. In the same year he attended the Coventry miracle plays.

Henry VII's great task was the settlement of the country; people craved for peace, law and order after nearly two centuries of intermittent disturbance and war. The king made great use of ecclesiastics; indeed, until the new race of educated laymen could mature, he had little option. The natural leaders in the council, the nobles, had almost disappeared in mutual slaughter. Henry was a good judge of men. When Cardinal Bourchier died in 1486, he appointed John Morton, Bishop of Ely, to be Archbishop of Canterbury. He had shared the king's exile. He was a wise counsellor, and Thomas More, who was brought up in the archbishop's household, has left us an attractive portrait of him in *Utopia*. Morton did not allow his heavy state responsibilities to let him forget his pastoral duties. He did much to reform and improve the clergy of his diocese. It was by Morton's tactful approach to the pope, Innocent VIII, that Henry was able to check the long-standing abuse of the right of sanctuary. Churches were places of sanctuary and a criminal or fugitive could gain protection, or at least a breathing space, by taking shelter in one. Sometimes, as at Westminster Abbey, the privilege covered a considerable area round the church. The name Broad Sanctuary is a reminder of this ancient right. Needless to say, rogues found ways of abusing what was intended as a means of mercy. The clergy defended this ancient custom but Morton agreed with the king, and a bull from the pope set limits to the right of sanctuary. Morton was made a cardinal in 1493 and died in 1500. He was succeeded as archbishop by William Warham, who had been trained in the law and had proved to be a skilled diplomatist. It was a wise choice, for Warham was also a good churchman.

Another who had shared Henry's exile was Richard Fox, one of the great men of his times, whose advice was appreciated by the king. Although Fox was for many years engaged closely in state affairs and carried out several important diplomatic missions, he gave careful attention to his dioceses — Exeter, Bath and Wells, Durham and finally Winchester. We know that in his first two sees he had as suffragan Thomas Cornish, titular bishop of Tine. Fox is best remembered now as the founder of Corpus Christi College, Oxford, and of a lectureship in Greek in the university.

Henry was a sincerely religious man; in this he owed much to his mother, that great Lady Margaret Beaufort. Did she at some time comment on her son's choice of bishops? For the most part they were canon lawyers and diplomatists. Certainly the king was conscious that the chief reason for nominating a bishop had been the needs of the State rather than of the Church. This comes out in a letter he wrote to his mother when, at the suggestion of Bishop Richard Fox, he appointed her confessor, John Fisher, to be Bishop of Rochester in 1504. He wrote,

'I have in my days promoted many a man unadvisedly, and I would now make some recompense to promote some good and virtuous one which I doubt not should please God.'

It may be noted here that the king simply says that he is responsible for the appointment of a bishop; this may have not been technically correct, but it was a statement of what now became the actual practice. If the pope objected to a nomination, the king could reply by witholding the temporalities. There were occasions when the king found it useful to have someone with the ear of the pope; this explains the appointment of Italians to English sees, such as Giovanni Gigli, Bishop of Worcester, and his nephew Silvestrio who succeeded him at Worcester. Both were Henry's diplomatic agents at Rome, and the popes were well satisfied with the relations with England. Innocent VIII had issued a bull (27th March 1487) confirming Henry as lawful king and securing the succession to his children; this was perhaps a face-saving gesture as the power of the popes over secular princes was on the wane. In 1489 the pope sent the sword and cap of maintenance to the king; this mark of approval was also conferred by Alexander VI in 1496 and by Julius II in 1505.[1]

John Fisher had been confessor to the Lady Margaret Beaufort for several years before being appointed to Rochester. In 1501 he became vice-chancellor of Cambridge University and, shortly before becoming bishop, had been elected chancellor, a position he held for thirty years, the same length of time as he was Bishop of Rochester. He used his influence with the Lady Margaret to promote the two causes he had most at heart — religion and learning. In 1502 he obtained a papal bull giving the University the power to

[1] One of these caps is preserved at Exeter.

appoint twelve preachers who had the privilege of preaching anywhere in the country. A year later the Lady Margaret endowed readerships in divinity at both universities, Fisher being the first reader at Cambridge. Then in 1504 she endowed a special preachership at Cambridge; the holder was to give six sermons each year at Paul's Cross or at St. Margaret's, Westminster. During her lifetime she re-endowed Godshouse, Cambridge, as a new college to be named Christ's College, and the foundation of St. John's College was due to her. In all this John Fisher was the directing mind, for these good works furthered his desire to train scholarly priests who would be good preachers.

We are fortunate in having a foreigner's impressions of religious life at the end of Henry VII's reign. Andrea Trevisano was Venetian Ambassador to England, and in one of his reports he wrote,

> 'They all attend Mass every day and say many Pater-
> nosters in public — the women carrying large rosaries in
> their hands, and any who can read taking the Office
> of Our Lady with them, and with some companion
> reciting it in church, verse by verse, in a low voice after
> the manner of churchmen. They always hear Mass on
> Sunday in their parish church, and give liberal alms . . .
> nor do they omit any form incumbent on good Christians;
> there are, however, many who have various opinions
> concerning religion.'

It would, of course, be unwise to read this as generally applicable, but the ambassador was reporting what he himself had observed in London and thereabouts. Perhaps the most suggestive sentence is the last.

CHAPTER 15

The Break from Rome

HENRY VIII was not quite eighteen when he succeeded his father in April 1509. Two months later he married Catherine of Aragon, the widow of his eldest brother Arthur. Henry inherited several wise councillors whom he retained in his service. William Warham, Archbishop of Canterbury, was Chancellor; Richard Fox, Bishop of Winchester was Keeper of the Privy Seal, and Thomas Ruthall, Bishop of Durham, was the king's secretary. Although Henry spent long hours in hunting and sports, in dancing and in elaborate entertainments, he was not a play-boy king; his interest in state affairs during the early years of his reign was intermittent. For the time-being he was enjoying his vigorous youth, but, like the other Tudors, he had a good brain though his thinking did not go far below the surface. He had been well educated, and, it was said, while he was still the second son, he was intended by his father to be Archbishop of Canterbury and he had some instruction in theology; certainly he always took an interest in theological questions and could talk about them intelligently, but an amateur theologian is a dangerous person. The Venetian ambassador reported, 'He is very religious and hears three Masses daily when he hunts and sometimes

five on other days. He hears the Office every day in the
Queen's chamber, that is to say, vespers and compline.'

From the beginning of his reign Henry was a supporter
of the pope, from whom he received the golden rose in 1510
and the sword and cap of maintenance in 1513. This
attitude of loyalty to the papacy was still strong when in
1521 he wrote his *Assertio Septem Sacramentorum* in answer
to Luther. The manuscript was vetted by experts and then
handed to Sir Thomas More to get it ready for printing.
He warned the king that his support of the pope's authority
went too far since the pope 'is a prince as you are and in
league with all other Christian princes.' The king would
have none of this. 'We are so much beholden unto the See
of Rome that we cannot do too much honour to it.' Sir
Thomas then tried another approach; he reminded Henry
'of the statute of praemunire whereby a good part of the
pope's pastoral care was pared away.' To which the king
replied, much to More's astonishment, 'We will set forth
that authority to the uttermost for we received from that
see our crown imperial.' Presumably he was here referring
to the bull of Innocent III which confirmed Henry VII as
King of England.

The second Parliament of the reign met in February 1512,
and the Convocations, according to custom, at the same
time. That for the Canterbury Province gathered in St.
Paul's Cathedral for Mass and a sermon. The preacher was
the Dean, John Colet. He pointed out the evils among the
clergy — their pride in their dignities, 'carnal concupiscence'
banqueting and hunting, covetousness in seeking more and
richer benefices; such wrong-doings meant that the clergy
were dishonoured and despised. He inveighed against 'the
continual secular occupation wherein priests and bishops
nowadays doth busy themselves, the servants rather of men
than of God.' He then turned to the way of reform. 'This
reformation and restoring of the Church's estate must need
begin with you our fathers, and so follow in us your priests,
and in all your clergy.' He pointed out that there was no
need for new canons; all that was required was to enforce

the decrees made by synods and councils time and time again. Some of these he recalled to their minds: let only worthy men be ordained; let promotion come by merit; let simony be abolished; let priests reside in their parishes and bishops in their dioceses; let monks observe their rule, and let the wealth of the Church be spent, not in buildings and pomp and feasting 'but in things profitable and necessary to the Church.'

Among Colet's listeners was Thomas Wolsey, Dean of Lincoln, his feet now firmly placed on the ladder he was to mount so rapidly. Only four years were to pass before John Colet was called upon to preach in Westminster Abbey on a very different occasion. It was the official reception of the cardinal's hat conferred on Wolsey by Leo XI with the king's approval. The new cardinal organised a magnificent spectacle in his own triumph described by an onlooker as only equalled 'at the coronation of a mighty prince or king.' The preacher gave a warning of the danger of Wolsey's new authority, a warning that fell on deaf ears.

'Let no one in so proud a position, made most illustrious by the dignity of such an honour, be puffed up by its greatness. "He who exalts himself shall be humbled, and he who humbles himself shall be exalted." '

Wolsey's own conception of his dignity was shown when the procession left the Abbey. No cross was borne before the Archbishop of Canterbury, but the new Cardinal had two — one as cardinal and the other as Archbishop of York.

There is some truth in saying that the history of the Church in England for the next fourteen years was the history of Cardinal Wolsey, provided we bear in mind that the essential inner life of the Church, the administration of the sacraments, the worship and prayers of the people subsisted in parishes up and down the land. Ordinary folk in country places (where the majority of the population lived) would not be aware of Wolsey's autocratic rule over the higher clergy, but they would see him as the outstanding example of some of the abuses at which they grumbled. He was, for instance, the great pluralist of his day. At the time of his fall in 1529 he was at one and the same time, Archbishop of York, Bishop of Winchester, and, though not a monk, Abbot of St. Alban's, the richest monastery in England, besides holding other benefices. His nepotism may not have been widely known. His bastard son Thomas Wynter was made Dean of Wells when below canonical age; he held seven prebends and two archdeaconaries besides other benefices.

Wolsey became a papal legate in September 1515 at the instance of the king and in May 1518 he was appointed *legatus a latere*, and, by exceptional provision, was later granted that position for life. A *legatus a latere* was usually sent on a special mission and when that was completed the commission lapsed. As we have noted, the Archbishops of Canterbury had long been given the status of *legatus natus* but this carried with it precedence but no special powers. It will be recalled that when Henry Beaufort was appointed a legate by the pope in 1417, Henry V would not allow him to exercise such authority in England and a writ of praemunire had been issued against him. Did this come to Henry VIII's mind in later years?

Wolsey had become Lord Chancellor at the end of 1515; he thus controlled the secular courts and as legate the ecclesiastical courts; no man before or since has been given such wide powers in this country. Here we are concerned with his relations with the Church. At first he showed some concern with the need for reform but as he became more and more absorbed in foreign affairs so the early intention waned. This meant that urgently needed reforms were postponed until it was too late. People noticed that his actions, such as suppressing monasteries that were failing for want of subjects or money, tended to add to his financial resources; his colleges at Ipswich and Oxford benefited but they were expressions of his pride; thus his cardinal's arms were carved on every vantage point at Cardinal College (now Christ Church). So it went on; he rode roughshod over any opposition so that at his fall there was no man of influence to plead for him.

He used his legatine powers to push the Archbishop of Canterbury into the background; he ignored the bishops in making visitations in their dioceses and even in filling benefices to an extent never allowed to the popes. He disliked the Convocations and synods as much as he disliked Parliament; whatever he did brought fees and perquisites. How far he demoralised the bishops and abbots cannot be assessed, but that they deeply resented this invasion of their powers is certain. He interfered with Church government far more than any pope had dared to do, and the ordinary people were quick to see that the Cardinal-legate was a greater menace than any pope had been. It has been well said that 'he rode papal jurisdiction in England to its death.' This in turn reflected on the popes whose standing was thus weakened.

Wolsey's attitude towards Lutheranism gives the impression that he was not seriously perturbed; he himself was not a theologian and he was beset with state affairs. He presided over a burning of heretical books at Paul's Cross in May 1521 when Bishop John Fisher was the preacher. This was in response to the papal bull *Exurge Domine* against Luther. Wolsey again presided at the abjuration in February 1526 at Paul's Cross of Friar Robert Barnes and four merchants of the Steelyard. These were official occasions. He knew so little of what was fermenting that in 1525 he arranged for some of the brilliant young Cambridge scholars to be transferred to his new College at Oxford. These men were nearly all attracted to Lutheran ideas and so they carried their influence from one university to the other.

Martin Luther's attack on the trade in indulgences in the theses he put forward in October 1517 took some time to make any impact on England. Erasmus sent a copy of one of Luther's pamphlets to Thomas More in March 1518 but neither left any comment on it. It was not among the factors that provoked anti-clericalism in this country because the government kept a tight control over papal collectors and there seems to have been no organised sale of indulgences here, certainly not on the scale that had roused Luther's justifiable indignation. The three pamphlets he issued in 1520 were a different matter; these were *The Babylonish Captivity of the Church*, *The Liberty of a Christian Man*, and *An Appeal to the Christian Nobility*. They do not appear to have been translated into English. It was the first of these pamphlets that gave rise to Henry VIII's *Assertio Septem Sacramentorum* (1521). Luther had argued that there were only three sacraments authorised in the Gospels — baptism, penance and the eucharist. Later he deleted penance. In the other pamphlets he questioned the powers of the papacy and put forward his distinctive doctrine of justification by faith alone.

It was naturally among scholars at the universities that these new ideas first circulated and were discussed, but there was also another group of inquirers among the London merchants and well-to-do tradesmen who had contacts with Germany and Antwerp through the Hansa head-quarters in London at the Steelyard. It was they who financed William Tyndale and others who had left England to sit at the feet of Luther and his disciples. It was these merchants who made possible the printing and marketing of Tyndale's translation of the New Testament in 1526, a date that is more important for this country than Luther's theses of 1517. The bishops did all they could to suppress the book; they even bought up copies until they realised that they were providing funds for further printings.

The story of the next twenty years is too complicated to set out in a few pages. Moreover we lack vital information. Heavily documented as Henry's reign is, we have few clues to help us understand why and how policies were devised or who was primarily responsible for them. Here we can do little more than indicate the main lines of development. Fortunately we need not unravel the tangled skein of the king's marriage proceedings; they had a direct bearing on the break with Rome but they had no direct doctrinal significance; this political severance did help to loosen men's attachment — already much weakened — to the Holy See.

Henry's claim to be 'protector and only Supreme Head

of the English Church' (January 1529) was central to the religious situation, or it would be more exact to say, to the governance of the Church in England. This was not conceded by the clergy in their Convocations without prolonged argument and protest. The crucial questions were — 'What exactly did "Supreme Head" involve? Did it imply spiritual authority, the cure of souls?' The precise distinction between 'temporals' and 'spirituals' was not obvious; it had to be worked out in practice. Though the king did not claim priestly functions, he did insist on his right to govern the Church in all other respects including its jurisdiction in its courts and the power of the Convocations to enact new canons. This was to transform the Church *in* England into the Church *of* England. In the end the clergy gave way. We should be better able to appreciate the position if there were full reports of the debates in the Convocations. Some may have thought that the king was doing little more than make explicit what had long been implicit in the royal authority in England. Others, more perceptive, may have feared that this was only the thin edge of the wedge. Yet others may have felt that it was hopeless to oppose the royal will. It may be that this surrender can in part be attributed to the demoralisation resulting from the undermining of episcopal authority under Wolsey's arrogant rule, and his unexpected and total disgrace probably unnerved the bishops and abbots; it was a warning of the power and ruthlessness of the king. The clergy were able to slip in a qualifying phrase, 'as far as is allowed by the law of Christ', but that was soon forgotten. The bishops lacked a forceful leader. Archbishop Warham was a tired man of eighty who could not face a new conflict. He died in August 1532. John Fisher was outspoken in his opposition; we do not know how much support he had in the discussions but it was not enough to win the day. His final comment was 'The fort has been betrayed even by those who should have defended it.' It should be noted that the acquiescence of the Convocations did not make the new title statutory.

The stages of the retreat from Rome must be briefly

recorded. An act in restraint of Annates (i.e. payments made of the first year's revenue of a benefice) was passed in 1532 but held in suspense; annates were an important item in the papal revenues, so the threat to cut them off could be used as one way of cajoling the pope into yielding to the king's wishes. The Act in Restraint of Appeals (1533) was the decisive statute; it forbade all appeals to Rome; in future such causes would be settled by the Archbishop of Canterbury; this Act, in effect, removed all ecclesiastical jurisdiction from Rome and lodged it with the Crown. The words of the preamble are significant. 'This realm of England is an empire . . . having the dignity and royal estate of the imperial crown of the same.' The purpose was 'to keep it from the annoyance as well as of the see of Rome, as from the authority of other foreign potentates.' An Act of Dispensations (1534) transferred to ecclesiastical authority in England powers that had hitherto been exercised by Rome, as well as the visitation of exempt monasteries by the heads of their orders. The Act of Supremacy (1534) made statutory the acceptance of the title by the Convocations.

Henry had married Anne Boleyn secretly in January 1533. Four months later the new Archbishop of Canterbury, Thomas Cranmer, annulled the marriage between Henry and Catherine and declared that between Henry and Anne to be valid. The Princess Elizabeth was born in July 1533; the pope then excommunicated Henry and declared the marriage with Anne to be invalid. On 23rd March 1534 the pope declared the marriage between Henry and Catherine to be valid. The news seems to have made little stir in England. Seven years had passed since the issue had been raised and this long delay further weakened the prestige of the papacy. It may be that people had become bored with the whole affair.

The sudden mention of Thomas Cranmer calls for some explanation as for twenty years he was to be a dominant influence in the religious life of the country; indeed his influence through the Book of Common Prayer is still pervasive. He first came to the notice of the king with his suggestion that the opinions of the universities on the king's marriage problem should be sought. Henry was not an originator of ideas but he was quick to seize on suggestions that fell in with his inclinations. At Cambridge Cranmer had moved towards Lutheranism but his religious beliefs never became static; he continued to ponder the theological and liturgical problems raised by the Reformers and it is difficult to define his position at any one period. He was not a fanatic nor a violent controversialist. He became chaplain in the Boleyn household where reformist, perhaps anticlerical, ideas were regarded sympathetically. He had some diplomatic experience which brought him to the favourable notice of the emperor and also of the pope; he was sent to make contact with the German princes and while in Germany he married the niece of Andreas Osiender who had started as a Lutheran but had soon got out of step as so many of the earlier adherents did. This marriage clearly intimated that Cranmer no longer accepted the discipline of the Church. It is not known how far Henry VIII was aware of Cranmer's divergence; presumably Cranmer's critics must have told the king of the marriage. The lady lived a retired life. There was one son and a daughter.

It may have been at the suggestion of Anne Boleyn that Cranmer was made archbishop; the proposal took him by surprise as indeed it took most people. The relations between Henry VIII and Cranmer are baffling to anyone who tries to understand the two men. One thing must be kept in mind; Cranmer shared with most of his contemporaries a deference to the kingship of the king; Henry was always conscious of his regality and it was part of his power. Not that Cranmer was obsequious; at times they differed in their interpretation of doctrine and in their religious policy; in the end Cranmer usually gave way simply because the king was the king, an attitude we find it difficult to appreciate. He could always count on the king's support in times of difficulty. It is tempting to think of them as friends if true friendship had come within the compass of Henry's personality. Thomas Cromwell once remarked to the archbishop, 'You were born in a happy hour, I suppose, for, do or say what you will, the king will always take it at your hand.'

During the first seven years of his archbishopric Cranmer had to work in harness with Cromwell whose appointment as Vicar-General (hitherto an ecclesiastical position) and Vicegerent in Church affairs in 1535 considerably limited the traditional authority of the archbishop and indeed of the bishops. Yet they appear to have worked together harmoniously. This appointment must have been a shock not only to the clergy but to reflective laymen; this lay-official was not conspicuously devout. Cromwell was discreet about his own beliefs, as indeed many found it prudent to be at that time. His sympathies were certainly with the Reformers, but it is more difficult to decide whether this was because of religious conviction or because he disliked muddle and indiscipline. John Foxe of the *Book of Martyrs* saw him as a precursor of Protestantism in England and in that respect Cromwell's advocacy of the English Bible can be brought in support. One accusation against him was that he had shielded heretics, but the details are lacking.

The first injunctions he issued (1536) were in part on the same lines as those issued by bishops to their priests in earlier times. He urged the need, for instance, for the instruction of the people in the articles of the faith. He put new emphasis on the responsibility of parents to provide for the education of their sons and of the wealthy to give financial support to schools and colleges. There was a reference to the superstitious adoration of images and relics. This last point was more strongly repeated in the second injunctions of 1538. The most important of the injunctions referred to the provision of the English Bible in every church. It seems that Anne Boleyn's influence was here at work and she may have persuaded the king, with the help of Cranmer, to moderate his opposition to the publication of an English Bible. We cannot go into the details of the various versions produced. The Great Bible, as it came to be known, was published in April 1539. It was largely the work of Miles

Coverdale, a former Augustinian friar. The second edition of 1540 contained a notable preface by Cranmer.

Cromwell's powers included the visitation of all monasteries and convents. Much has been written of the work of his commissioners. Their work was speedily done, too speedily to inspire confidence. Those who have no sympahy with the monastic ideal accept the commissioners' findings with some reservations. Others, who have some appreciation of what was lost to the religious and cultural life of the country when monasticism was swept away, are not so credulous. No one will deny that there were defects, some serious, that should have been, and could have been, corrected by the Church itself, but many of the scandalous charges were part of the human situation — men who had lost their sense of vocation, others perhaps who had never had a true vocation and so were more easily subject to the temptations of their human nature. Even so, the wholesale destruction of the system could not be justified. The process of dissolution began in 1536 with the smaller houses and was extended to all in 1539. The dissolution of the smaller monasteries was one of the causes of the Pilgrimage of Grace in October 1536, but this very serious threat to the government was far from being solely a religious uprising; it gathered together, so to speak, a number of grievances some of which were economic. It was ruthlessly suppressed.

Most of the confiscated lands, perhaps as much as two-thirds, were sold or leased. Only a fractional part was given away. Of the lands retained by the Crown little was left by the end of the reign of Elizabeth I. The buyers were, it should be remembered, Catholics, including such staunch adherents as the Arundells among the nobility, and William Roper among the commoners. The dispossessed monks and nuns were pensioned. According to the social attitudes of the day, abbots and priors received preferential treatment. Many of those who were priests were able to find benefices or other clerical employment.

Cromwell was the master-mind behind the well-planned legislation that gave statutory authority to the radical adjustments that were needed in the retreat from Rome. The first move was an Act of Succession (1534). This was far more than a simple statement of the line of succession. The long preamble dealt with the king's marriage. Throughout Queen Catherine was referred to as 'the Lady Catherine', and it was laid down 'that the said Lady Catherine shall henceforth be called and reputed only dowager to Prince Arthur, and not queen of this realm.' In her place appears the 'most dear and entirely beloved wife Queen Anne.' It was declared that 'according to the just judgement of Thomas, Archbishop of Canterbury' the marriage with Catherine was 'utterly void and annulled', thereby bastardising the Princess Mary. Further it was stated that in future all questions affecting marriage were to be settled not by 'the Bishop of Rome', but by 'any archbishops, bishops, or other ministers of the Church of England.' This was a sweeping decision, but, who were the 'other ministers'? The succession was settled on Henry's surviving eldest son or, failing a son, on the Princess Elizabeth. Everyone had now to take an oath to accept the whole Act, not just the part referring to the succession, but to the preamble repudiating Queen Catherine, and, by implication, the authority of the papacy.

This Act was followed by a new Act of Treason (1534); it was this that was to lead to the martyrdoms of fifty Catholics. The old law of Edward III had covered obvious cases of treason such as planning to overthrow the government or raising a rebellion. This new Act invented another kind of treason, that of wishing or willing by words or writing to deprive the king or queen of any of their royal titles. This effectively silenced those priests and laymen who had hitherto voiced their objections to the supremacy, either from the pulpit or in conversation. Prior to 1534, there was no law that could be invoked against those who voiced opposition unless there was open incitement to treasonous action. There had, in fact, been considerable grumbling up and down the country, but, apart from some local riots, it did not express itself in action. As 'Supreme Head' was one of these titles, to *say* that the king was not Supreme Head now became treason. It was a perversion of justice to make the spoken word treasonous unless there was also evidence of action being planned. It opened the door wide for the informer and blackmailer; a loose word in an ale-house might be sufficient. The common opinion of the Act was shown when within a few months of the death of Henry VIII it was repealed; by then it had become known as the 'Act of words.'

We can follow Thomas Cromwell's policy for he was a clear thinker and could plan the means to reach his objectives. It is far more difficult, indeed almost impossible, to see into the mind of the king; there were times when the Reformers had hopes that he was moving their way, but he always drew back from definite commitment. There was, for instance, the contact he made with the Lutheran princes in 1534–5 but the motive was more political than religious. There is nothing to tell us precisely how far the Boleyn Lutheran sympathies affected him; the publication of the Great Bible, it has already been noted, may have been due to Anne Boleyn's advocacy. The Ten Articles of 1536 can be taken as representing Henry's views at that date; these were imposed to establish unity of belief. The king gave much thought to this pronouncement which was issued over the signatures of Thomas Cromwell, Thomas Cranmer and the bishops. The Bible, the three creeds and the decrees of the Ecumenical Councils were to be accepted. Baptism, Penance and Justification were dealt with on traditional lines with small modifications. Images were to be allowed provided no superstitious ideas were attached to them. The established rites and ceremonies were to be maintained. Praying for departed souls was commended but doubts were expressed about their state since nothing definite was to be found on the subject in the Scriptures.

In the following year the bishops were responsible for *The Godly and pious Institution of a Christian Man*, usually known as *The Bishops' Book*. The king licensed it for three years but admitted that he had not had time to examine it.

The bishops at that date included some with Lutheran leanings such as Nicholas Shaxton (Salisbury), William Barlow (St. Asaph) and Edward Foxe (Hereford). Their views were reflected in this new statement of what a Christian should believe. It was an attempt to reconcile the divergent views in the episcopacy. Great emphasis was put on the king's authority, and, by contrast, on the usurped authority of the pope. The creeds, Scripture and the seven sacraments were set down as the basis of belief, and the sacramentals (holy water, the ceremonies of Ash Wednesday, Palm Sunday and the like) were commended as 'useful to turn our minds to God.' All this was submitted subject 'to the most excellent wisdom and exact judgment of Your Majesty.'

When the book was printed, Henry read it carefully and made his annotations; he exchanged comments with Cranmer and Tunstal. Some of the points made by the king were shrewd, but others showed an inadequate grasp of the theological principles involved.

Whatever modicum of encouragement the sympathisers with Protestantism may have been able to find in *The Bishop's Book* was abruptly removed by the Act of Six Articles passed by Parliament in 1539. Here, indeed, was the recognition that Parliament had authority in doctrinal questions. The final draft of these Articles was the king's. Among Protestants this Act became known as 'the bloody whip with six strings.' It imposed no penalties but it became the yard-measure of heresy. The first article reaffirmed the Catholic doctrine of the eucharist; the second stated that communion 'in both kinds is not necessary *ad salutem.*' The third declared that priests 'may not marry, by the law of God'; this is not Catholic teaching since celibacy is a matter of discipline and the rule could be abrogated at the will of the Church. The fourth article commended vows of chastity and widowhood. Henry seems to have been obsessed by the subject of marriage; it had even been dragged into the Act of Succession by a clause dealing with the prohibited degrees. The fifth article approved of private Masses; finally, 'auricular confession is expedient and necessary.'

This Act was not passed without difficulty. On the one side were such traditionalists as Tunstal and Gardiner; on on the other such 'modernists' as Thomas Cranmer and Hugh Latimer. The king himself presided over some of the debates in the Lords and displayed his theological learning and shortcomings. Cranmer objected to the statement that celibacy of the priest was 'the law of God' but Henry was quite certain he knew what was God's law about marriage. So Mrs. Cranmer had to lead an even more retired life. The archbishop also questioned the second (communion) and sixth (confession) articles, but the king was not to be moved. Two bishops did persist in their opposition; Hugh Latimer and Nicholas Shaxton had to resign their sees. There were also warm debates in the Commons especially on the doctrine of the eucharist.

The Act was a defeat for Cranmer; it was probably also a defeat for Thomas Cromwell. In the following year his enemies achieved his downfall; politically Henry's acquiescence was his most foolish action for he lost the clearest-headed and most efficient of his councillors and there was no one to replace him. He had no successor as Vicar-General and Vicegerent; by this time Henry seems to have been satisfied that the archbishop needed no layman to supplement him. Moreover the business of the monasteries was as good as settled. Cranmer was the only one to plead for Cromwell as he had been the only councillor who tried to prevent the executions of More and Fisher. This makes Henry's treatment of Cranmer all the more striking by contrast with his sacrifice of Cromwell. On more than one occasion the king saw to it that the archbishop was not harassed by his enemies, this was in spite of their theological differences, or was it that Henry enjoyed such arguments?

The *King's Book* of 1543 was the last attempt to reach agreement on doctrine. Henry took an active part in its preparation. It can be regarded as a revision of the *Bishops' Book*. The full title was *A Necessary Doctrine and Erudition for any Christian Man, set forth by the King's majesty of England*. Its exposition of the creeds and meaning of the sacraments is clearer than in its predecessor. One notable omission was its failure to expound the significance of the Mass, which is barely mentioned. What was in the king's mind? He later suggested to the French ambassador that the Mass should be abolished in both countries. This may have been but one indication that Henry's religious belief had an insecure foundation, and that, at times, even apart from political expedience, he was more attracted to Protestantism than his actions revealed. The impression is of a man with a somewhat muddled mind. The speech he made to his last Parliament reveals that he was getting wearied with all the battling between rival schools of thought. The following quotation is worth pondering.

'I see and hear daily that you of the clergy preach one against another without charity or discretion. Some be too stiff in their old Mumpsimus, others be too busy and curious in their new Sumpsimus. Thus all men almost be in variety and discord, and few or none preach truly and sincerely the word of God according as they ought to do ... How can poor souls live in concord when you preachers sow among them in your sermons, debate and discord? Of you they look for light, and you bring them to darkness. Amend these crimes I exhort you, and set forth God's word, both by true preaching and good example giving, or else I whom God hath appointed his Vicar and high minister here, will see these divisions extinct, and these enormities corrected, according to my very duty, or else I am an unprofitable servant and untrue officer.'

All this must have been very confusing to ordinary people and indeed to all thinking people. The king had certainly put his finger on the discord resulting from divergent interpretations of doctrine. The topsy-turvy state of affairs is well illustrated by the following incident. The date is 30th July 1540. The place is Smithfield. A gallows has been erected for the hanging of three victims; there are also three stakes with piles of faggots for the burning of three other victims. The first three were Catholic priests to be hanged for treason; the second three were heretics.

The Catholics were priests: Thomas Abel, Richard Fetherston and Edward Powell. Thomas Abel had been chaplain to Queen Catherine and her outspoken defender; Richard Fetherston had been tutor to the Princess Mary. These two showed how perilous it was to have been closely associated with the unhappy queen and her daughter. Edward Powell was a noted preacher. These three had refused to accept Henry as Supreme Head of the Church in England. They had been in the Tower for six years and had resolutely resisted every inducement to change their minds.

The heretics were: a former Austin friar, Robert Barnes, William Jerome, a former Dominican, and Thomas Garrard an Oxford Fellow.

Not one of these six had been brought to trial but had been condemned by Acts of Attainder; thus they had not been allowed to defend themselves. Robert Barnes, at the stake itself, complained that they had not been told the nature of their heresies.

As if to emphasis the eccentric nature of the occasion, each Catholic had been coupled with a heretic on the hurdles when they were dragged to Smithfield.

A foreigner in England at the time made the comment, 'What a strange country where papists are hanged as traitors and antipapists burned as heretics!'.

This incident shows the difficulty of tracing any well-conceived line of religious policy in the last twenty years of the reign. Henry must have been well aware of the rising tide of Protestantism ('their new Sumpsimus'). At court, Edward Seymour, later the Protector Somerset, and brother-in-law to the king, was high in favour though his Protestant sympathies were well known. So too Catherine Parr, Henry's last wife, favoured the new teaching. She was the most gracious and intelligent of his queens since Catherine of Aragon. At one stage her religious opinions brought her dangerously near being sent to the Tower, and she is said to have persuaded the king to mitigate the application of the Six Articles. Henry would know that some of the Protestant clergy had left the country; they were moderates when they went, but extremists when they returned in the next reign. The king was sufficient of a realist to see in what direction men's thoughts were turning. His discussions with Cranmer would have been a warning that the old paths were being left by the new people.

It must have been considerations of this kind that led the king to appoint as tutors to his son scholars who were moderate Protestants. Such were Richard Cox and John Cheke, while the boy's French tutor, John Belmain, was a Calvinist. The only interpretation that can be put on this choice is that the king sensed the religious changes that were coming and wanted to prepare the Prince Edward for them. This may have been politically prudent and far-sighted but it was not a service to orthodox Catholicism.

As if to accentuate this policy, the Council of Regency to guide the boy should his father die within the next few years, was predominantly Protestant in character. The intention was that the sixteen members should have equal powers though it may be wondered if Henry really believed such an arrangement workable; someone would have to be at their head if only for administrative purposes. As things turned out it was the boy's uncle, the Protestant Edward Seymour, who was to take the lead and become Protector. The members of the Council were either avowedly Protestant or were willing to go along for want of strong religious principle. The omission of such an experienced and able statesman as Bishop Gardiner was significant; while he approved of the break from Rome, he remained stubbornly conservative in his faith.

It is a hazardous task to try to see into the workings of Henry's mind, but what has just been said seems a reasonable interpretation of this final phase of his policy.

Henry VIII died on 28th January 1547, his hand pressing that of Thomas Cranmer. That too seems appropriate.

CHAPTER 16

The Henrician Martyrs

THE first victims of the Act of Succession were the Carthusians of London. Surely, no body of men could have been chosen who were less likely to talk of or even imagine political action. They were widely respected for the strictness with which they observed their rule. When they were asked in May 1534 to take the oath prescribed by the Act, their prior, John Houghton, replied that the king's affairs did not concern them; but he and his fellow monks were persuaded, after some hesitation, that there was nothing in the Act contrary to the faith; so they took the oath. It may be doubted if, at this stage, they had studied the Act or even have heard of it, so completely apart were they from public life. Indeed it would be probably true to say that a large majority of people who took the oath were unaware of the implications of the long preamble dealing with the king's marriage. It was unlikely that all this was explained by the commissioners when they put the oath, nor that all those taking it troubled to read through the whole Act; for most, the fact that it was the king's wish as declared by Parliament, was sufficient.

When the Carthusians came to think things over and to study the Act more closely, their doubts grew. They were again brought face to face with the problem when commissioners visited the monastery in the spring of 1535 to demand that the monks should specifically acknowledge the king's Supremacy. It might have been thought that the acceptance of the Supremacy by the Convocations in 1531 was sufficient as far as the clergy were concerned. This new title was not yet statutory so only the clergy were involved at this stage. The move may be regarded as the first step towards the dissolution. The subsequent harsh treatment the Carthusians received was, in part, an expression of Cromwell's annoyance at their evading his first demand; acceptance was a hindrance to his anti-monastic policy. The Friars Minor (Observants) of Greenwich had already been imprisoned or dispersed for refusing to accept the Supremacy; they were the first to suffer, no doubt because they had been under the patronage of Queen Catherine to whom they were devoted.

Meanwhile the Act of Supremacy and the Treason Act had become law; it now became treason even to say that the king was not Supreme Head. Two fellow Carthusian priors came to consult John Houghton in the spring of 1535. They were Robert Lawrence of Beauvale and Augustine Webster of Axholme. They were troubled in their minds and consciences about the Supremacy for this was not a civil matter like the king's marriage but one that touched the authority of the pope. So ignorant were they of the political world, they ingenously sought an interview with Thomas Cromwell to beg that they might be excused from taking this new oath. They were quickly disabused. They must conform or suffer the consequences. On their refusal they were committed to the Tower. They must have been three very bewildered men so remote had their lives been from state affairs. They were brought to trial on the 28th April on a charge of treason since they had refused to accept one of the king's titles. Could the injustice and absurdity of the Act have been better demonstrated? Here were three Carthusian monks, the last people in the world to bother themselves with what went on outside their enclosure, accused of treason because they could not in conscience recognise the substitution of the pope by the king. At the trial the jury was at first reluctant to convict, but, after some threats from Cromwell, the required 'Guilty' was pronounced.

On the 4th May 1535 they were dragged on hurdles from the Tower to Tyburn. With them was Richard Reynolds, a learned Bridgettine monk who was an intimate friend of Thomas More; also John Haile, parish priest of Isleworth. They were watched as they left the Tower by Sir Thomas More and his daughter Margaret. No doubt this had been arranged in the hope that the plight of these five priests might shake Sir Thomas's resolution through his daughter's distress. He was, however, encouraged by their serenity, saying, 'Lo, dost thou not see, Meg, that these blessed fathers be now as cheerfully going to their deaths as bridegrooms to their marriage?'

The crowd that assembled along the route to Tyburn was shocked to see that these victims still wore their religious habits. The custom had always been that a cleric handed over to the civic authorities for a criminal offence, was first degraded and then defrocked. A group of courtiers had assembled at Tyburn; among them were the Dukes of Norfolk and Suffolk, the Earl of Wiltshire (Anne Boleyn's father), and the Duke of Richmond, the bastard son of Henry VIII. Rumour said that the king himself was there in disguise; there is no confirmation of this and it is unlikely, but the rumour is significant.

Three more of the London Carthusians were hanged on the 19th June: Humphrey Middlemore, William Exmew and Sebastian Newdigate. For two years every kind of pressure was brought to bear on the remaining monks and lay-brothers; they were lectured and preached at and forced to read books justifying the king's proceedings. Eventually eleven, including five lay-brothers, were sent to Newgate prison where they were chained and manacled so that they could not move hand or foot. They were, as one of Cromwell's commissioners said, 'to be despatched by the hand of God.' Margaret Giggs, the adopted daughter of Sir Thomas More, did what she could to succour them, but her efforts came to an end when the authorities found that the prisoners were not dying fast enough. They were not brought to trial, but died of starvation during the summer of 1537.

A comment by a modern historian, Dom David Knowles, himself a Benedictine, is worth quoting.

'They had left the world, as they had hoped, for good; but the children of the world, to gain their private ends, had violated their solitude to demand of them an approval and submission which they could not give. They had long made their austere and exacting Rule a means to the loving and joyful service of God; pain and desolation, therefore, when they came, held no terrors for them. When bishops and theologians paltered and denied, they were not ashamed to confess the Son of Man. They died faithful witnesses to the Catholic teaching that Christ had built His Church upon a rock.'[1]

During the last twelve years of Henry VIII's reign, fifty Catholics were martyred; one bishop, thirty-two religious, nine secular priests, seven laymen and one woman; she was Margaret Pole, Countess of Salisbury, a niece of Edward IV and a close friend of Queen Catherine and, for twelve years, governess of the Princess Mary. Although Henry had once described her as the most saintly woman in England, he did not scruple to have her beheaded when she was close on seventy years of age. She was convicted by Act of Attainder on the flimsiest evidence and kept in the Tower in distressing circumstances. She was beheaded on 28th May 1541.

Of the laymen the most eminent was Sir Thomas More. Few men have had to face such a crisis of conscience or have given up so much. It is worth examining this aspect of his life as it brings out so clearly the problems that beset him and his contemporaries.

It is worth emphasising how intimate Thomas More had been with Henry and Catherine during the four or five years

[1] *The Religious Orders in England* (1959), III, p. 236.

after he had become a councillor in 1517. He was with the court as it moved from manor to manor like a swarm of locusts eating up supplies at one place before passing on to the next. More was one of the small group of councillors in attendance on the king, and there are a number of letters written by More on behalf of the king to Wolsey. Henry and Catherine found More's company so congenial that he could rarely get away to see his family. He had no delusions about Henry's character after this close association. Some years later, after one of the king's visits to Chelsea, William Roper remarked to his father-in-law how proud he must be of such familiarity. To which the reply came, 'If my head could win him a castle in France, it should not fail to go.'

We must go back to 1526 when the king first put before Thomas More his doubts on the validity of his marriage. Henry regarded his lack of a male heir as a divine judgment on him for marrying his brother's widow contrary to the injunction in Leviticus 20, 21, 'If a man takes his brother's wife, it is impurity.' Henry's argument was that even the pope could not dispense with God's law; as we have seen the king became more and more convinced that he knew what was God's law on religious problems. Thomas More asked for time to consider the question; he read the Early Fathers and consulted the leading theologians and canon lawyers. As a result he told the king that in his opinion, the marriage was valid. This was not what Henry hoped to hear, but he took no offence as he was confident that he could get what he wanted from the pope. As the cause dragged on year after year, so the king's feelings towards those who would not support him, became soured. A few years later Sir Thomas spoke to the emperor's ambassador 'of the liberty he had always used in speaking boldly to King Henry in those matters which concerned the Emperor Charles and Queen Catherine.' There is no indication of the extent to which More was aware of the infatuation of Henry with Anne Boleyn. No doubt the king may have hoped that when More became chancellor, he would be more compliant.

The increasing strain of the campaign against the clergy and the whittling away of the pope's authority in England led to More's resignation in 1532. His persistent silence on the marriage problem was as eloquent as many words.

The time came when Thomas More knew he must declare himself. The occasion was the coronation of Anne Boleyn on Whit Sunday 1533. He refused to attend. Friends tried to persuade him to change his mind but he warned them that their attendance would be only the first step on a slippery slope. Events were to prove how right he was. The new queen took the absence of the former chancellor as a personal rebuke and he thus incurred her implacable enmity. He knew now that there could be no going back, and he knew, too, that the king would sooner or later exact the penalty for his opposition. 'If my head . . .' It had not been easy for him to make his great decision. He once told his daughter Margaret that he had spent many sleepless nights counting the cost to his family, so dear to him, as well as to himself.

The crisis came with the passing of the Act of Succession in 1534. More was summoned to Lambeth Palace on the 13th April 1534 to take the oath before a special commission of councillors. When he left his Chelsea home that morning, Thomas More knew that there was little hope of seeing it again; he recognised that the die had been cast. As they were rowed down the river, he said to his son-in-law, 'Son Roper, I thank Our Lord the field is won.' When they arrived at Lambeth they found that Bishop John Fisher was already there, for, in spite of the aged bishop's frail health, he too had been summoned. Fisher was also well aware that there could be no going back. Before he left Rochester he distributed his goods saying, 'You may doubt of the time of my return hither to you again.'

Thomas More refused to take the oath after he had read through the Act. He was willing, he said, to accept Parliament's decision on the succession, but he could not accept the contentious matters also covered; he had in mind, the implied repudiation of papal authority. He refused to give

197

his reasons or to go in to details. The commissioners must have realised to what he objected.

Bishop John Fisher took exactly the same stand. It should be noted that, at this stage, the question of the king's Supremacy had not yet become legal. Fisher and More were given time to reflect, but at a second summons, they again refused to take the oath and were sent to the Tower; this was on the 17th April. Under the Act they were guilty of misprision of treason for which the penalty was imprisonment for life and the forfeiture of goods. They were both condemned by Acts of Attainder in the next session of Parliament in the autumn of 1534.

It was while Fisher and More were in the Tower that the Acts of Supremacy and Treason were passed. This now meant that anyone refusing to recognise one of the king's titles, such as Supreme Head, would be guilty of treason with the death penalty to follow. The intention was to get the two prisoners to say that the king could not be a Supreme Head. If they did that, they were trapped. At several interrogations the two prisoners were urged to express an opinion on the Supremacy; both refused to answer such a question and so incriminate themselves. Fisher was tricked into saying the fatal words. The solicitor-general, Sir Richard Rich, came to see him; he was, he claimed, the personal emissary of the king who was still not satisfied in his conscience that he could be Supreme Head. He therefore begged John Fisher to give his real opinion, on the understanding that whatever he said would not be used against him. Fisher felt that, as a priest he must answer this appeal, so he solemnly declared that 'by the law of God, the king could not be, and was not, Supreme Head.' In spite of the promise made, these words were reported by Rich at Fisher's trial on the 17th June 1535, and so brought his condemnation. He was executed on the 22nd June.

Rich then tried to trap Thomas More but he was now dealing with the foremost lawyer of his day. More treated the questions put to him as an exercise in legal fencing rather like the moots held in the Inns of Court. He skilfully avoided making any direct statement on the Supremacy. Nevertheless at the trial on the 1st July, Rich asserted that More had denied the king's right to the new title. This blatant perjury made More angry, the only sign of disturbed emotion that he showed. So he was condemned.

After the expected verdict of 'Guilty', More felt that he was free to speak his mind. He pointed out that the Acts were 'repugnant to the laws of God and his Holy Church, the supreme government of which belonged to the see of Rome, a spiritual pre-eminence.' No single member-country of that Church could legislate for the whole body contrary 'to the general laws of Christ's Universal Church, no more than the City of London might make a law against an Act of Parliament; no more might this Realm of England refuse obedience to the see of Rome than might a child refuse obedience to his own natural father.' He added that he knew that at the root of his condemnation was his opposition to the king's separation from his lawfully married wife.

On the scaffold on the 6th July 1535 he declared that he died the king's good servant and of God first of all.

The other Catholic martyrs of the reign of Henry VIII could have said the same words. They died for the unity of the Church under the pope. They were aware of the need for reform; they were also aware of the unworthiness of the popes of their day; they were far from ignorant of the corruption and venality that besmirched the Roman Curia. These considerations make their stand all the more impressive.

There were others of integrity who could not take the same position. One of More's closest friends, Cuthbert Tunstal, successively Bishop of London and of Durham, was not able to go with him. He had spent some years in Padua and Rome and had not liked what he saw. His considered opinion was that the papacy was of human, not divine, institution, and he found it impossible, to separate the office from the holder of the office. More believed that the Petrine claims were transmitted from pope to pope whether saint or sinner. He made this point in his controversy with Luther. He wrote, '... the case of a

man and his office, of conduct and authority, of virtue
and power, is so distinct that, even though the heavenly
life which God has promised to virtue is taken away
from wicked and criminal men, nevertheless the earthly
authority which God has joined to their office is not taken
away.' And again, 'How much more should we desire God
to make such men popes as well befit the Christian commonwealth and the dignity of the apostolic office, so that, freely
spurning riches and earthly honours, they may breathe a
wholly heavenly spirit, promote piety among people and
procure peace.'

There was another consideration that weighed with those
like More and Fisher. They believed that the rejection of
papal authority would inevitably lead to the disruption of
the Church and to civil discord. Nor was this just theory;
they could see around them the results of Luther's defection,
for his own followers soon split into rival groups until it
seemed that Luther would be the last Lutheran. No one was
more aware than More of the dangers to the social order of
the break-up of the Church. The extravagances of some of
the extremists who refused both Church and Luther, and
the horrors of the Peasants' War were a grim commentary.
The remarks of a martyr of our own times, Dietrich Bon-
hoeffer, himself a Lutheran pastor, are to the point.

'One wonders how it was Luther's action led to consequences which were the direct opposite of what he had
intended, and which overshadowed the last years of his
life and work so he doubted the value of everything
he had achieved. He desired real unity for the Church and
for Western Christendom, but the consequence was the
ruin of both. He sought the "Freedom of Christian Men",
and the consequence was apathy and barbarism. He hoped
to see the establishment of a genuine social order free
from clerical privilege and the outcome was the Peasants'
War, and soon afterwards the gradual dissolution of all
cohesion and order in society.'

The martyrs of Henry VIII's reign were not put to death

for denying any doctrine of the Christian faith; they were not heretics; they did not plot against the state, but their fate was to be beheaded or hanged, drawn and quartered for a newly invented kind of treason that involved the repudiation of papal authority.

CHAPTER 17

Protestant—Catholic

So in January 1547 a boy of nine became Supreme Head of the Church of England. Many must have felt that this was grotesque. The bishops were made aware that the Supremacy was not in abeyance when their appointments lapsed with the death of Henry and had to be renewed by letters patent in the new reign. Religious policy was now firmly in the hands of Cranmer with the full support of the Protector Somerset. Neither was by nature an extremist nor a persecutor but they were not entirely free agents. Protestantism had taken a firm hold in London; it had been restrained by the power and fear of the old king, but now it could make its voice heard. Outbreaks of image breaking were difficult to control. A spate of controversial books and pamphlets poured from the presses. Preachers at Paul's Cross were openly Protestant in their sermons. 'Hot Gospellers', as the more zealous were called, preached and lectured at will. We must, however, remind ourselves again that the centres of this agitation were the big cities; the countryside was largely unaffected and Somerset and Cranmer knew that to carry the people with them would mean a cautious handling of the majority of the population who went to Mass in their village churches.

Some of the bishops urged that there should be no religious changes during the king's minority, but such a stand-still was impracticable in view of public opinion. The conservative leaders were Stephen Gardiner (Winchester) and Tunstal (Durham) and Bonner (London). Gardiner was undoubtedly sore at not being a member of the council; he had been deliberately omitted by Henry who did not trust him but his steady opposition was based on conviction. Tunstal was one of the executors of Henry's will as well as being a member of the council so that he was in a position of prestige. The bishops fell into three groups. Ten of them were opposed to any change; about the same number were intent on promoting Protestantism under the guidance of Cranmer. Of this group, Nicholas Ridley (Rochester) was the most radical and he had considerable influence over Cranmer. The rest of the bishops, eight of them, could not unfairly be described as careerists who would swim with the tide.

In July 1547 injunctions ordered that in addition to copies of the English Bible, copies of Erasmus' *Paraphrases* (these had to be completed) and Cranmer's *Book of Homilies* were to be available in all churches. These injunctions were on much the same lines as those issued by Cromwell; images were to be destroyed, processions and the use of candles were regulated and anything savouring of super-stition, such as some of the popular devotions, were to be avoided. At the same time a general visitation by royal authority was to be carried out. As Bonner was obstructive when the visitors came to St. Paul's he was imprisoned in the Fleet for two months. Gardiner objected to the *Para-phrases* and *Homilies*, so he too was imprisoned.

When Parliament met in November 1547 its first task was to repeal several Acts of the previous reign. These included the dreaded Act of Treason (the Act of words) and all statutes concerning religion such as that of the Six Articles. It was further enacted that those who 'shall unreverently speak against the sacrament of the body and blood of Christ' would be subject to imprisonment. Communion in both kinds was allowed since, it was claimed, this had been primitive practice. Yet another statute decreed that in future the appointment of bishops would be by royal letters patent and not by election. This Parliamentary activity, so much done in such a short time, may be compared with the work of 1534–5. This early Edwardian legislation really pleased very few; Catholic conservatives were alarmed, while the radicals thought that Parliament had not gone far enough. Somerset and Cranmer were evidently set on a policy of *festina lente*, or, one might say, of clearing the decks.

An Act was also passed dissolving chantries, hospitals, guilds and fraternities. A previous Act at the end of Henry's reign had not been implemented owing to the king's death. This dissolution hit the towns far more than was done by the sweeping away of the monasteries. It affected schools and hospitals that depended for support on chantry bequests. Some of the schools were retained, and some of them now bear the name of Edward VI. For the most part the funds went into the exchequer and the lands were eagerly bought up.

Meanwhile Cranmer was recruiting the Protestant forces from abroad. Peter Martyr, a former Austin friar of Italy, became Regius Professor of Divinity at Oxford. Martin Bucer, an early disciple of Luther, was given the similar position at Cambridge. Bernardino Ochino, another Italian and a famous preacher, joined Cranmer's entourage. Besides these three notable Reformers, several lesser known divines accepted Cranmer's invitation to come to England to strengthen the Protestant cause. Support also came in correspondence with such leaders as Melancthon, Bullinger and Calvin himself. Against such a body of learned preachers Catholics in England could not muster defenders of equal learning and reputation. Gardiner was the most resolute opponent of the new order. Somerset and Cranmer tried to bring him to their way of thinking, but he was inflexible. After his few months in the Fleet in the autumn of 1547, he was allowed to return to Winchester, but he soon showed that he was irreconcilable; he was sent to the Tower in June 1548 where he remained until the end of the reign.

He was deprived of his bishopric in February 1551. Tunstal, too, was soon out of favour. His duties as President of the Council of the North during the Scottish disturbances kept him away from London for months at a time, but his opposition to the religious changes was absolute. He was called to London in May 1551 and put under house arrest; during this period he wrote a defence of the Catholic doctrine of the Eucharist. Six months later he was sent to the Tower and in September 1552 he too was deprived of his see. Both Gardiner and Tunstal, the two leading survivors of the Henrician episcopacy, changed their views on the Supremacy when, as they considered, advantage was being taken of the king's minority to further Protestant views. Tunstal may have reflected that, perhaps, after all, his old comrade Thomas More had been right. Gardiner's *De vera obedientia*[1] was constantly being brought up against him; the bishops were, in fact, in a difficult position. Those accused of heresy were quick to point out that they were being arraigned for opinions the bishops themselves had recently avowed.

The second session of Parliament met in November 1549 and its legislation was crucial. An Act was passed permitting priests to marry. Eight bishops voted against the bill. By the end of the reign a number of the bishops had married. The proportion of the clergy who did so varied from about thirty per cent in the south-east to ten per cent in the north. The great measure discussed in this Parliament was the Act of Uniformity which made *The Book of the Common Prayer* the only permitted form of public worship. The bill was thoroughly debated in both Houses. In the Lords the main point of discussion was the nature of the Eucharist; it was then that Cranmer admitted that he no longer accepted the Catholic doctrine of transubstantiation. At the final vote eight bishops were against the bill. It was passed on 21st January 1549 and it was ordered that the new service was to come into use by the next White Sunday, the 9th June. It was in print, in folio, early in March; unbound copies

[1] Printed in 1535. It was a defence of Henry's Supremacy.

cost two shillings and twopence, and copies in boards three shillings and eightpence. Such orders could be issued from Parliament but it was not a simple matter to get them carried out as the administrative machinery did not exist and visitations took time and were infrequent. To hasten matters, further instructions were sent out for the destruction of the old missals and other church-books. Enforcement was easier in the big towns, but it took time for remote villages to come into line. As far as the records show, most people accepted the new services, and 'most people' included the majority who were Catholic. There were evasions and some passive resistance; for instance, a priest might use the new wording but would add, contrary to the instructions, the gestures of the Mass. Others would say Mass privately for those who wished for it. In some churches there were what amounted to riots, but these were rare. The general mood was acquiescence and many must have asked, 'How long will this last?' The reading of Cranmer's *Homilies*, not aggressively Protestant in tone, was obligatory. So for four years the people grew accustomed to this English service. There were some minor revolts. The Welsh, the Cornish and the Irish objected to the English because to them it was as foreign as the Latin to which they were accustomed. The trouble in Wales and Cornwall was soon put down, but Ireland proved unyielding. The Act did not compel attendance at church; penalties were reserved for recalcitrant priests who were liable to increasing penalties leading to imprisonment for repeated failures to use the new services. One result of the Act of Uniformity was the emigration of those Catholics who could not bear to be deprived of the Mass. Among them were members of the More circle, such as his nephew William Rastell.

The preliminary work for *The Book of Common Prayer* must have been done during the later years of Henry VIII; he, however, was not ready to permit such an innovation which would have amounted to a declaration in favour or Protestantism. The farthest he would allow Cranmer to go was the publication in 1544 of an English Litany. It is not necessary to give here an account of Cranmer's correspondence on the liturgy with foreign Protestant leaders, nor of his discussions with English bishops. He strove to satisfy as many scholars and theologians as possible so that the new services would be widely acceptable to those who were not extremists. The first Prayer Book was therefore less radical than Cranmer himself may have wished. In his preface he made two points. Over the centuries the services of the Church had become more and more complicated, in the course of which the reading of the Bible had become less systematic. Secondly, there had grown up in England a number of local variations, 'some following Salisbury (Sarum) use, some Hereford use, some the use of Bangor, some of York, and some of Lincoln. Now from henceforth all the realm shall have but one use.' In fact the differences were not great and did not affect the central act of worship. The need for greater uniformity had been recognised by the Church, and Cardinal Quiñonez had carried out a simplification of the medieval uses in 1535 and Cranmer owed something to this pioneer work which was ultimately superseded by the breviary of Pius V after the Council of Trent (1568). Cranmer's laudable objectives could have been reached without giving the book a Protestant character. This new orientation is most clearly shown in 'The Supper of the Lord and the Holy Communion commonly called the Mass.' Thus the priest after the consecration was instructed, 'The words before rehearsed are to be said, turning still to the Altar, *without any elevation or showing the Sacrament* to the people.' At the Communion, 'Then shall the priest first receive the *Communion in both kinds* himself, and next deliver it to other Ministers and after to the people.' The words used were, 'The body [blood] of our Lord Jesus Christ which was given for thee, preserve thy body and soul unto everlasting life.' Communion was to be received 'all kneeling humbly upon their knees. 'The last rubric enjoins that *Communion is to be received by the people 'in their mouths, at the Priest's hands,'*[1] although it is said earlier,

[1] The most significant phrases are here italicised.

'And although it be read in ancient writers, that the people many years past received at the priest's hands the Sacrament of the body of Christ in their own hands, and no commandment of Christ to the contrary. Yet forasmuch as they many times conveyed the same secretly away, kept it with them, and diversely used it to superstition and wickedness: lest any such thing hereafter should be attempted, and that an uniformity might be used, throughout the Realm: it is thought convenient the people commonly receive the Sacrament of Christ's body, in their mouths, at the Priest's hands.'

There are a number of variations from Catholic usage which may at first have escaped the notice of many. Prayers invoking the saints were omitted and the calendar of saints drastically pruned. Our Lady was mentioned only once, and a significant sentence in the consecration read, 'Grant this, O father, for Jesus Christ's sake, our only mediator and advocate.'

The Book did not satisfy the more zealous Protestants such as John Hooper, Bishop of Gloucester, who had caused considerable trouble with his scruples about wearing vestments. It became apparent that a revision would be needed to meet criticisms. How this was done is not known; it was certainly not done by the Convocations; it seems probable that Cranmer alone was responsible. The revised Book, known as the Second Prayer-Book of Edward VI, was authorised by Parliament in April 1552 in a second Act of Uniformity. A comparison between the two Books shows how much farther along the Protestant road the authorities were prepared to go, but it should be noted that it was Parliament that gave the necessary permission; it was no longer a matter solely for the ecclesiastics.

The changes in the Communion service were significant. The sub-heading 'commonly called the Mass' was dropped. The altar is banished; instead,

'The Table having at the Communion time a fair white linen cloth upon it, shall stand in the body of the Church,

or in the chancel. . . . And the Priest standing at the
north side of the Table. . . .'

The words used at the Communion 'in both kinds' were
changed to,

> 'Take and eat this [Drink this] in remembrance that
> Christ died for thee, and feed on him by faith, with
> thanksgiving.'

It was now directed that *the Communion should be given 'to the
people in their hands, kneeling.'* Note — *'in their hands'* not as
before 'in their mouths.' The prayer before consecration
left out the name of Our Lady. Even while the Book was
printing, some members of the council raised new objections
to the rubric that the people should kneel when receiving
Communion. So the printing was stopped and a final
paragraph added. This became known as the Black Rubric.
Its importance lies in its outright rejection of Catholic
teaching on the eucharist. It reads,

> 'Lest yet the same kneeling might be thought or taken
> otherwise, we do declare that it is not meant thereby,
> that any adoration is done, or ought to be done, either
> unto the Sacramental bread or wine there bodily received,
> or unto any real and essential presence there being of
> Christ's natural flesh and blood. For as concerning the
> Sacramental bread and wine, they remain still in their
> very natural substances, and therefore may not be adored,
> for that were Idolatry to be abhorred by all faithful
> christians. And as concerning the natural body and blood
> of our saviour Christ, they are in heaven and not here.
> For it is against the truth of Christ's natural body, to
> be in more places than in one, at one time.'

A further change was in the kind of bread used. In the
earlier Book, it was to be 'unleavened and round, as it was
afore, but without all manner of print, and something much
larger and thicker than it was.' This became, 'such as is
usual to be eaten at the table with other meats, but the best
and purest wheat bread.'

As the boy-king died within eight months of the date when the Second Book was to come into use, it did not have time to make much impact, but the present authorised Book of Common Prayer of the Church of England is substantially the same; even part of the Black Rubric is retained.

Cranmer produced a series of forty-two articles in 1554. This statement of belief had not been discussed by the Convocations but was issued under letters patent. There were two notable points: the seven sacraments were reduced to two (baptism and confirmation), and the doctrine of transubstantiation was condemned. The importance of these articles was that they were the basis of the thirty-nine articles of 1571 that are still to be found in the Anglican Prayer Book.

These Church affairs must be seen against the background of the deplorable struggle for power among the magnates. The Protector was a strange mixture of genuine sympathy with the lot of common folk and a personal lust for self-aggrandisement. His chief opponent was John Dudley, later Duke of Northumberland, a man of coarser fibre with few redeeming qualities. The tale of intrigue and perfidy that resulted in the execution of Somerset in 1552 cannot be told here. Protestants hoped that their cause would be furthered by Northumberland and at first it seemed they had good reason but he was a man who had no religious convictions and he used the Protestants as long as they seemed useful to him. He followed Somerset to the scaffold in 1553 after the abortive attempt to put the Protestant Lady Jane Grey on the throne.

The six years' reign of Edward VI marks a dividing line between a Catholic and a Protestant England, for, as we shall see, the attempt to return to the old religion during the five years of Mary Tudor's reign proved a tragic interlude that set back Catholicism permanently. This is not to say that the nation was Protestant by the end of Edward's reign; far from it; London and the south-east was more markedly so than the rest of the country. Protestants had been given sufficient encouragement by Somerset's rule to take a firm hold in some sections of the people, but the majority were more bewildered than convinced and had no interest in abstruse discussions on the nature of faith and of the Eucharist. There was a strongly Catholic element and a strongly Protestant element but in between most people were passively waiting to see how things moved. Had a more prudent policy been followed in the reign of Mary, the nation's religious history might have developed on other lines.

Mary Tudor came to the throne at the age of thirty-seven. Until she was fifteen she had enjoyed all the privileges of a princess; then came the separation of her parents; mother and daughter had to live apart; her formidable father alternately favoured her and neglected her. She was twice declared illegitimate. Her Catholic faith was her main consolation and, during her brother's reign, she resisted as long as she could the orders of the council that she should give up the Mass. By the time of her accession, the nervous strain of those twenty years or more had taken its toll of a woman who, by nature, was of a kindly disposition. She had been forced to lead a secluded life, and could have had few contacts with the outside world; consequently, when she was enthusiastically greeted by the people in the streets of London at her accession, she undoubtedly misinterpreted the welcome the received. Public opinion had not supported her claim to the throne because she was a Catholic, but for her clear hereditary right. She may have thought that Lady Jane Grey had been rejected as a Protestant; she was soon to discover, to her consternation, that London was a stronghold of Protestantism. Part of her tragedy was that she had no wise counsellor at hand to guide her and to warn her. The council, far too large, was at sixes and sevens and were mostly second-rate men. As chancellor she had Bishop Stephen Gardiner; he was an embittered old man, but he had considerable influence until his death at the end of 1555. The queen relied most, unfortunately, on the imperial ambassador, Simon Renard, for she looked to her cousin, Charles V, for advice. He was not interested in the welfare of England but in safeguarding his vast dominions, but he too passed from the

political field when he abdicated in October 1555. By then
he had the satisfaction of having brought about, indeed of
having insisted upon, the marriage of his son Philip to Mary.
To make sure of this marriage, the emperor had delayed the
arrival in England of Cardinal Reginald Pole who had been
appointed legate by Julius III. There had been a movement
in favour of the marriage of Mary to Reginald Pole (he was
not yet in deacon's orders); from a dynastic point of view
it had much to commend it. He was a grandson of George,
Duke of Clarence, brother of Edward IV. Once the suggestion that she should marry Philip was made to her, Mary
became obsessed with the proposal. Gardiner and some of the
council opposed this Spanish match; they knew how unpopular it would be. Wyatt's rebellion at the beginning of
1554 was more anti-Spanish than pro-Protestant. The
marriage took place in July 1554, and Cardinal Pole arrived
in England four months later.

Queen Mary was determined from the first to restore
Catholicism in England and to heal the breach with Rome.
The title of Supreme Head was obnoxious to her but, on her
own authority, she could not do away with it. The first
Parliament repealed the church legislation of Edward VI's
reign; the intention was to return to the position as it was
when Henry VIII died; this left the question of papal
authority in the air. Among Acts repealed was that permitting priests to marry; in consequence some 1,500 priests
were ejected, but many found ways round the new decree.
Parliament was not to be rushed into a more radical reversion
to the past. There was the thorny question of monastic and
church lands to be faced. The queen would have liked them
returned as an act of reparation, but the holders, most of them
Catholics, were naturally opposed to giving up what they had
legally bought. Moreover, since some of the lands had
changed hands more than once any attempt to unravel the
legal complications would have created a lawyer's paradise.
It was not until assurances had been given that there was
to be no resumption of these lands, that Parliament was
prepared to consent to reunion with Rome. So on the 30th

November 1554, Cardinal Pole, in a solemn ceremony, absolved the nation and restored it to the unity of the Church. Parliament then went on to repeal all ecclesiastical legislation back to 1529.

The aspect of Mary Tudor's reign that must always excite strong emotions was the bitter persecution of heretics. Between February 1554 and November 1558, two hundred and seventy three were burnt. If we except the bishops — Cranmer, Hooper, Latimer, and Ridley — the majority were of the artisan class. Foxe's *Book of Martyrs* (1563), which was a household book for generations second only to the Bible, and of which copies were chained in many churches, did more than anything alse to perpetuate the memory of those four years so that hatred of Catholicism became part of the English outlook. The main facts collected by Foxe need not be disputed though some of his em- bellishments must be read with reservations. For instance, his characterisation of Bishop Bonner of London is open to question. As the majority of the victims were in the diocese of London, which at that time included Essex, the impression is given that Bonner was the leading persecutor; but any Bishop of London would have been faced with the same concentration of Protestantism. Foxe's charge of sadism against Bonner is not supported by independent evidence, indeed it is clear from some of the accounts that he spent much time trying to persuade heretics to recant, as many of them did. Moreover there is a letter written to Bonner in May 1555 from the queen and the king rebuking him for being too lenient and not sufficiently co-operative with the magistrates who had the duty of delating suspected heretics to the bishops.

It may be doubted if the Smithfield fires excited so much horror at the time as we imagine. Catholics and Protestants alike accepted burning as the due penalty for heresy. In an age when hanging was so common — it has been estimated that some 12,000 victims were hanged every year — the dreadful fate of some three hundred heretics in four years would not have seemed so horrible at that time as it does to us, though, God knows, we, in this century, have no right to cast the stone at our forebears; our scientific progress has brought greater horrors. This is not to excuse the burnings; it proved a disastrous policy that was to stifle Catholicism for several centuries.

Whose policy was it? Dates are here important. Up to 1554, the time of Wyatt's rebellion, the persecution of heretics had not been exceptional. At the beginning of the reign, Mary declared that she would force no one to go to Mass, but that those who wished to do so must not be prevented. The outbreaks of sacrilege and blasphemy with the inevitable hooliganism that followed the revival of the Mass, must have come as a shock to the queen. In that same year she married Philip of Spain, and, a few months later, Cardinal Pole arrived in England; the old heresy laws were re-enacted. We have no means of knowing how far Philip or Pole was responsible for the queen's change of policy; there can, however, be no doubt that she countenanced the persecution. A more powerful influence behind her was probably exerted by the Spanish chaplains who arrived with Philip. Bartolomé Carranza, later Archbishop of Toledo, a Dominican, was the most important; later he boasted that 'I have no other object in life than that of suppressing heresy.' Supporting him were three other Spanish priests. The queen was particularly susceptible to Spanish influence; she was herself half-Spanish. This does not exonerate Pole and Gardiner; of the two the Cardinal was the more implacable and there are no indications that he exerted a restraining influence. This policy was in keeping with the spirit of the age; the heretic was regarded by all religious parties as a moral outcast who threatened not only religion, but the state itself.

In fairness to the queen it must be admitted that during the second half of her reign she was in a highly neurotic condition. Her vain expectations of a child, and her long separations from her husband who had to take up great responsibilities on the abdication of his father in October 1555, combined to undermine a spirit that had been already sorely strained by the unhappy years after she had been separated from her mother. To this must be added in her last year the awareness that the attempt to eradicate Protestantism had failed and that she would be succeeded by a Protestant; she was clear-sighted enough to see that, although Elizabeth went to Mass, she was not at heart a Catholic.

The pope who sent Pole to England died in 1555 and was succeeded by Paul IV (Carafa). In his prime he had been a leader of reform from within the Church, but he was also a zealous supporter of the Inquisition. He became pope at the age of seventy-nine; his political ambition was to humiliate Spain. So it was that in 1557 Spain dragged England into war against France and the pope. It must have been a bitter day for Mary when her husband went to war against the pope and was excommunicated. The disastrous consequence for England was the loss of Calais in January 1558; it was our last foothold in France and its loss was felt as a national disgrace. It was probably his anger at England's alliance with Spain that led the pope to withdraw Cardinal Pole's commission as legate and to summon him to Rome on a vague charge of heresy. It would seem that by this time Paul V had allowed his anger to disturb his mental balance. Queen Mary showed there was something of her father in her. She wrote to the pope that, as for the charges against Pole, 'she would, in observance of the laws and privileges of her realm, refer them to the cognizance and decision of her own ecclesiastical courts.' Nor would she allow the publication of the papal letters. In fact she acted as if she were Supreme Head. This conflict with the pope dragged on and it had not reached a conclusion until both queen and cardinal were dead. They died on the same day, the 17th November 1558.

The reign of Mary Tudor had a tragic outcome for the Roman Catholics of England. When she came to the throne, the majority of the people were Catholic in upbringing. The four years during which the Book of Common Prayer had been enforced had not produced the intended uniformity. Many Catholics tolerated it as having some affinity with the old services, but many Protestants denounced the Book as a Laodician compromise. It might have been possible for a wise and prudent successor to Edward to have brought back Catholicism as the predominant religion of the country. Protestantism could not have been suppressed but it could have been contained. Unhappily Mary Tudor lacked the experience of men and affairs to frame an acceptable policy. There was no one she could trust among the power-greedy councillors who had produced a state of near anarchy by the time she became queen. So she took her lonely and tragic road. The legacy of her reign was a hatred of Catholicism that was kept alive for several centuries by *The Book of Martyrs*.

CHAPTER 18

How did the Reformation happen?

'REFORMATION' is defined in the Oxford English Dictionary as 'the great religious movement of the sixteenth century, having for its object the reform of the doctrines and practices of the Church of Rome, and ending in the establishment of the various Reformed Protestant Churches of central and north-western Europe.' The term has been established by custom just as 'the Divorce' is accepted for the rejection of Queen Catherine by Henry VIII, and it would be doctrinaire to avoid their use. At the same time it is allowable to question the accuracy of calling the schism a 'reformation.' Whether the innovations in doctrine constituted a reformation depends on one's religious convictions, but, as for some of the abuses so loudly condemned, they were not corrected for several centuries. Thus the ecclesiastical courts continued their leisurely and expensive proceedings until 1857; even benefit of clergy was not abolished until 1779, and tithes were a source of friction until 1836. Pluralism and absenteeism were not brought under control until a hundred years ago. A married clergy meant a great increase in nepotism until it became a public scandal during the nineteenth century.

There is no simple answer to the question, 'How did the

Reformation happen?'. Historians have varied in their assessments of the conditions that brought about the great change. A number of so-called 'causes' have been touched upon in the previous pages, but it will be useful, at the expense of some repetition, to bring these together so that the over-all picture can be seen. The order in which these factors will be noted is not intended as an indication of relative importance; it should be kept in mind that all these factors were operative at the same time; sometimes one, sometimes another, would predominate, but not to the exclusion of the others.

1. *The Papacy*

Sufficient has been said already about the declining prestige of the papacy — the years at Avignon, the Great Schism, and the scandal of the Renaissance popes. From being religious leaders they had contracted to being Italian princelings, making alliances and waging wars like other secular rulers. Their position was further eroded by the development of states under kings and princes who insisted on liberty to follow their own national and dynastic policies.

2. *The Bishops*

As we have seen, during the fifteenth century and on into the sixteenth, many bishops were ministers in the king's government or were employed as diplomatists, and a bishopric was regarded as a normal way of rewarding or paying a cleric who had given outstanding public service. Such men were qualified not by their learning or their holiness but by their administrative gifts. Moreover their training was more often in canon or civil law than in theology. While it is true that the duties of these absentee bishops were delegated to suffragans, they did not themselves know their dioceses nor their clergy, and some were more intent on enriching themselves than on the spiritual welfare of their people.

3. *The Priests*

There were undoubtedly many priests who had not gone beyond the grammar school, and some had not even done that. Episcopal registers tell us of the failures but little of the successes. There must have been great numbers of these good or competent priests who served their parishes with faithfulness; the very existence of the Church depended on their apostolate. Scandals were mostly connected in the towns with the semi-employed chantry priests and footloose friars. The need was for a well-trained clergy.

4. *The Monasteries*

No responsible historian now accepts as the whole truth the reports made by Cromwell's commissioners. Yet there was undoubtedly a decline in fervour; the greater houses were often too involved in the care of their estates, and their abbots had become more like landed gentry than monks. The lesser houses too had their failures. These weaknesses could have been remedied, but the purpose of the dissolution was not cure but confiscation. It has been argued that the gentry and rising mercantile class coveted the monastic lands; no doubt some of them did, but without the connivance of Cromwell, acting for the king, there was little they could have done about it, and there is no evidence that Cromwell was under pressure from the land-hungry, though he was besieged as soon as land became available. It is worth noting that right up to the dissolution, lands were being bequeathed to the Church, and chantries being endowed.

5. *The Laity*

It has been maintained that one reason for the inertia of the laity was lack of an informed understanding of their faith. There is no means of testing this, though the fact that bishops, or their officials, sent out suggestions on the instruction of the parishioners shows that the problem was not neglected but taken seriously. Many, then as now, would have what Cardinal Newman called 'a material faith,' which he described as 'that sort of habitual belief which persons possess in consequence of having heard things said in this or that way from their childhood, being thoroughly familiar with them, and never having had difficulty suggested to them from without or within.' Now clearly a 'material faith' such as this is not likely to stand up to attack. The Catholic layman is neither a theologian nor a philosopher; he accepts the teaching of his priest and the catechism, and is content. How many Catholics to-day could defend the doctrine of the Trinity or expound the nature of the Eucharist? Faith does not, fortunately for most of us, depend on a deep intellectual understanding of doctrine.

Perhaps the best description of the state of the ordinary Catholic in those days was that it was one of bewilderment. Suddenly he was told to make first one and then another change in his way of worship; he was told to renounce the pope, then to use the new English service, only to be told next to return to the Mass and his allegiance to the pope, and following that to revert to the English worship and once more renounce the pope. All this in the space of twenty years or so. In the end he probably shrugged his shoulders and left things to his betters and those with book-learning to sort it all out. Yet there must have been many humble souls who felt that something precious had gone out of their lives; they must have looked back nostalgically to the days when there was no dispute about Christian beliefs. They were not of the stuff of martyrs; they endured what authority decreed; they were Chesterton's 'secret people' who 'never have spoken yet.'

This is one reason for not trying to estimate how many Catholics there were in the country at any one time after the break from Rome. We do not know, and any estimates are little better than guess-work. The 'secret people' were never counted; had things turned our differently, they would have resumed their Catholic lives with the Mass and their beads. As the years passed, so the old loyalties became weaker and people had to make their own decisions, for, as we shall see, the Church failed to give them any lead.

6. *Anti-clericalism*

There was strong anti-clerical feeling especially in the towns. It was based on legitimate grievances which the Church should have met, such as the delays, costs and inter-ference of the ecclesiastical courts, the fees exacted by the clergy, the scandalous lives of some clerics and the wealth of some of the higher clergy. To use modern language, there was a growing feeling that many of the clergy, monks and friars were unproductive. A kind of lethargy had settled on the Church, and, although the Convocations had discussed these complaints, it all ended in talk. Even John Colet's 1512 sermon had failed to persuade the clergy to reform themselves. Yet, while admitting that this anti-clericalism had a sound basis, it could not alone effect a reformation and its importance has been exaggerated. As was pointed out in the first paragraph of this chapter, the Reformation failed to put right some of the very defects of which people complained.

7. *The Divorce*

It should be recognised that Henry VIII's break from Rome was a political act, even a self-regarding act by the king. He had probably not thought out the larger consequences; it was the one way in which he could get what he wanted. While it did not lead to any marked official divergence from orthodox teaching, it did raise the expectations of Protestants and give them more confidence in the ultimate success of their cause.

8. *The Mental Climate*

This rather vague term connotes those changes of outlook that mark the late fifteenth and the sixteenth centuries as a turning point in history. It was not a sudden happening; it had been building up slowly in the late medieval world. The New Learning, the Renaissance, are names we give to one aspect of the change. There were other contributory factors. In England there had been important social changes; feudalism had faded out; a rising trading class, important for its growing wealth, was taking over from the nobility, even absorbing the old aristocracy by marriage and by the purchase of estates. Towns were increasingly gaining extensive powers of self-government giving to the leading burgesses a new sense of authority and independence. Schools and universities were expanding. Printing had meant a rapid increase in literacy and the pamphlet became a means of disseminating ideas. At the same time venturesome navigators were widening man's knowledge of his world, and the old discovered the new. The spirit of inquiry and curiosity was stirring men to explore not only the seas but their own minds. They came to resent former restraints and to question long-accepted beliefs. If it had not been Luther who canalised this tendency, it would have been someone else. At the time no one could assess the significance of all these changes in outlook, otherwise the Church might have faced the new problems with more understanding and wisdom.

These notes — for they are little more — on the many influences at work in the first half of the sixteenth century, will serve to show how complex the circumstances were in which the unity of the Church was broken. From 1558 onwards our story will be of how the Catholics of England struggled to keep the faith alive and how they had to endure as a sequestered and proscribed community.

CHAPTER 19

The Elizabethan Persecution

WHEN Elizabeth I came to the throne in November 1558, the climate was more favourable to Protestantism than even in the days of Edward VI. She does not seem to have had any strong personal religious convictions but she was anxious to avoid a head-on clash between Catholic and Protestant. Mary had wished to drop the title of Supreme Head; Elizabeth made a verbal change and in the Supremacy Act of 1559 she was described as 'only Supreme Governor of this realm . . . as well in all spiritual as ecclesiastical things or causes, as temporal.' The term 'Governor' sounded less pretentious than 'Head', but she found that Parliament was not going to be left out of decisions about the Church. When the Thirty-nine Articles were published in 1571 an attempt was made to define what 'Governor' meant.

'We give not to our Princes the ministering either of God's Word, or of the Sacraments, the which thing the Injunctions also lately set forth by Elizabeth our Queen do most plainly testify; but that only Prerogative, which we see to have been given always to all godly Princes in holy Scriptures by God himself; that is, that they should rule all estates and degrees committed to their charge by God,

whether they be Ecclesiastical or Temporal, and restrain with the civil sword the stubborn and evildoers.'
(Article XXVII).

The Act of Uniformity which was passed at the same time as
the Act of Supremacy, restored the second Edwardian Book
of Common Prayer with some modifications. Of the sixteen
bishops, only one, Kitchen of Llandaff, took the oath
prescribed by the Act.[1] The others were deprived and kept
in confinement or under house-arrest. As there were already
ten vacant sees, the reign began with a new bench of bishops.
We are not here concerned with the details of the Anglican
Settlement save in as much as they directly affected Catholics
who did not accept it.

By the Act, priests who did not use the Book of Common
Prayer were penalised; for a first offence a priest went to
prison for six months; for a second, one year with the loss
of his benefice, and for a third offence he faced life imprisonment. The laity were penalised if they spoke against the
Book of Prayer; first offence, one hundred marks (say £60)
second offence, four hundred marks, and for the third offence,
loss of goods and life imprisonment. These were heavy fines
even for a well-to-do offender. There was, however, another
provision that hit the individual more harshly. Everyone had
to attend his parish church every Sunday; for each absence
he had to pay a fine of one shilling. Our way of life is so
different that it is impossible to give equivalent values, but a
rough indication is that a skilled carpenter could in those
days earn tenpence a day. The churchwardens had to
collect these fines and use them for the relief of the parish
poor.

The great majority of the clergy, perhaps four out of five
conformed; they and their congregations, for the most part,
followed suit. Many Catholics attended the parish churches
as a matter of prudence; they came to be known as Church
Papists. There may have been up to five hundred priests

---

[1] Presumably he took the oath, but this is not recorded. He certainly came to
terms with the government.

throughout the land who refused to conform. Some fled abroad. Others found a refuge in the houses of Catholic gentry who were less likely to be harassed; yet others led a vagrant life taking the Mass and the sacraments to Catholics wherever they could be found. As the utmost secrecy was necessary, it is not surprising that we have few records of these priests. One example comes much later in the reign but it is probably typical of what had gone on from the beginning.

A priest named James Stonnes, affectionately known as 'Uncle James', was arrested at 'a very poor man's house' in November 1585. He was seventy-two years of age and had been ordained by Bishop Tunstal in 1539. The report tells us that,

> 'he hath said Mass as often as the opportunity of time, place and company have given leave, and so is of mind to continue, but where he said Mass last and who were present thereat, he utterly denieth to acknowledge or confess, because, saith he, I am not to accuse myself, neither will I accuse any other.'

His 'Massing attire', as it is called, included vestments, a portable altar, small pewter flasks for wine and holy oils, two boxes of 'singing bread' (wafers), a chalice and paten of tin, three crucifixes and 'an old Mass book.' It would be interesting to know how he transported all these things. Unfortunately, the fate of this indomitable old priest is not recorded.

If the Act of Uniformity had been rigorously enforced, Catholicism would have been suppressed, but there was no police force and much depended on the local magistrate who might be unwilling to trouble men with whom he had always lived on friendly terms. So too, the churchwardens would be unwilling to pester their neighbours, though, occasionally, spite would lead to a delation to the magistrate or bishop. The Council or Parliament might insist on the more efficient application of the laws; at such times the bishops would make enquiries and pursuivants, sent by the

Council, would urge the magistrates to action. While it is true that many Catholics, especially poor ones, escaped being penalised, the law was always there as a menace to their peace of mind. In the early years of the reign, the hope of the Council was that, with the dying off of the old priests, Catholicism would wither away; this might well have happened but for the more active missionary work set going in the Spanish Netherlands.

Parliament in 1563 stiffened the law by increasing the penalties for upholding the authority of the pope and for refusing to take the oath to the Supremacy, and by extending the obligation to take the oath to more office-holders, lawyers, and so on. Death was the penalty for a second refusal of the oath. The queen, however, through Archbishop Parker, instructed the bishops (who were responsible for exacting the oath) that they were not to offer it a second time without the archbishop's consent. The oath was now to apply to Members of Parliament, but not to the peers. So the next Parliament was the first without an avowed Catholic member but, no doubt, some were Church Papists.

The year 1568 was crucial. It saw the founding of the English college or seminary at Douai, commonly called Douay. This was the work of William Allen (1532–94). He was born at Rossall in the Fylde, Lancashire. It was a strongly Catholic region with such landed families as the Southworths, the Hoghtons, and the Towneleys as the leaders of the opposition to the religious changes. Allen entered Oriel College, Oxford, in 1547 and became a Fellow. In 1556 he was principal of St. Mary's Hall. After the death of Queen Mary, he found it impossible to remain at Oxford as a Catholic, and he crossed to the Netherlands in 1561. He made a visit to his home county in the following year and later to Oxford and Norfolk. Wherever he went he he was dismayed to find how many Catholics were going to their parish churches to satisfy the law. He could see that, if this tendency continued, Catholicism would steadily decline. On his return to Louvain in 1565, he was ordained priest, and it was then that he conceived the idea of a college in the Spanish Netherlands where young Englishmen could be educated on Catholic principles. Out of this purpose grew the further idea of providing training for the priesthood for those who had vocations. Such young priests could then return to their native land to fill the dwindling ranks of the Catholic clergy. So at Douay he established his first seminary which was to prove the main source of priests for the English mission until the French Revolution: 'mission' because, in the eyes of Rome, England had now lapsed into heresy.

Before the death of Elizabeth nearly 450 priests were sent from Douay. The example of this first successful seminary led to the establishment of others at Lisbon, Madrid, Seville and Valladolid, and finally in 1579 of the English College (the Venerabile) at Rome. It should be noted that all these, apart from the one at Rome, were in Spanish territory, a fact that was to be of increasing moment in England as anti-Spanish feeling grew; thus the seminarians became linked in people's minds with the national enemy. This was the period of the raids of Hawkins and Drake on the Spanish Main, and stories were soon going round of the treatment of English prisoners by the Spanish Inquisition.

Catholics were more harassed as events moved against them. Mary, Queen of Scots, fled to England in 1568, the same year as the foundation of Douay. As a Catholic, and also as a possible successor to Elizabeth, she immediately became the focus for conspiracies. A rising that year in the north failed to win sufficient support; it was ruthlessly put down and some hundreds of Catholics, mostly of the labouring class, were hanged. Thomas Percy, Earl of Northumberland, was beheaded on the 23rd August 1572. Then came the Ridolfi plot of 1571 which was uncovered before it could get going; the intention was to depose Elizabeth, put Mary on the throne and marry her to the Duke of Norfolk, in spite of the fact that he was not a Catholic. He was executed in 1572; his eldest son, Philip, was then fifteen years of age.

The rising in the north coincided with the issue of the papal Bull of Excommunication against Elizabeth. The Bull,

Regnans in Excelsis, listed the crimes of the queen and added,

> 'Moreover the nobles, subjects and people of the said
> kingdom and anyone else who has taken an oath to her
> are freed from that and from every obligation to allegiance,
> fealty and obedience.'

The pope, St. Pius V, issued this without consulting, for
instance, Philip of Spain, who refused to implement it. It
could not be promulgated in England, but John Felton, a
man of property, got a copy and affixed it to the gate of the
Bishop of London's palace outside St. Paul's Cathedral.
He was tracked down, tried, and on the 8th August 1570,
hanged in front of the cathedral. The wisdom of issuing
such a Bull has been warmly debated, but its effect on
Catholics can be exaggerated. News spread very slowly and
there must have been many out-of-the-way places where
no one had heard of the papal Bull. The most serious result
was that the Bull put a powerful weapon into the hands of
the government. A Catholic's loyalty to the throne could
now be questioned. Which did he choose — the queen or
the pope? There can be little doubt that the majority of
Catholics remained loyal to the queen, but they were faced
with a dilemma of which the government took full advantage.
The Massacre of St. Bartholomew of Protestants by Catholics
in France in August 1572 deepened opposition to the
Catholics in this country. This was intensified two years later
by the sack of Antwerp by Spanish troops in the 'Fury'
which led to the revolt of the Netherlands.

Inevitably the law against Catholics was made more
stringent. An Act of 1571 made it treasonous to introduce
or implement any papal Bulls or other instructions received
from Rome, or to reconcile anyone to that Church or to
give absolution; and those who brought in 'tokens, crosses,
pictures, beads, or such like vain superstitious things' would
be subject to the statutes of praemunire. The Catholic
response came from Douay; its first priests landed in England
in 1574.

Two years later St. Cuthbert Mayne came on the mission.

As a native of the west country, he went back there to carry out his dangerous assignment. He himself was a convert having been born at Barnstaple in Devon where his uncle was a conforming priest. He hoped that his nephew would succeed him in his benefice; with this in mind he sent Cuthbert to Oxford. There he took his B.A. in 1566 and became a chaplain at St. John's College. This was the year in which Edmund Campion was one of the disputants before Queen Elizabeth on her visit to the university. Campion was a member of St. John's as was Gregory Martin, the future translator of the Douay Bible. It seems likely that it was under their influence that Cuthbert Mayne was 'reconciled.' When both Campion and Martin had finally gone to Douay they wrote to their young friend urging him to join them. One of their letters was intercepted by the Bishop of London who sent a pursuivant to Oxford to bring Mayne to London; he, however, was warned in time by a friend and so made his escape and joined his friends at Douay where he had Campion as one of his tutors. Cuthbert Mayne took his degree in divinity and was ordained just before he left for England in April 1576.

He settled at Golden, the manor house of Francis Tregian, a few miles east of Truro. The Tregians were a wealthy, landed family and firm Catholics. Francis was the grandson of Sir John Arundell of Lanherne, among the most powerful families in Cornwall. Cuthbert acted as steward to his host and carried out his priestly functions as discreetly as possible. This became a common practice among Catholic landowners as it gave a plausible cover to a priest. If there were children, a priest might be engaged as tutor. Generally speaking the Catholic gentry at this period were seldom disturbed if they lived quietly. It is difficult for us to appreciate the deference shown to social status and rank. The nobility were regarded with special respect. There were Catholic lords at the court of the queen; they were not expected, for instance, to take oaths like ordinary people. As the drive against the Catholics became more determined, so the Catholic gentry lost much of their immunity. Trouble could arise when there was rivalry or even hostility between landed families, and this was undoubtedly one of the factors that led to the arrest of Cuthbert Mayne and of his patron Francis Tregian. This rivalry seems to have been particularly fierce between such Cornish families as the Arundells, Grenvilles and Tregians. The Grenvilles were represented by Richard. His later fame as commander of *The Revenge* has thrown a veil of romance over his true character; he was a proud and ambitious man whose violent temper was a by-word. Basically this case was not one of religion but of rivalry between powerful families.

Richard Grenville had been appointed sheriff in the year in which Cuthbert Mayne had gone to Golden. In a case of piracy there had been a clash between Grenville and Sir John Arundell and Francis Tregian. The rumour that there was a priest at Golden gave Grenville just the opening he needed. There happened to be a hue and cry against a malefactor named Bourne who had escaped from London and was believed to have reached Cornwall. So Grenville arrived at Golden in June 1577 in company with several magistrates and a posse of nearly a hundred men in search, so he said, of Bourne. Francis Tregian assured Grenville that he had no knowledge of the man, but Grenville, in one of his rages, and despite his lack of a search warrant, insisted on searching the house. So Cuthbert Mayne, who made no attempt to conceal himself, was eventually captured. He was found to be wearing on a cord round his neck an Agnus Dei[1] in a locket, one of the 'vain superstitious things' of the Act. Among his papers was a copy of a papal Bull, not indeed the *Regnans in Excelsis* but for the Jubilee of 1575.

Both Tregian and Mayne were imprisoned, fettered, in an underground dungeon of Launceston Castle in company with common criminals. There they remained until the Michaelmas Assizes four months later. Mayne was then arraigned with seven others who were accused of aiding him; they included a schoolmaster, a yeoman and a tailor.

[1] A wax medallion stamped with the figure of the lamb, and blessed by the pope.

Later sixteen more were brought to trial; they were mostly tenants or servants of Francis Tregian. They received varied sentences of imprisonment and fines.

The charges against Cuthbert Mayne were that he had introduced a papal Bull into the country and had published it at Golden, that he adhered to 'the Bishop of Rome', that he had brought in an Agnus Dei, and that he had said Mass at Golden. The evidence was not conclusive apart from the Agnus Dei; the Bull was outdated and had no reference to the queen, and no proof was given that the prisoner had said Mass, not even that he was a priest. The presiding judge, Sir Roger Manwood, declared that 'where plain proofs were wanting, strong presumptions ought to take their place' — a dangerous maxim. The jury accepted this hint and brought in a verdict of guilty. Grenville had interfered at one point in the hope of getting evidence against Tregian, thereby revealing his true purpose. One of the judges, John Jeffery, had doubts about some technical points — as well he might — and he put his problem to the Council at Westminster. Grenville went up to London to counter these scruples; the Council decided, though not unanimously, that the verdict should stand as a warning to other Popish priests. Grenville was then knighted for his services.

Cuthbert Mayne was hanged at Launceston on the 30th November 1577, the first of the seminary priests to suffer martyrdom. He was thirty-three years of age. On the scaffold he was asked if 'Mr. Tregian and Sir John Arundell did know of these things which thou art condemned for, and also what dost thou know of them?' He answered, 'I know nothing of Mr. Tregian and Sir John but that they are good and godly gentlemen, and as for the things I am condemned for, they are only known to me and to no other.' He had to suffer the full agony of being cut down while still alive, disembowelled and quartered. His skull is preserved at Lanherne convent, the old home of the Arundells.

Francis Tregian was kept in the foul conditions of Launceston for some months; he was condemned under the Acts of Praemunire to life imprisonment and loss of goods. Some irregularities in the proceedings were brought to the notice of the Council at Westminster, but the verdict was confirmed. Sir George Cary, to whom the lands were leased, at once went down to Golden, turned out Mrs. Tregian, her children and relatives, and entered into occupation. Francis Tregian's mother retrieved part of her own property that Carey had also without warrant seized, and with this and the help of the Arundells her son's position was somewhat relieved by what money they were able to send him. His wife petitioned the Council for better conditions for him than Launceston could provide, and he was brought up to London, and first put in the Queen's Bench prison and later in the Fleet where his wife was allowed to join him. He petitioned several times for some mitigation of his sentence but he was thwarted by Sir George Cary who had become Lord Hunsdon. He had the queen's ear as he was the grandson of Mary Boleyn, the sister of Anne Boleyn. It was not until 1601, twenty-five years after his arrest, that Tregian was permitted to live in Chelsea under house arrest. Both the queen and Hunsdon died in 1603, and three years later James I gave Francis Tregian leave to go abroad. He went first to Douay and later to Lisbon where he lived in the Jesuit house of San Roque on a pension from King Philip. Tregian died on the 25th September 1608 and was buried in the church. Twelve years later the grave was reopened for a fresh burial and it was found that the body was incorrupt; for a time there was a cult. In 1626 English Catholics in Lisbon had him reburied, upright, in the wall near the pulpit where an inscription can still be read.

This is not the end of the Tregian story. There were two sons, Francis and Charles. Both were sent to Douay for their education but neither became a priest. They proved to be scholars and later went to Rome in the household of Cardinal Allen. Francis paid a visit to England in 1594 to see his parents, and then returned to Rome. On his father's death (the date of his mother's is not known) he again came to England doubtless to see to family affairs. He was arrested under the recusancy laws and imprisoned in the Fleet. He was not only a scholar but a musician and he spent his enforced leisure in making a collection of Elizabethan and Jacobean music. Three volumes are extant; one in the Fitzwilliam Museum at Cambridge, a second in the British Museum and the third in New York. But for Francis Tregian's industry, our knowledge of the music of his times would be scanty. He included, for instance, some seventy pieces by William Byrd who has been described as 'one of the greatest musicians England has produced.' He was a Catholic and he illustrates the fact that Catholics who were connected with the court were not unduly harassed as recusants. He was organist at the Chapel Royal and that protected him. Another instance is that of William Roper, the son-in-law of St. Thomas More. He lived until 1578, and, although he suffered at least one short term of imprisonment and had to pay fines, he was too valuable as protonotary of the Queen's Bench to be discarded. He did much to help Catholics and he was regarded at Douay as a benefactor. His son succeeded to the same office and, though a declared Catholic, escaped serious trouble.

Francis Tregian junior died in the Fleet in 1619. His brother Charles then came to England probably to settle affairs, but he too was arrested as a recusant and put in the Fleet. While there he wrote a biography of his father; the manuscript is at Oscott. Thus father and sons spent fifty years in all in prison; the family in the male line came to an end with the death of Charles; every acre of the family estates had been taken from them.

It has seemed worth while telling at some length this story of Cuthbert Mayne and the Tregians as it gives a more vivid picture of how Catholics were treated than would be conveyed by a series of general statements. We do not know how many Catholics endured years of imprisonment, but, from such records as have been studied, it is clear that the total must have amounted over the years to tens of thousands. Many, unable to pay their fines, or condemned under praemunire, died in prison, and others, on release, from the effects of prison conditions. They form an unnumbered army of martyrs.

Owing to the stress of the war in the Netherlands, the college of Douay had to move to Reims in 1578 where it stayed for five years until it was possible to return to its original home.

An early problem that faced Douay was the placing of priests on arrival in England. Some, like Cuthbert Mayne, went to their own parts of the country, but others were not able to do so for want of means. When they landed they had very little money and their clothes would be of a foreign style and so aroused suspicion. Any obvious stranger was always liable to be stopped and questioned. These priests usually made their way to London, and, in their ignorance, could soon betray themselves. Thus Everard Hanse was arrested soon after his arrival in March 1581 and was hanged that July.

It was with such needs in mind that a group of young men, some of whom had studied at Douay, banded themselves together in an informal association for the purpose of looking after newly arrived priests. They supplied them with money and suitable clothes and directed them to reliable Catholics who could shelter them. If they were to go beyond London, as most of them did, there would be horses and guides to put them on their way. The first leader of this band was George Gilbert and his companions bore such well-known Catholic names as Vaux, Throgmorton, Brooksby, Titchborne and Stonor. Most of them, if not rich, were well-to-do and they were glad to provide funds for this service to the mission. At the same time they were aware that they themselves were in danger of arrest as recusants or for aiding seminary priests. Gilbert left the country in 1581 as his part in the work was becoming too well known to the authorities. He went to the English College, Rome, where he died two years later. It is not known how long this association was active; as time passed, so the arrangements from Douay and other centres became more efficient. Some of the work was taken over by certain families and their womenfolk were particularly devoted to this service. An outstanding example was the Vaux family.

As the number of priests entering the country increased, the Council became more alert. Both Sir William Cecil (Lord Burghley) and Sir Francis Walsingham were alive to the threat that this influx of young enthusiasts meant to the State religion. English ambassadors had instructions to gather all the information they could by their own spies. A few seminary students and even priests were seduced into betraying their fellows, but the number was minute compared with that of the unwavering priests. After a few years little could happen in the seminaries that was not soon reported to Westminster; the names of priests setting off for England were supplied so that a special watch could be kept for them at the ports, but they soon learned to avoid these and were set ashore on secluded parts of the coast. Needless to say there were spies in London whose business it was to watch for suspicious looking young men who might be priests. The houses of known recusants were also under surveillance to see what visitors they had, especially anyone who might be a priest going there to say Mass. The priests led a kind of cloak-and-dagger existence. They accepted this dangerous life and also the prospect of a savage death from the moment they took their vows at the seminary. Nor did the news of the martyrdoms of priests who had been fellow students daunt them; it rather stimulated their ardour and devotion.

It was not only seminary priests who slipped into the country; books were also smuggled. William Allen regarded the writing of polemical and apologetic works as a parallel method of sustaining Catholicism in England and of rebutting Protestant propaganda. At Douay and Louvain there were a number of distinguished exiled English scholars, particularly from Oxford, who devoted their pens to this work. Such were Thomas Harding, John Rastell, S.J., and Thomas Stapleton whose translation of Bede's Ecclesiastical History was aimed at the queen herself, to show her how different the church of St. Augustine of Canterbury was from that of 'the pretended reformers.' She probably never saw the book, but many Catholics were glad to have it. During Elizabeth's reign some two hundred volumes were produced ranging from pamphlets to learned folios. Devotional books were also printed such as Laurence Vaux's catechism and Robert Parson's The *First Book of the Christian Exercise*, which came to be known as *The Christian Directory* and was adapted to Protestant use. The practical problem was how to get these books into England. The government issued many proclamations against importing them and customs officers were alerted and the houses of recusants searched. The constant traffic between Antwerp or Dunkirk and England provided opportunities for smuggling books concealed in other merchandise. Priests sometimes risked taking a parcel with them when they came on the mission. One of them described what happened when the books were safely landed.

'They were distributed by hundreds or fifties to the priests so that they may be published all together in all parts of the realm. And the next day, when pursuivants begin to search the Catholics' houses, it is too late, for during the night the young gentlemen have introduced copies into the houses, shops, and mansions of the heretics, and even into the court, and the stalls in the streets, so that Catholics alone cannot be accused of possessing them.'

This suggests pamphlets and small books rather than bigger volumes that would be more difficult to handle. 'The young gentlemen' were, presumably, the Gilbert association. An example of a less successful transaction is given by the experience of Fr. William Weston, S.J., and his companion, a lay-brother named Ralph Emerson who had also been a companion of Edmund Campion. His previous unhappy visit did not deter him from returning. The two were put ashore somewhere between Yarmouth and Lowestoft in September 1584. They had with them some cases of books; we are not told how many volumes there were, but 'cases' suggests a fair number. Fr. Weston went on to London leaving Ralph Emerson to arrange for the transport of the books by a carrier. When he got to London he deposited the books at an inn, but a sharp-eyed searcher (had he been given the tip-off by the carrier?) became inquisitive and had the cases opened. The books were at once confiscated and Ralph was arrested; he spent the next twenty years being moved from prison to prison until at length he was exiled.

One production of the Reims-Douay period calls for mention. This was the translation of the Vulgate Bible. The New Testament was published at Reims in 1582; for lack of funds the Old Testament could not be printed until 1609. The translation of the New Testament had some influence on the King James version of 1611.

A lot of money was involved in all this printing and distribution. The funds were in part contributed by Catholics in England. Thus in July 1568 William Roper was brought before the Council 'for having relieved with money certain persons who have departed out of the realm, and who, with others, have printed books against the Queen's supremacy and government.' He entered into a bond to be of good behaviour, but does not seem to have been further molested.

The seminary students had a very thorough training in polemics and seem to have had moots reminiscent of the Inns of Court. When they set out for England they were warned against verbal controversy with non-Catholics unless a Catholic could assure them that the inquirer was genuinely seeking the truth. We do not know how many converts were made, but some indication is that out of 264 martyrs between 1570 and 1680, forty-three were certainly converts and others may have been.

Between 1570 and 1581 there were only eight martyrs; from 1581 to 1603 there were 182. This considerable increase reflects the state of almost panic that possessed the government in regard to Catholics. The threat from Spain was growing more serious, but there were no indications that Catholics as a body were pro-Spanish. They had no kind of organisation and were scattered about the country. For forty years they were left without a bishop to guide them.

In 1598 Rome at last appointed George Blackwell with the odd title of archpriest but without episcopal authority. So during all these years the Catholics had to get along as best as they could; undoubtedly the lack of clear guidance led to many defections; people conformed because Rome seemed to have lost interest in them. Although the seminaries were able to send over some hundreds of priests, they were far too few to cover the country effectively and people living in areas where they never saw a priest had to be very firm in their faith to resist the temptation to conform. By and large they were loyal to the queen and shared the national suspicions of Spain. The tragedy was that in the mounting tension of foreign affairs, the public could not believe that these priests coming from Spanish territory, some from Spain itself, were concerned solely with the spiritual welfare of their countrymen. The two or three priests who allowed themselves to get sucked into the political whirlpool inevitably drew suspicion on the others. It is no exaggeration to say that the public regarded the seminary priests as what we should call fifth columnists. Nor could they be blamed for such an attitude which is understandable. This does not, however, excuse the kind of brutal treatment with which Catholic prisoners were treated.

Considerable alarm was caused to the government at the news that a Jesuit mission was coming from Rome in 1579. The Society had at last agreed to let some of its priests come on the mission. The party left Rome in a blaze of publicity. They were accompanied outside the walls by many of the English exiles. Spies had already warned the government of this new development and the movements of the party were duly reported as they made their way from Rome to Reims. There were fourteen members made up of priests from the English College with some lay-brothers and the two Jesuits St. Edmund Campion and Robert Parsons (or Persons). Special but unavailing precautions were taken to prevent the two Jesuits from landing in England. There was talk of 'Jesuit invasion', but there were already upwards of four hundred seminary priests in England, and two Jesuits would have made little difference had it not been for their outstanding qualities and the unwarrantable alarm of the government.

Why was it that the Jesuits were regarded with such apprehension within a generation of their foundation? The extension of their influence is one of the most striking facts about the Counter-Reformation following the Council of Trent; they became the spear-head of the Catholic recovery. Allied to this question is another, 'Why had they gained such an unfortunate reputation?' The very name, according to the Oxford English Dictionary, came to have the slur meaning of 'a dissembling person, a prevaricator.' Their rigid organisation, almost military, had resulted in an efficiency in operation that was the greatest threat to Protestantism. So their coming to England, even two of them, put the Council on the alert more than ever. It was also unfortunate that many secular priests eyed the Jesuits with suspicion, though others admired their achievements so warmly that they sought admission to their ranks.

No one can question the high value of what was accomplished by the first two Jesuits to work in England. In a brief period of little more than a year, they gave fresh inspiration to those priests with whom they came in contact and they revivified Catholic life in those parts they were able to visit. The full story of this first mission cannot be told here. Edmund Campion's holiness, single-mindedness and courage made a deep impression on his contemporaries. Indeed it could be said that the government would have been wiser to have ignored him and his companion. The resulting publicity must have enheartened many a lonely Catholic. Robert Parsons was a more enigmatic character; he had a deep devotion to the English mission for whose cause he was to labour for thirty years after leaving the country. He long hoped that he would be allowed to return, but his superiors decided that his great abilities could be better used in other ways. Even a false rumour that he had returned was enough to alarm the government. At this stage we must forget how he later became involved in political projects.

The Jesuits brought with them two important rulings from the pope. The first was that the Bull of Excommunication did not bind Catholics until circumstances changed and it became practical politics. This relieved Catholic consciences, but it put another weapon into the hands of the government; the loyalty of Catholics was not absolute but conditional; they were waiting for the right opportunity — that was the interpretation by those in authority. The second ruling struck at the Church Papists who attended their parish churches to meet the requirements of the law; such attendance was now forbidden as a 'great impiety'. Undoubtedly some Church Papists fell away at this time; indeed successive tightenings of the law had the same effect. It meant, however, that those who chose Catholicism rather than Anglicanism were all the more staunch in their determination to hold to their faith.

The work of the Jesuits and of all other priests was made more dangerous by the expedition sent under papal patronage to invade Ireland in 1579. Spanish troops followed in the next year. The rising was ruthlessly suppressed. The English party that left Rome that year were not fully aware, if aware at all, of what was being planned, and it was with dismay that they heard the news before they crossed the Channel. They themselves had been warned, as all priests were, not to get entangled in political projects. Now they found themselves in an equivocal position. The government made the most of the situation and popular opinion inevitably linked the arrival of the Jesuits with the Irish rising. Here was the pope, with the aid of Spanish troops, actually encouraging rebellion. Rome had, in effect, let down the priests and the Catholics alike, and it was they who had to suffer the consequences. A further stiffening of the law against them was the outcome.

An Act was passed in 1581 'to retain the Queen's Majesty's subjects in their due obedience.' Those who were reconciled to the 'Romish religion' and those who were the instruments of such reconciliation, were now guilty of treason. For saying or hearing Mass the penalty was by fine or imprisonment.

The celebrant was fined 200 marks and the hearer 100 marks. Recusancy, that is refusal to attend the parish church, meant further fines. To the former one shilling weekly was now added a £20-a-month fine which had to be paid until the recusant conformed. If he could not meet the demand out of income (and relatively few could do so) his goods and chattels were forfeit to the amount due; this would mean, for the landowners, the seizure of lands. Those who could not pay the fines for lack of goods or property were imprisoned. This could mean perpetual imprisonment for many Catholics. All this new system of fining took some time to get into working order as the fines had now to be paid into the exchequer. By the end of Elizabeth's reign, the exchequer was receiving over six to seven thousand pounds a year from recusant fines. Informers, or 'promoters' as they were called, were rewarded by a third of a convicted recusant's fines. Even this did not satisfy the authorities who were now clearly determined to destroy the Catholic religion since it refused to lie down and die. An additional Act in 1586 tightened up the law and made evasion more difficult. There was sometimes one way of evasion still open; informers were often blackmailers, and pursuivants sent down by the Council did not despise hush-money. An informer could make a good living out of his profession, as it could be called.

As the likelihood of a Spanish invasion drew near, the numbers of imprisoned priests and layfolk increased until the ordinary prisons could not contain them. So new places of detention had to be found. Castles and other suitable buildings became prisons, or, should we say, concentration camps? Such were Wisbech, Kimbolton, Ely and a dozen others in various centres over the country. Some were used for priests only and others for the gentry. A typical case of the treatment of a landowner is that of John Towneley of Lancashire. Under his portrait, painted in 1601, is this inscription.

'For professing the Apostolical Catholic Roman Faith, he was imprisoned first at Chester Castle, then sent to

the Marshalsea, then to York Castle, then to the Block-
houses in Hull, then to the Gatehouse in Westminster,
then to Broughton in Oxfordshire, then twice to Ely in
Cambridgeshire; and so now, seventy-three years old and
blind, is bound to appear and to keep within five miles
of Towneley his house; who hath since the statute of
23rd Elizabeth [1581] paid into the Exchequer £20 a
month, and doth still, that there is paid already about
£5000.'

It will be noted that paying the monthly fine did not mean
that the unhappy victim was necessarily left in peace; he
could still be kept in prison until he conformed. It is difficult
to understand why recusants were shifted about from prison
to prison; perhaps it was to make conspiracies among the
prisoners more difficult.

Anti-Catholic feeling was further aggravated when William
of Orange was assassinated by a Catholic in June 1584. In
the following year, Elizabeth sent an army to help the
Dutch against the Spaniards. Popularly this was regarded
as an armed conflict between Catholics and Protestants,
but it was not as clear-cut as that, for independence from
Spanish rule was the primary aim. A Bond of Association
was drawn up by the Council for all to sign who wished
to safeguard the life of the queen. An assassination plot was
uncovered in 1585; the conspirator, William Parry, was a
dubious Catholic. Elizabeth had now established for herself
a position such as no other queen had attained; people were
dismayed at the thought of what might happen after her
death. Her successor, if right of descent counted, was
Mary, Queen of Scots, and the prospect of a second Catholic
Queen Mary was alarming. Not all Catholics supported her,
but she inevitably became the hope of others and the centre
of plotting. The Council was greatly worried, especially
when the Queen of Scots took refuge in England in 1568.
The queen would make no move against another queen,
especially one so near the throne. Lord Burghley, the
leader of the Council, and Sir Francis Walsingham, the

Secretary of State, were particularly concerned with this embarrassing problem.

The Babington Plot played into their hands. Some would, with reason, prefer to call it the Walsingham Plot, but he did not make the first move; the conspirators gathered together and he used them. Anthony Babington, a wealthy young man in his twenties, had a romantic notion of rescuing Queen Mary. He was the last person in the world to make a successful conspirator; he was guileless, and, one is tempted to say, somewhat stupid. A seminary priest, John Ballard, encouraged Babington to get together half a dozen young men to share his wild project. One of them, possibly himself, may have spoken rashly in company; news of what was happening was at once passed on to Walsingham, who planted among these naïve plotters a skilled spy, Robert Poley, who became 'sweet Robin' to Babington. The details are too involved to give here. The upshot was that Babington was persuaded to write to Queen Mary to obtain her approval for the scheme which now included 'the dispatch of the usurper' by six gentlemen. It was amateurish of Babington to assume that such a letter would escape Walsingham's notice; he had, in fact, organised an apparently secret means of communication between Queen Mary and her supporters. If Babington was foolish, Queen Mary was more foolish or reckless for writing that she accepted the plan for the 'dispatch' of Elizabeth. Here at last was the evidence the Council wanted. The sequel was inevitable; Mary, Queen of Scots, was executed on the 8th February 1587. Anthony Babington, the priest, John Ballard and five others had been hanged six months earlier. The fact that one of the conspirators was a seminary priest added to the popular suspicion of Catholics.

When the Armada was imminent, Catholic gentry were rounded up and put in prison or under supervision. Their weapons and horses were confiscated. In that year, 1588, twenty priests, eight laymen and one laywoman were hanged. The laywoman was St. Margaret Ward who had rescued a priest, Richard Watson, from the Bridewell. She was tortured in prison and hanged at Tyburn on the 30th August.

It was in anticipation of the Spanish invasion of England that Cardinal Allen had penned his *Admonition to the Nobility and People of England*. The defeat of the Armada made publication pointless as it was intended for distribution when England was defeated. A copy had been secured in Antwerp by a spy and passed on to the government. In the controversial bad manners of the day, it was an abusive attack on Queen Elizabeth, 'an incestuous bastard.' This intemperate diatribe provided the government with more ammunition against Catholicism. Exiles abroad were also concerned about who should succeed Elizabeth; they naturally hoped a Catholic would succeed her. Some thought that James VI of Scotland, the probable heir, would at least be sympathetic to Catholics as the son of a Catholic, but others preferred a Catholic and picked upon the Infanta Isabella of Spain as a descendant of Edward III. Fr. Robert Parsons was concerned with this project. Exiles, as the years pass, get out-of-touch with the public opinion of their own countrymen. It was unrealistic to imagine that the English, even most Catholics, would have welcomed a Spanish Princess as their queen.

In 1591 a Proclamation was issued entitled *A declaration of great troubles pretended against the Realm by a number of Seminary Priests and Jesuits, sent, and very secretly dispersed in the same, to work great Treasons under a false pretence of Religion.* This lengthy document reiterated the dangers to the kingdom of harbouring priests who, 'under a false colour and face of holiness' were 'a secret infection of treasons in the bowels of our Realm.' To root them out and all disaffected Catholics, special commissioners were to tour the country to track down these 'wilful destroyers of their Native country and monstrous traitors.' It may be noted that in that year there were only five Jesuits in the country and one of them, Fr. William Weston, was in Wisbech.

The occasion for this new attack was that a second Armada was expected to sail in 1592. The fact that a new proclamation was thought necessary is evidence that the previous Acts, severe as they were, had failed to destroy Catholicism. An immediate reply, *An Humble Supplication to Her Majesty*, was written by St. Robert Southwell, S.J. This could not be printed at the time but was circulated in hand-written copies, one of which came into the hands of the government.

Robert Southwell, poet and martyr, born in 1561, was a member of one of those knightly families that rose under the Tudors. His grandfather, Sir Robert, had refused to perjure himself at the trial of St. Thomas More. Like so many others he had adapted himself to the religious and political changes of the times. Robert's mother was Bridget Copley of the Sussex Catholic family; in her younger days she had been a companion of the Princess Elizabeth. Her brother, Sir Thomas, passed the last twelve years of his life abroad rather than live in a Protestant England. Robert spent part of his boyhood in Sussex where there were a number of Catholic families such as the Montagues of Cowdray, the Gages of Firle, the Shelleys of Michelgrove and Warming-hurst, and the Cottons of Warblington on the Hampshire border. It was from one of the creeks there that Robert and John Cotton slipped away from England for Douay in 1576. Two years later, Robert went to Rome to enter the Jesuit novitiate. The Jesuit training was long and searching and it was not until July 1586 that Robert Southwell and another Jesuit priest, Henry Garnet, landed in England. The government was well aware of their coming but they came ashore at a deserted part of the Sussex coast and so evaded capture. By separate routes they made their way to London.

It was a dangerous time for Catholics. The threatened Spanish invasion was awaited and the Babington plot was about to be uncovered. Seven priests had been hanged in the first six months of the year and seven more were to follow in the second half. St. Margaret Clitherow had been pressed to death for harbouring priests. Southwell remained in London, sheltered by layfolk. For a time he moved about freely, but soon the hunt was up and it became necessary to be more cautious. He found a refuge in Arundel House where the Countess was living while her husband, St. Philip Howard, was in the Tower for being 'reconciled.' There Southwell remained for over a year, going out at dusk to minister to Catholics and to keep in touch with other priests. The Countess was evicted in 1591, and from then onwards Southwell moved from sheltering house to house in London. It was at this period that he wrote his *Humble Supplication*. He countered the statement that priests were of 'very base birth' by pointing out that many of the Jesuits came from well-established families and included men of learning from the universities. He went into some detail about the Babington plot and claimed, with some justification, that it had been 'a snare to entrap' the victims and that Walsingham had 'laid and hatched all the particulars thereof.' Next he took up the point that priests were condemned for treason and not on account of their religion. He protested that they were in fact loyal to the queen; 'we daily in our lives and always at our executions, unfeignedly pray for your Majesty.' On the question of the oath taken by a priest at ordination, he wrote, 'And as for oaths and promises in receiving holy orders, we neither take nor plight any, but one common to the priests of all nations, which is a solemn vow of perpetual chastity, a thing rather pleasing than offensive to a virtuous Queen, who hath herself made choice of a single life' — a nicely made point! To the charge that the priests encouraged rebellion, he replied simply, 'The weapons of our warfare are spiritual not offensive.' Then he appealed to 'the softness of your merciful hand' on behalf of imprisoned Catholics subject to 'the extremist tortures.' He described what was happening in the Tower and elsewhere. The passage is too long to quote here in all its grim details, and the opening sentence must suffice. 'Some are hanged by the hands, eight or nine or twelve hours together, till not only their wits, but even their senses fail them, and when the soul, weary of so painful an harbour, is ready to depart, they apply cruel comforts, and revive us, only to martyr us with more deaths; for eftsoons they hang us in the same manner, trying our ears with such questions which either we cannot, because we know not, or without damning our souls, we may not, satisfy.' He mentions the flogging of the naked victims, lying in dark dungeons, starved of food, 'consumed with vermin and most stifled with stench.' Some were kept awake day and night before being questioned. 'Some have been tortured in such parts, as is almost a torture to Christian ears to hear it.' There is, alas, a modern ring about all this.

The *Supplication* goes on to deal with the talk of a Catholic rising. Southwell pointed out that the numbers of Catholics were so small that such fears were baseless, but, more than that, 'what army soever should come against you, we will rather yield our breasts to be broached by our Country's swords than use our swords to the effusion of our Country's blood.' He was not concerned solely with the persecution of the priests, and the last part of his appeal dealt with the plight recusants suffered 'by the merciless searching and storming of pursuivants and such needy officers. They build their houses with the ruins of ours, tempering the mortar of their foundations with our innocent blood . . . We can bring the consumption of our goods, the poverty of our estates, and the weeping eyes of our desolate families for the palpable witnesses of the truth of these complaints.'

It was disarming, if prudent, to write as if the queen knew little of the ways in which Catholics were persecuted. After a reign of more than thirty years, Elizabeth had established her authority so firmly that no official dared to act contrary to her wishes, and she kept herself fully informed of what was going on. Southwell would know to what extent torture was being used beyond customary procedure, though his own Gethsemane was yet to come. Under common law, torture was strictly controlled; it was limited, at least officially, to suspected cases of treason, and the purpose was to extract from the victim the names of his accomplices. Such examinations were carried out in the Tower in the presence of at least two councillors. This limitation was not always observed in dealing with priests. The two leading priest-hunters were Richard Young, a Middlesex magistrate, and

Richard Topcliffe. To say that either was motivated by religion would be a libel on both Catholicism and Protestantism. Both men were sadists, and Topcliffe was the greater monster of the two. They were allowed to torture priests in the Bridewell House of Correction and also in a nearby house they used for that purpose. This was permitted with the queen's knowledge. Topcliffe was referred to as 'Her Majesty's Servant', but his exact status is not known. He sent reports direct to her nor were they lacking in grim detail.

Robert Southwell fell into the hands of Topcliffe in June 1592; in his triumph he wrote to the queen to assure her that he would extract all the Jesuit's secrets 'if he be rightly used.' He failed and the queen called him a fool; nor did his subsequent efforts succeed. Southwell had to suffer the wall torture, 'hanged by the hands' as he called it, ten times, but no word had been wrung from him. Sir Robert Cecil, a distant relative of Southwell, witnessed one of these torturings; afterwards he said, 'They boast about the heroes of antiquity, but we have a new torture which it is not possible for a man to bear. And yet I have seen Robert Southwell hanging by it, still as a tree-trunk, and no one able to drag one word from his mouth.' When even his inquisitors had to confess they could get nothing from him, he was transferred to the Tower. He was kept in close confinement for two and a half years. His old father petitioned the queen that the son of her former girlhood companion should either by brought speedily to trial, or, 'if not, as he is a gentleman, that her Majesty might be pleased to order that he should be treated as such, even though he was a Jesuit.' Perhaps as a result of this appeal, Robert Southwell was removed to Newgate in readiness for his trial which took place on the 22nd February 1595. The proceedings cannot be followed here in detail but one incident is worth noting. Southwell complained that his memory had been affected by more than two years of prison. He added, 'I wish when by torture nothing can be got, I wish there might be some measure therein, lest by extremity of pain a man be driven, if it were possible, to despair.' Topcliffe tried to bluster at this reference to his methods; he declared that he had the Council's permission for what he did. Southwell's comment was, 'Thou art a bad man.' One result of this confrontation in open court was that Topcliffe lost face; the hearers were shocked by the prisoner's revelations. The verdict was inevitable. St. Robert Southwell, aged thirty-four, was hanged at Tyburn on the 21st February 1595. Lord Mountjoy, who may have been prompted by the queen, was present with other nobles. He insisted on the priest hanging until death was certain so that the ghastly disembowling was not carried out on a quivering body. As he left the scene, Lord Mountjoy exclaimed, 'I cannot answer for his religion, but I wish to God my soul may be with his.'

That year, 1595, was to see also the hanging of St. Henry Walpole at York and the death in the Tower of St. Philip Howard. The remaining years of Elizabeth's reign brought the martyrdoms of thirty-nine Catholics including sixteen laymen and one laywoman. She was St. Anne Line who was condemned for harbouring priests. At her hanging at Tyburn she declared 'I am sentenced to die for harbouring a Catholic priest, and so far I am from repenting for having done so, that I wish, with all my soul, that where I have entertained one I could have entertained a thousand.' Two priests, a Benedictine and a Jesuit, suffered with her.

The end of the reign was to see one of those wrangles within the ranks of the clergy that threatened to undermine the Catholic witness. We have noted that George Blackwell was appointed archpriest in 1595 — Rome's first attempt to bring some kind of authority to guide the priests in England. By this time there had grown up in some quarters an antagonism between the secular clergy and the Jesuits, and, unfortunately, Rome had instructed the archpriest to consult the Jesuit superiors. The feud — for it was nothing less — was carried on acrimoniously by the secular priests who were in prison, either in one of the regular prisons or in such concentration camps as Wisbech. Part of the trouble was that these unfortunate priests had nothing to do and they could brood over imagined wrongs. At the end of

Elizabeth's reign there were probably some four hundred secular priests on the mission and about forty Jesuits. There may have been something of the feeling expressed by the Prodigal's elder brother, 'Lo, these many years I have served you'; the Jesuits had come comparatively late into the field and had stolen the limelight though that was far from their wish. Letters and pamphlets and appeals to Rome followed one another in an unending and muddy stream. It was an unedifying business. Such dissensions were encouraged by the government and the disputants were unwittingly playing its game. Fortunately these argumentative and opinionated priests were a minority and a warped impression of the true state of the mission is gained if we pay too much attention to this paper warfare. The great majority of the priests were content to carry on their apostolate in the seclusion that was their safety.

The last martyr of the reign was a seminary priest, William Richardson, who was hanged at Tyburn on the 17th February 1603, five weeks before the death of the old queen in her seventieth year. In her last days she named James VI of Scotland as her successor.

CHAPTER 20

Catholics in Penal Days

CATHOLICS of penal days can be conveniently grouped under four headings: the gentry, urban Catholics, scattered Catholics, and vagrant Catholics.

Gentry

The great houses of the Catholic gentry were the centres of resistance to Protestantism. Such a house was a self-contained unit with a host of Catholic servants and tenants. Many of these mansions were in out-of-the-way places; even to-day the sites of some of them are isolated. In Elizabethan times, with the poor roads and wide-spread forests, they must have been all but inaccessible in winter. A stranger, such as a pursuivant, would be noticed at once. It was therefore possible for a priest to live in such a house, ostensibly as a steward or tutor, with a fair degree of safety, and it was even secure enough for several priests to come together at times in conference. A further precaution was the construction of hiding-places. For some twenty years from 1587, Nicholas Owen[1] ('Little John'), a Jesuit lay-

[1] St. Nicholas Owen, after dreadful torturing, died in the Tower on 2nd March 1606.

brother, and a carpenter by trade, made this work his form of service to the Church. When priests were taken in such houses, it was often through betrayal by a disgruntled servant or tenant such as George Eliot who was responsible for the capture of St. Edmund Campion at Lyford in Berkshire in 1581. These houses were not evenly distributed about the country. They were numerous in Lancashire where, it was claimed, they were so widespread that it was possible to move about the County without leaving Catholic ground. There was another cluster across the south Midlands especially in Worcestershire, Warwickshire and North-amptonshire. A third group in West Sussex has already been mentioned.

It was a tragedy when the head of these families conformed, or when the family died out. This meant that the services of a priest were no longer regularly available, and, as a consequence, the servants and tenants fell away. These great families were also an important source of vocations to the priesthood and they contributed generously to the support of the seminaries and for the relief of recusants in prison who lacked means of their own.

Urban Catholics

Those Catholics who lived in the greater towns such as Norwich, Bristol and York were able to get together dis-creetly to hear Mass; they were also able to shelter priests. London with a population of 300,000 (Norwich, the next largest city, had 17,000) was in a class apart. A few Catholics would dare to go to Mass occasionally at the Ambassadors' chapels, but they were watched and liable to arrest on leaving. The very size of the sprawling city made it possible for priests to be sheltered but there were eager pursuivants and informers who made life on the mission in London precarious. London Catholics had one advantage; there were so many parishes (ninety in the City itself) that they could more easily evade statutory attendance than in a village where everyone knew everyone. It seems strange to us that the prisons were centres of Catholicism; bribery could effect almost anything save liberty; Mass was said regularly and visitors were able to enter without much supervision. Conversions among the prisoners were not infrequent. Cases are known where a newly arrived priest would go to the nearest prison in order to be put into touch with Catholics and to get advice from priests who had been captured.

Scattered Catholics

This term may be applied to Catholics living in the country but too far from a Catholic mansion to be able to get there except occasionally in summer when they might stay a night or two. Otherwise they had to rely on itinerant priests. The difficulties were considerable, not least to inform a priest of their existence. Many of these Catholics fell away simply because they might have to go for years without the sacraments. Perhaps the parents, with memories of a Catholic England, clung to their faith, but the children would have no such links with the past and as they grew up the very meaning of Catholicism would fade out except for the consciousness that its adherents were looked at askance by their neighbours, or were harried by the churchwardens or parson. The growth of Puritans must have meant that the rather tolerant local attitude would change to harsh antagonism especially if the parson became a 'hot gospeller' himself.

Vagrant Catholics

This was a recognised category. To evade church attendance, such Catholics would move from parish to parish.

There was the risk of being taken up as a vagabond, but if a man wanted work, especially if he had some craft or skill, he could usually make a living, however meagre, for himself and his family. It should be kept in mind that except at times of crisis, such as the Armada threat, the application of the penal laws was intermittent and a man and his family could return safely to their own parish once the storm had passed. It was a precarious existence at best, and there are records of some Catholics living in rudely made huts in the wilder parts.

We know little of the third and fourth of these groups; only an incidental reference here and there gives us an inkling of how such Catholics survived. The strength of attachment to the old religion depended on some contact, even at long intervals, with a priest; where that was impossible these lonely folk might lapse in the long run.

Some priests, as we have seen, had settled stations in the houses of the gentry and could serve the neighbourhood and even farther afield. Many more priests were itinerant. Some would have an agreed territory in which to work, but others had a roving commission and went from place to place keeping in touch with their scattered flock and trying to trace those who had lapsed. The life was a hard one. They had to face all weathers and could not always be sure of shelter for the night, nor of the next meal, but, like 'Uncle James' mentioned earlier, they plodded the countryside and brought the sacraments to many who otherwise would never receive them. At times, when the priest-hunt was vigorous, such priests would have to take to the wilder country and find shelter with a shepherd or in a cave. There must have been an efficient grape-vine to give warning of the presence of pursuivants, as well as to let people know that a priest would be available at such and such a place. We have no record of the numbers of such priests nor even of their names, but many were able to evade capture for years at a time. Some indication of the length of such apostolates is given by the records of three who were eventually captured and hanged in 1679. St. John Wall was on the mission in Worcestershire for twenty-three years; St. John Kemble for fifty-four years in Herefordshire, and St. David Lewis (a relative of Augustine Baker) for thirty years in South Wales.

Secular priests were largely on their own; for many years they had no superior to whom they could refer their problems. Those in or near London had a fairly regular means of communication with their seminaries, but those farther afield would be out of touch as their very whereabouts had to be kept secret. Very occasionally it was possible for the priests in one region to get together, though it meant much organising. When together they could make their confessions one to another, discuss their problems and exchange any news they had of Catholic affairs. It was a solitary life without the means of spiritual refreshment that all priests have to-day. It says much for the soundness of the seminary training that so few, a handful at most, fell away. There are no indications that they took any part in political discussions; the two or three who did become involved were betraying their own brethren by breaking the rule laid down in every seminary.

Priests dressed in such a fashion as to be inconspicuous; those who were stationed in the houses of the gentry would dress according to their assumed station in the household. In the towns a priest would look like a small tradesman or clerk, while in the country he might appear to be a farmer. An interesting detail is that it was only in prison that they dared to wear the cassock. Those who were settled were able to follow the full liturgy. There would be a room in one of the rambling houses of the times where Mass could be said; after Mass, vestments and everything else were kept concealed. Even in out-of-the-way parts it was prudent to have someone on the watch during Mass to give warning of the approach of any stranger. At the alarm all signs of the Mass would be whisked away according to a well-practised drill. Neighbours who came to Mass would not draw attention to themselves by all arriving at the same time. Occasionally a hunting party or some family celebration would be a cover for the real purpose. The sermon after Mass was important and greatly valued.

Itinerant priests, out in the field, could not have such regularised methods. Each would, like 'Uncle James' carry his Massing equipment with him; presumably a pony or a mule would be used when not too conspicuous. Rome recognised the practical problems that had to be faced and allowed these priests considerable discretion. In necessity they could use an ordinary table even without an altar stone; they could omit some of the vestments and have only one candle and even omit the crucifix. An unblessed tin chalice was permitted. Women could serve the altar.

We can picture the priest arriving at the cottage of a simple Catholic. He would be welcomed as an honoured guest. If there were other Catholics within reach they would be warned and a time arranged for them to see the priest. The Mass, which might be said to small groups at a time, would be the central event of the visit. Unless danger threatened, the priest would stay for a week or longer. Receiving the sacrament was a solemn and precious moment in the lives of these scattered Catholics. A day or so would be allowed for the examination of conscience before confession, and after communion there would be a thanksgiving that would not be hurried. The children as well as the grown-ups would be catechised. These children must have been well warned of the need for prudence, for there is no example of a priest being betrayed by a child's thoughtless chatter.

There were a number of practical difficulties that had to be faced by scattered Catholics when a priest was not available or could come to them at only long intervals. Baptism presented no problem as the sacrament is valid when administered by a layman in default of a priest, and we may be sure that the priests taught the people the right way and the right words. Under James I baptism by law had to be in the parish church. There were ways of avoiding this; a mother expecting a baby might go to relatives at some distance in another parish, have her child there and privately baptised and later return home without questions being asked. Some

257

parsons were willing to ignore the law and say nothing.

Marriages were a more serious difficulty. During the period here covered, there could be no question of Catholics marrying in the parish church; this did, however, become more common in the eighteenth century. If a priest was not to be had, the old rule prevailed: a clandestine marriage by consent, even without witnesses, was allowed by the Church to be valid; then, when a priest came that way, he would bless the marriage.

Confirmations were impossible without a bishop, but, as we have seen, in medieval times not much stress was put on this sacramental. Rome at last appointed a bishop for England in 1623; he was appropriately named William Bishop; he died within a year, but in this brief time he confirmed some two thousand in or near London and four hundred at Cowdray in Sussex. Then came another long interregnum without a bishop.

Burials also presented a problem. Catholic recusants were, *ipso facto*, excommunicate by the Anglican Church and so could not be buried in the local graveyard. After a Mass at home when possible, burial was often carried out at night, sometimes with the parson agreeing to look the other way. Prayers for the dead would be recited. In this and other ways there was much give and take in country parishes during the earlier Elizabethan period. Neighbours were neighbours. Of course someone with a grudge might prove a nuisance, but it was not until Puritanism became a force that the laws were rigidly applied in these private matters.

How did Catholics, lonely ones in particular, nourish their spiritual life? Prayer was the essential foundation. In addition to the familar prayers, there was the Rosary, the beads. Douay and Reims and St. Omer printed a number of books of prayers as aids to devotion. The most used was *A Manual of Prayers*, the forerunner of a long series of such books and leading to the small missals of later times. The *Manual* included the Jesu Psalter, and, in later editions, the Litanies, a summary of Christian doctrine and 'the order to help at Mass.' The Jesu Psalter had long been a

treasured devotion. Richard Whytford, 'the wretch of
Syon', the friend of More and Erasmus, is believed to have
been the author. Mention has already been made of the
catechism composed by Lawrence Vaux, and of Fr. Parson's
Christian Directory. Fr. Parson had a printing press at Rouen
and later at St. Omer and issued many books for the use of
Catholics. These new books did not replace the Book of
Hours, or Office of the Blessed Virgin Mary. This book goes
back to the ninth century and there are many beautifully
illuminated copies to be seen in museums and libraries.
I have before me a copy printed at Salamanca in 1588,
the year of the Armada. It belonged to Giles Poyntz, one of
a well-known Catholic family. He was born in 1601, fought
for the king against parliament and was declared to be a
'Popish recusant in arms'. He died in 1666. Some details
of the family are written in the calendar at the beginning
of the book. Books of Hours contained besides the Hours of
the Virgin, the Seven Penitential Psalms, the Fifteen Gradual
Psalms, the Litanies and the Office of the Dead. It is interesting to note that the most thumbed part of this volume
before me is the section giving the Penitential Psalms and
the Litanies. Such volumes were expensive, and were, of
course, in Latin, so would probably be found only in the
houses of the gentry.

Catholics were then much stricter than ourselves in the
observance of the days of obligation, and the rules for
fasting and abstinence; this was part of the discipline they
accepted in preserving the faith. There were thirty-seven
days of obligation; the weekdays of Lent and all Fridays
were fast days. Abstinence was observed on Sundays in
Lent, Saturdays outside Eastertide, and on three days before
the Ascension. It must have been difficult to keep the days of
obligation in a Protestant country, but priests would give
dispensations to ease the problem.

Such was the faithful remnant that kept the faith. 'A remnant has remained true; grace has chosen it.' (Rom. 11.5). We
naturally and rightly give the martyrs and the forty-two
martyr-saints special honour, but we should not forget the

many thousands of ordinary folk who clung to their religion; still less those who suffered in prison but were not called to make the final sacrifice. One of the heaviest burdens the ordinary Catholics had to bear was the suspicion with which they came to be regarded as the threat from Spain drew near.

The religious atmosphere changed after the first half of Elizabeth's reign. In the early days the authorities hoped that gradually all would become accustomed to the new services and be willing to conform. The clergy who had conformed had been Catholic priests, some of them old enough to recall days when there was no thought of a Royal Supremacy. While they themselves were not prepared to run hazards, they had a respect for the old religion and were not anxious to trouble those of their neighbours who would not conform. Gradually the outlook changed. The obligatory reading of authorised homilies at every service ensured that a Protestant belief would be regularly put before the congregations. Among the pastors who had spent the years of Queen Mary's reign at Geneva or some other protestant centre, were some who regarded the Book of Common Prayer as too much like the old Catholic services. They began to advocate more radical changes. So the government was faced with a new development, the beginnings of the Puritan movement for whom Rome was the Scarlet Woman and the pope Anti-Christ. It now became the practice of Anglican bishops to insist on Catholic recusants having conferences with the Anglican clergy. Such conferences soon proved ineffective, but one unexpected result was that Catholics learned the need for understanding their own faith so that in these disputes they could hold their own. So it came about that in the second half of Elizabeth's reign, Catholics were better grounded in the faith than many of their fathers had been. The numbers decreased as Church Papists dropped away with each successive increase in the severity of the penal laws. Parallel with this loss was the building up of a Catholic community firmly holding to beliefs they now understood better than ever before and ready to face the trials that lay ahead.

CHAPTER 21

The Gunpowder Plot and afterwards

AT the accession of James I, Catholics had reason to hope for some amelioration in their treatment. Apart from some vague promises before he was sure of the succession, James made a statement in his first Parliament that seemed to endorse this. 'I acknowledge,' he said, 'the Roman church to be our mother church although defiled with some infirmities and corruptions. My mind was ever so free from persecution.' Such a declaration must have alarmed his listeners; he clearly had little idea of the strong Protestant and increasingly Puritan feeling of his new realm, nor of the power of Parliament. A later remark revealed his true attitude. 'Na, na,' he said, 'we'll nae need the Papishes now.'

The disappointment of Catholics found an outlet for the more reckless of them in plots. The Bye Plot of 1604 to kidnap the king was devised by an unstable priest named William Watson, the same who had been helped to escape from the Bridewell in 1588 by St. Margaret Ward. He had already caused trouble among his fellow-priests and it is charitable to regard him as addle-pated. The scheme came to the knowledge of Fr. Henry Garnet, S.J. and other priests and they warned the government. Watson and two others were hanged. This gave Parliament reason to pass an Act 'for the due execution of statutes against Catholics.' All priests were ordered to leave the country. Unhappily this first crack-brained plot was followed by a far more serious affair that was to inflame anti-Catholic feeling.

We shall never know the full facts about the Gunpowder Plot of 1605. The available evidence comes from government sources and we are more sceptical of confessions extracted by torture than our forefathers were; in fact we have become suspicious of all official publicity. It seems probable that the government was early aware that some kind of plot was in the making, but this particular one was not fostered with the skill Walsingham had used in the Babington Plot. Doubts have been raised as to the genuineness of some parts of the documents, and there are a number of inconsistencies that call for explanation, and a whole literature has recorded various speculations. For want of key evidence, it is impossible to reach a firm conclusion. Nor does this affect the plain fact that there was a plot made by Catholics. It was both criminal and irresponsible. Criminal, because it could have resulted in the killing and maiming of innocent people, though some contemporaries might have found dubious justification for such acts; irresponsible, because it gambled with the future treatment of Catholics. Conspirators at that period seem to have deluded themselves into thinking that they had only to raise the standard for thousands to flock to their support. They had, in fact, no way of testing this assumption. It would have needed a widely-spread and efficient organisation to have ensured success. Secrecy was the primary requirement but there was always someone who got cold feet and blabbed, or, more likely, there would be a spy planted by the government at the first sign of a conspiracy. These plotters learned nothing from experience. The Essex rising of 1601, though not of Catholic origin, should have warned them of the dangers ahead. Three of the Powder Plot conspirators had been concerned with that rising and were lucky to have escaped the gallows. They were, Robert Catesby (aged 32), Francis Tresham (aged 38) and John Wright (aged 37). They were not headstrong young men but, for their period, middle-aged. They had witnessed the Earl of Essex marching to the City in expectation that the people would rally to him only to see the citizens gape. As these three must have been marked men from then onwards, it was all the more foolish to start scheming again; their movements and associates would be closely observed and reported.

Thomas Winter, Catesby's chief abettor, had had military experience in the Netherlands, where he had known Guy Fawkes, the son of a Yorkshire landowner. Robert Winter helped his brother in the enterprise. John and Christopher Wright, also Yorkshire gentry, joined the plot. Most of the conspirators were related to one another; indeed, it was almost a family affair.

The head of the Jesuit mission at this time was Fr. Henry Garnet; he had come over in 1586 with St. Robert Southwell. Gradually Fr. Garnet had brought in more Jesuits and he accomplished a great work in organising his own priests and in helping seminary priests; his success made the government all the more anxious to get hands on him. It was in June 1605 that he had a first vague hint from Robert Catesby that there was something in the wind; Garnet, knowing his man, suspected some desperate enterprise; he at once took steps to get from Rome an injunction against any kind of violent movement, but this did not restrain the plotters. Then Fr. Oswald Tesimond (alias Greenway, or Greenwell) told Fr Garnet in confession of the plot, knowledge of which had also come to him in confession. He had done all he could to dissuade Catesby from going forward with his plans. The lips of both priests were thus sealed. The two Jesuits could only hope that after the serious warnings they had repeatedly given the plot would be abandoned.

There is no need to retell here the well-known story of the Plot. The intention was to blow up the Parliament house when it reassembled on the 5th November. The neighbouring house of one of the conspirators, Thomas Percy, proved a convenient point of attack by way of the cellars. On the 26th October Lord Monteagle received a letter warning him not to go to the meeting of Parliament. This letter may have come from his brother-in-law Francis Tresham. Monteagle had himself been involved in the Essex rising but not to the same extent as the other three; he had been a Catholic but had recently conformed. The letter led to the capture of Guy Fawkes. The other conspirators fled and were at length run to earth at Holbeach, near Wolverhampton. In the subsequent fight, Catesby and Percy were killed; the others were captured, tortured and hanged. It has already been noted that there are a number of difficulties in accepting the official version of what happened; the facts were dressed up for publicity purposes, but the main facts cannot be explained away.

In the course of the investigations after the Plot, three priests were named, John Gerard, Henry Garnet and Oswald Tesimond. Fr. Gerard, who certainly had no knowledge of the plot, and Fr. Tesimond managed to get out of the country, but Fr. Garnet was taken at Hinlip Hall, Worcestershire, in January 1606. He refused to give any information during the early interrogations, but after the first torturing he told what he knew. Fr. Tesimond, when he had made his confession, had said that if Fr. Garnet were threatened with torture, he could break the seal of confession. Fr. Garnet waited until he had been actually tortured before making a statement, which showed that he had not in fact known the details of the plot, and his inquisitors learned nothing new from him. He was hanged in front of St. Paul's on the 3rd May 1606.

The trial of Fr. Garnet is of peculiar interest because a much stressed aspect of it had a permanent effect on the popular attitude towards Catholics and especially towards Jesuits. Shakespeare's *Macbeth* was written in the year of Fr. Garnet's hanging; it has a reference to his trial. At the beginning of Act 2, scene 3, the Porter, posing as the porter of hell-gate says,

'Faith, here's an equivocator, that could swear both the scales against either scale, who committed treason enough for God's sake, yet could not equivocate to heaven: O, come in equivocator.'

'Equivocation' is defined in the Oxford English Dictionary as 'the use of words or expressions susceptible of a double signification, in order to mislead,' and gives the date for its use as 1605. The claim of the Crown was that priests, especially Jesuits, avoided giving straight-forward answers by evasion and by twisting words from their true meaning. In rebuttal, the defendants argued that situations do arise, quite apart from religious beliefs, where the obligations of charity would warrant the withholding of the full truth, or the wrapping up of the truth in an easily accepted form. This is a common dilemma; it may, for instance, be prudent to avoid telling a sick man that he has cancer. At his trial in 1595 St. Robert Southwell had put this case to his accusers:

'Suppose that the French King should invade Her Majesty's realm, and that she (which God forbid) were enforced to fly to some private house for safety from her enemies, where none knew of her being but Mr. Attorney. Suppose that Mr. Attorney, being taken, were put upon his oath to say whether she were there or not. And suppose that Mr. Attorney's refusal to swear should be held as a confession of her being in the house. Would Mr. Attorney refuse to swear? Or, would he say, 'She is not there,' meaning, 'I intend not to tell you.'

Mr. Attorney (the redoubtable Sir Edward Coke) made no reply.

There is no need to discuss the finer points of this problem since it is one we all have to solve at some time or another. What is of concern is that this charge of equivocation was used by the government to throw doubt on the veracity of all Catholics; the argument was that whatever lies they told could be covered by a dispensation from the pope. So the idea spread that the word of a Catholic was not to be trusted.

Guy Fawkes night became an annual commemoration of the escape of King and Parliament. For more than two centuries it was definitely anti-papist, and, usually, an effigy of the pope was burned. Much of this meaning has been lost and the effigy ('a penny for the guy') now represents Guy Fawkes. Later, this celebration was combined with a commemoration of the landing of William of Orange at Torbay on the 5th of November 1688. A special thanksgiving service was added to the Book of Common Prayer and an annual Gunpowder Plot sermon was preached. In the communion service thanks were given that 'this day miraculously preserved our Church and State from the secret and hellish malice of Popish conspirators.' This special service was not abandoned until 1859.

Of more immediate consequence to Catholics was the tightening up of the penal laws. A new oath of allegiance was devised. The first part of the oath declared that,

'the pope, neither of himself, nor by any authority of the church or see of Rome . . . hath any power or authority to depose the king.'

A later paragraph read,

'And I do further swear that I do, from my heart, abhor, detest, and abjure, as impious and heretical, this damnable doctrine and position — that princes, which be excommunicated by the pope, may be deposed or murdered by their subjects, or any other whatsoever.'

James I and Charles I seem to have been particularly sensitive on this matter of the pope's powers to depose kings and princes; they were needlessly so since the claim was no longer practical politics. The power of deposition had been an effective weapon in medieval times, but it had become blunted as had been shown when it was used against Queen Elizabeth. A world that was now part Catholic and part Protestant could no longer be controlled

266

by powers that were applicable when all Europe was Catholic. Most Catholics in Stuart times would probably have been willing to accept this disavowal but the wording of the oath was so offensive as to make it repugnant. It seems that the government, on the principle of divide and rule, was intent on splitting the Catholic community, and this it succeeded in doing. Some Catholics, including priests, saw no objection to the oath and subscribed to it. The question was fiercely debated with deplorable effects on the unity of Catholics. George Blackwell, the archpriest, took the oath and was deposed by the pope in 1608 two years after Rome had condemned it. So there was revived the contention among the clergy to which reference has already been made. Further examination of its character is necessary.

There were three main issues.

1. *The need for a bishop to have full authority over all clergy*

The secular priests were surely right in appealing for a bishop. Their work was hampered in many ways for want of one. It was not just a question of organisation but of those sacraments that could be administered only by a bishop. Unfortunately the Jesuits were opposed to such a measure. In effect this meant Fr. Robert Parsons, whose prestige at Rome was decisive. There was as we have seen, a bishop, William Bishop, during 1623–4; after his death came arch-priests without episcopal authority until 1631. Apart from this interlude, Catholics in England had no bishop for 125 years. In spite of all the arguments advanced by the Jesuits against such an appointment, it is difficult to under-stand why Rome failed to provide for some kind of interim organisation.

2. *The authority of the Jesuits*

We have seen how the Jesuit mission, until towards the end of Elizabeth's reign, never numbered more than a few active priests. Fr. Garnet gradually built up the number. Even so, they constituted less than a tenth of the number of priests in England. The Jesuits were better organised than the bishopless seminary priests could be. Unfortunately

267

they became the focus of government attack and the people at large must have got the impression that there were Jesuits all over the country. It has already been pointed out that some of the secular clergy resented this undue emphasis on the Jesuits, but was there not also a touch of arrogance among the Jesuits? There are expressions in some of Fr. Garnet's reports to Rome suggesting that until the Jesuits arrived, the mission was disordered. He could not have known many of the hundreds of seminary priests, least of all those who were working in remote parts which he never visited. Indeed, so cut off were many of the itinerant priests from outside contacts, it may have been a long time before some of them knew that there were Jesuits on the mission. This 'hiddenness' had its advantages; it meant they could keep out of the wrangling of the quarrelsome imprisoned priests.

3. The James I oath

It has been noted that some priests, chiefly those in prison, took this oath in spite of its condemnation by Rome. They must have been disagreeably surprised that they were not set at liberty, but their confinement was made as easy as possible; indeed, the government went so far as to allow a delegation to go to Rome where their reception was far from cordial.

The Act of 1606 imposing the oath included a new requirement. Not only must everyone attend his parish church regularly but communion must be taken once a year. Parliament during Elizabeth's reign, had several times voted from compulsory communion, but the queen, on each occasion, vetoed the proposal. In addition, under the new Act, the head of a household was made responsible for paying the fines not only for his family but for his servants and for his guests if they were absent from church. One result of this was that many Catholic servants were discharged. Yet another Act banished all Catholics from court and restricted their movements. Catholics could no longer be lawyers, doctors, or officers of any public corporation, nor have commissions in the army or navy; they could not be executors and their rights of inheritance were threatened. In future only baptisms and marriages in the parish church would be valid under the law, and burials outside the churchyard were forbidden. Catholic recusants were excommunicated so could not have recourse to the law and their homes could be searched at any time without warrant. All this meant that henceforth a Catholic was a social outcast. It is from this date, 1606, that the Catholic community ceased to play an active part in the life of society. Inevitably some found it impossible to endure this ostracism and conformed.

An indication of the ebb and flow of the persecution of Catholics is to be found in the exchequer receipts from recusant fines.

1603	£7,115
1604	£1,414
1605	£2,213
1606	£10,210
1607	£8,321
1608	£8,537
1609	£12,965

Neither James I nor Charles I was a persecutor by nature, and they used the royal prerogative to release priests on condition that they left the country. Many of these banished priests returned after an interval and thereby ran the risk of summary penalties. Whenever Parliament met, the Commons, becoming increasingly Puritan, demanded that the penal laws should be more efficiently enforced. St. John Roberts is a good example of the way in which a priest could be affected both by royal clemency and by Parliamentary rigour. He was arrested, banished, and returned, no less than four times before his final arrest in London on Advent Sunday 1610. Unfortunately Parliament was then sitting so there was no hope of a reprieve followed by yet another banishment. He has the additional interest of being a Benedictine. During one of his interludes in the

Netherlands, he helped to establish St. Gregory's Benedictine monastery at Douay; this was the precursor of Downside Abbey.

This leads to a note on a development during the first half of the seventeenth century. A number of English monasteries and convents were established abroad. The list is a long one and cannot be given fully here; one or two examples must suffice. Another Benedictine foundation was St. Laurence at Dieuluard, now at Ampleforth. A Benedictine convent was founded at Brussels in 1598 by Mary Percy, the daughter of Bl. Thomas Percy, Earl of Northumberland. A number of daughter convents were established in other towns, such as Cambrai, now Stanbrook, and Dunkirk, now Teignmouth. An interesting example is St. Monica's, Louvain. Margaret Clement, daughter of John and Margaret Clement, was one of the original nuns. Her parents had exiled themselves again, with William Rastell, after the passing of the Elizabethan Act of Uniformity. She became prioress and died in 1616. She brought to the convent the hair shirt of St. Thomas More; this is now the treasured possession of the convent at Newton Abbot. The Carmelites, Franciscans and Dominicans and other orders also established communities abroad. Benedictines and Franciscans sent priests to work on the English mission.

George Blackwell, the dismissed archpriest, was followed by George Birkhead who decided to petition the pope for the restoration of episcopal government for the Catholics of England; he collected the written support of some two hundred secular priests. This appeal was successfully opposed by the Jesuits in Rome under the leadership of Fr. Robert Parsons. Birkhead died in April 1614 and was followed by William Harrison. Four years later, he sent a report to Rome on what he had observed of the condition of Catholics. One paragraph reads,

'With regard to our affairs, they are in the same state as usual. The pillaging of property, the squalor of prisons, the intimidations of magistrates, the raids of officials, the snares of false brethern; and though trials of this sort can test Catholics more thoroughly (which is the goodness of God) they cannot withdraw them from the Faith. The officials, or, as we call them, pursuivants, are troublesome everywhere to an extraordinary degree, but, especially lately, they swoop upon Catholics, ruin them, plunder them, and when possible carry them off to prison. As to the priests, if they discover any, they drag them there, and after examination, send them to the dungeons. Besides many others elsewhere, at least thirty have been captured in London since the last banishment and thrust into prison. The rest press on with their duties, as is proper, with much praise and toil, and God giveth increase lest they should seem to labour in vain.'

A new factor in the situation was the result of James I's foreign policy. He wisely ended the war with Spain which was not getting anyone anywhere, but he went further in seeking a Spanish Princess as a wife for his son Charles. The negotiations meant some relaxation in the penal laws; the Spanish ambassador, for instance, would suggest, as evidence of good faith, the release of recusants and priests from prison. It is said that when James agreed to do this in 1621, some four thousand recusants were set free. This figure, which may be just a round number, is one of the few indications we have of how many of the Catholic laity were imprisoned. The exaction of fines was not relaxed; the Stuarts were always hard up and could not afford to forgo any source of income.

The country was still anti-Spanish and the proposed marriage once more strengthened anti-Catholic feeling. The king promised, as a condition of the marriage, that the penal laws would be gradually repealed. Such a promise he could not possibly carry out. The Spanish match fell through much to the rejoicing of the populace. Eventually a marriage was arranged with another Catholic Princess, Henrietta Maria, daughter of Henry IV of France. Secret clauses in the marriage agreement provided for the suspension of the penal laws. It is astonishing that James and Charles should have assumed that they could change the law at will; they must have been out-of-touch with the religious sentiment of the country and with the House of Commons, which was to prove a fatal error. Far from modifying the law, the Commons insisted, yet again, that the laws against papists must be enforced, and a proclamation was made ordering all priests to leave the country, and urging that measures should be taken to see that the children of recusants were brought up as Protestants. Once more the pursuivants, and informers, got busy.

The marriage was celebrated in May 1625; King James died two months later. The new queen's Catholic household and chaplains soon excited criticism. Papal agents, Gregorio Panzani, George Conn and Count Rossetti, in succession, were accredited to her and were popularly believed to have too much influence at court and even on the king himself. The queen's palace of Somerset House soon became a Catholic rallying place and Mass was openly said there and attended by many outside the court. A number of noble ladies and a lesser number of nobles and gentry were converted, but it is difficult to know how far this was from deep conviction and how far it was a passing fashion in court circles. All this was sufficiently provocative, but it should be linked with Archbishop Laud's High Anglicanism that to many seemed more Roman than Anglican. It was even rumoured that the pope had offered Laud a cardinal's hat if he would go the whole way to Rome.

The Catholicism manifested at Somerset House and at the court increased the suspicions of the Puritans and this was reflected in Parliament which, in 1628, passed an Act penalising parents who sent their sons abroad for their education. It was in this year that St. Edmund Arrowsmith, S.J., was hanged at Lancaster. At the time it was felt that the trial and execution had been indecently hurried by the judge, Sir Henry Yelverton; had there been time for an appeal, it was thought that the king would have granted a reprieve.

During the eleven years that Charles I governed without a parliament, no Catholics were condemned to death, but the Long Parliament which met in November 1641 acted as its predecessors had done and insisted on the laws being enforced, while a new Proclamation once more banished all priests.

At the end of 1641, rebels in Ireland, driven desperate by the injustices they suffered, massacred four or five thousand Protestants, and probably as many died of hunger and exposure. The popular belief in England was that the rebellion had been encouraged by the pope. Two years later, a new oath was prescribed; papal supremacy and the doctrines of transubstantiation and purgatory had to be renounced. James I had believed that any loyal Catholic could take the oath of 1606 with an easy conscience as it involved no doctrinal statement, but the Long Parliament oath was one that no Catholic could possibly take since it meant denying fundamental doctrines. It was during the early years of this Parliament that St. Ambrose Barlow and St. Alban Roe were martyred, the first in 1641 and the second a year later. Both were Benedictines; Alban Roe was a convert.

When the Civil War broke out in August 1642, the Catholic gentry rallied to the king. Many gave not only their possessions but their lives in the royal cause. Loyal Catholics had to pay special taxes; their arms and horses were confiscated and two-thirds of their estates forfeited in addition to the disabilities suffered by all who fought for the king.

CHAPTER 22

Puritans and Catholics

ONE of the early Acts of the Rump Parliament of 1650 repealed the law requiring all to attend their parish churches. This was not intended as a measure of relief for Catholics but as a step towards the abolition of the Anglican Church. It allowed Puritan sects liberty of worship. Nonetheless it was a considerable alleviation for Catholics. The test of recusancy under the Commonwealth became the refusal to take the oath of allegiance. By the Instrument of Government (1653) which made Cromwell Lord Protector, all 'who profess faith in God by Jesus Christ though differing from the doctrine, worship or discipline publicly held forth' were granted liberty in the exercise of their religion 'provided this liberty is not extended to popery or prelacy.' 'Popery' meant the Catholics, and 'prelacy' the Anglicans. Four years later the Humble Petition and Advice again gave liberty of worship to all save those guilty of 'popery and prelacy.' There was no renewal of the persecution of priests. As we have seen 'Popish recusants in arms' and Catholics not in arms were heavily mulcted under the Commonwealth. One example out of thousands may be given. In 1652 a Catholic named Hammond appealed to the commissioners for sequestrations for relief. He had not taken up arms

against Parliament, but his whole estate had been sequest-
rated; he begged he might be allowed a fifth of its value as he
had no other means. The appeal was dismissed. A return of
1655 shows that nearly sixteen hundred Catholic estates
were under sequestration. It was in that year that Cromwell
had the Long Parliament's two-thirds rule repealed. The
authorities were too busy with the war to give more than
occasional attention to the hunting down of priests. In
royalist areas they were safe. Only two were martyred under
the Commonwealth.

The first was Bl. Peter Wright, a convert who became a
Jesuit priest. After his ordination he became chaplain to
Sir Henry Gage, the son of Margaret Gage, cousin to St.
Robert Southwell. In 1630 Sir Henry was appointed colonel
of an English regiment in the service of Spain in the Nether-
lands. When he crossed to England in 1644 to join the royalist forces, he took Fr. Peter Wright with him. Sir Henry was
killed in the following year. His chaplain then moved to
London for work on the mission; there he was betrayed by
Thomas Gage, the apostate brother of Sir Henry. He was
inevitably found guilty. Many efforts were made, especially
by the Spanish ambassador, to get a reprieve, but as it was
Whitsun, neither the Council nor Parliament was in session.
Fr. Peter Wright was hanged at Tyburn on the 19th May
1654.

The second priest to suffer under the Commonwealth
was St. John Southworth, and, as his life was so typical of
that of seminary priests of the seventeenth century, it is
worth a detailed account.

He was born in 1592 in Lancashire of a notable Catholic
family whose extensive property centred on Samlesbury,
east of Preston. The Elizabethan head of the family, Sir
John, spent the greater part of twenty years in prison as a
recusant. As a result of the payment of fines and of support
given to the royal cause, most of the estate was lost by the
end of the century. A number of the great Catholic houses
of Lancashire had resident priests as tutors, and, probably
the boy John Southworth received his early education from

one of them, but he may have attended Blackburn Grammar School where the headmaster Lawrence Yates was himself a recusant but so strong was Catholicism in the district, he was left undisturbed. His life illustrates the fact that the penal laws operated fitfully in some parts of the country, but the big landowners were the main targets as their fines were wanted. In his boyhood and youth John Southworth must have grown familiar with the means used by Catholics to practice their religion — the covering of the movements of priests, leading them to safe hide-outs up on the moors when hotly pursued, the removal of all signs of the Mass at a warning of danger, and the passing of messages to Catholics in the vicinity.

He entered Douay on the 4th July 1613 at the age of twenty-one. He was thus somewhat older than most entrants but this gave him the advantage of greater first-hand experience of the practical problems Catholics had to face. At the end of his first year, he received the tonsure and in December 1615 he took the College oath which ended, 'Therefore I say and I swear to Almighty God that I have the prompt intention, so far as God's Grace shall help me, of receiving sacred orders in due time, and of returning to England to gain the souls of my neighbours, wherever it shall seem good in the Lord to the superior of this College, for the purpose of this institution, to order me to do so.'

It was at this period that the argument about the King James oath was most acute, and the Douay students attested that the oath 'was damnable, execrable, and involving open perjury.' They certainly did not mince their words in those contentious times! John Southworth subscribed to this declaration, but, when he was on the mission, he was too busy to get involved in further argument. He was ordained priest at Cambrai in 1618 and on Easter Day offered up his first Mass. He seems to have tested his vocation as a Benedictine at St. Gregory's, Douai, but he found that this was not his calling. At the end of 1619 came the great day when 'John Southworth, alumnus and priest of this College (Douay), with the usual faculties for the winning of souls, was chosen for the vineyard of England.' He was twenty-seven years of age.

For the first five years of his ministry he worked in or near London, but, apart from that bare fact, nothing definite is known of his labours. At this period (1619–24) the persecution of Catholics was relaxed while King James was trying to negotiate a Spanish marriage for Prince Charles. Only a few months before John Southworth landed, sixty priests had been collected from several prisons and banished. He must have met some of them at Douay and from them he would learn of the kind of life that lay ahead of him. After this apprenticeship period in London, John Southworth returned to Douay in March 1624; this was a result of a proclamation of that year banishing all priests at the demand of the Commons. John Southworth remained at the College for five months and then spent a year as chaplain to the English Benedictine nuns at Brussels. In July 1625 he returned to England and, this time, went to his own part of the country. He was arrested there two years later and imprisoned in Lancaster Castle. There are no details of his trial; he was condemned but reprieved; it should be noted that he was not pardoned; this meant that for the rest of his life, twenty-seven years, he had the sentence of death hanging over him. He was joined in prison by St. Edmund Arrowsmith who had served on the mission for fifteen years. Later they were joined by St. Ambrose Barlow. So these three priests, a Secular, a Jesuit and a Benedictine, were able to strengthen one another in prison.

The contemporary account of Edmund Arrowsmith's last hours (August 1628) gives us a glimpse of John Southworth.

'As he was carried through the castleyard, there was a reverend and worthy priest, Mr. Southworth, who had been condemned for his function a year before, and stood then reprieved, who shewed himself at a great window. And the blessed man, who was now on his way to the hurdle, no sooner saw his face, but he lifted up his hands towards him with great humility for absolution (for this was the sign whereof they were agreed before) and so that priest absolved the other in sight of the people.'

Ambrose (or Edward) Barlow was released but it is not known for what reason; he was imprisoned several times before his final arrest in 1641 when he was hanged at Lancaster on the 10th September.

The next certain information we have about John Southworth is that he was in the Clink prison, Southwark, in 1630. A royal warrant dated 11th April gives a list of sixteen priests, including him, who were to be handed over to the French ambassador for banishment. It is doubtful, in fact, if John Southworth left the country. In 1643 that irrepressible Puritan pamphleteer, William Prynne, published his *Popish Royal Favourite* in which he collected all the examples he could find of leniency being shown to Catholic priests owing to the influence of a Catholic Queen. He included the following:

> 'John Southworth, one of the sixteen priests released by the King's aforesaid warrant of 11 April, to be sent beyond the seas as was pretended; continuing a dangerous seducer after his release, was afterwards committed to the Clink prison by the Lords of the Privy Council's warrant; but yet for all that had free liberty to walk abroad at his pleasure (as most priests during their imprisonment had, the more safely to seduce His Majesty's subjects, and open Masses in their prison to boot.)'

This complaint about the easy-going conditions at the Clink is no doubt an exaggeration, but it had a basis in fact. If a priest had to go to prison, he would prefer the Clink as bribery could gain greater relaxations of rules there than in any other prison. The variation in treatment depended on the keeper who had leased the prison and was intent on making as much money as he could. As the Clink was on the south bank of the Thames it was rather out of the way and could be conducted in a more lax (and profitable) manner. The next easy-going prison was the Gatehouse outside

Westminster Abbey. The Tower was for state prisoners or those suspected of active treason, while Newgate was usually the prelude to trial and the gallows.

For twenty-five years John Southworth was able to carry on his mission in London, sometimes from prison, usually the Gatehouse, or from hidden lodgings. A contemporary note tells us that in prison he had a 'silver key to get out and exercise his priestly ministry.' The 'silver key' was another name for bribery. From the few indications we have it would seem that John Southworth's ministry was carried out in and around Westminster. We first think of the court at Whitehall and of the Abbey precincts when we picture the Westminster of those days, but there was a chaos of misery round them little different from the description written by Cardinal Wiseman two centuries later; 'labyrinths of lanes and courts and alleys and slums, nests of ignorance, vice, depravity and crime as well as of squalor and disease.'

It was not surprising that when plague struck, it found its greatest number of victims in this slummery. An outbreak in 1636 brought together the Jesuit priest St. Henry Morse and the secular priest St. John Southworth. The former was labouring in a similar area of destitution round about St. Giles-in-the-Fields. The two priests dared to print and circulate to Catholics an appeal for funds; it begged them 'to open the bowels of mercy towards their poor and desolate brethren, who have no expectation or hope of relief from any but from them alone.' The response was generous; the queen headed the list with a gift of over a hundred pounds, and she continued her support. This charitable work was not to go unchallenged. The curate of St. Margaret's, Westminster, Robert White, petitioned the Archbishop of Canterbury against Henry Morse and John Southworth.

'This Southwell (*sic*), under a pretence of distributing alms, sent from some of the priests in Somerset House and other papists, doth take occasion to go into divers visited houses in Westminster. . . . And Southwell doth fee the

279

watchman and other poor people thereabouts, that they should affirm he comes only to give Alms. And thus under pretence of relieving the bodies of poor people, he poisons their souls.'

This resulted in John Southworth's closer confinement in the Gatehouse. At this period he seems to have been in want of aid himself. His family had no doubt helped him from time to time and he may have had a small patrimony which was exhausted by his frequent imprisonments. So he was forced at last to make another appeal this time addressed to 'the Queen's most Excellent Majesty'; it was really an appeal to the king and was made through the Secretary of State, Sir Francis Windebank.

'May it therefore please your Excellency to move his Majesty that seeing the petitioner laboured only to preserve the poor from perishing (which he thought would neither offend his Majesty nor the State) it would graciously please his Majesty to give the petitioner leave to go to his friends for means; that he himself may not now perish in prison.'

According to Prynne the appeal was successful and John Southworth was released 'to the great discontent of the people.' One may doubt the truth of the last statement; certainly the poor and needy must have welcomed the return of their benefactor. The 'cat-and-mouse' policy continued; John Southworth was again in the Clink later on and remained there until July 1640 when he was freed on a warrant signed by Windebank who was a secret Catholic, and according to a Parliamentary report, had, on his own authority, stopped proceedings against seventy-four recusants and to have ordered the release of sixty-four priests. When summoned to justify his actions, Windebank fled to France.

There is a gap in our knowledge of Southworth's movements between 1640 and 1654. The turmoil of the times made it easier for a priest to evade capture in spite of Proclamations.

As he was ultimately arrested in Westminster it seems likely that he continued to make that district his field of labour. St. Henry Morse was less fortunate. He was banished in 1641 but returned two years later when he went to the north of the country; there he was recognised and brought to London. He suffered at Tyburn on the 1st February 1645.

John Southworth was arrested on the 19th June 1654 and tried five days later before the Recorder of London. As he had already been condemned at Lancaster twenty-seven years earlier, he was, as a banished priest who had returned, without hope of a further reprieve. A contemporary account tells us that the Recorder begged him to plead Not Guilty to being a priest as there was no evidence before the court that he was one, but he would only plead 'Not Guilty to treason' rather than betray his priesthood.

Appeals were made to Oliver Cromwell by several ambassadors and the Protector said, 'God forbid my hand should be consenting to the death of any for religion.' He promised a reprieve, but his Council would not give its consent, and Cromwell could do nothing further.

John Southworth was hanged at Tyburn on the 28th June 1654 in the company of ten common criminals. An onlooker recorded that 'he was clothed in a priest's gown and had a four-cornered cap.' On the scaffold he was allowed to speak to the crowd; the onlooker noted that there were 'two hundred coaches and a great many people on horseback.' After declaring that 'my faith is my crime, the performance of my duty the occasion of my condemnation' he went on,

'It has pleased God to take the sword out of the King's hand and put it in the Protector's. Let him remember that he is to adminster justice indifferently and without exception of persons. For there is not exception of persons with God whom we ought to resemble. If any Catholics work against the present Government, let them suffer; but why should all the rest who are guiltless (unless

conscience be their guilt) be made partakers in a promis-
cuous punishment with the greatest malefactors?'

He rightly resented being hanged with men who had been
condemned for common crimes. His body was cut down
before he was dead and the customary butchery carried
out.

That, however, was not the end of John Southworth's
story. The Spanish ambassador bribed the executioner to
let him have the head and the quarters. He arranged for
some leading Catholics, including Philip Howard, grandson
of St. Philip Howard, and later a cardinal, to have the body
sewn together and embalmed; it was then taken overseas
to Douay where it was placed in the chapel. When the
French Revolution came, the National Guard took possession
of the College. Fortunately there was a brief warning and
this made it possible for the priests to bury the body of John
Southworth. After Waterloo efforts were made to recover
the buildings and they were sold to the French in 1838.
A search for the body of the martyr and for the College
treasures failed. In 1927 the Douai municipality decided
to pull down the College buildings to make way for a new
road. In the course of the digging a leaden coffin was
discovered. Cardinal Bourne of Westminster at once sent
out a representative to make an investigation. The identity
of the body was established without doubt. It was brought
to England and on May Day 1930 was transferred to
Westminster Cathedral to the Chapel of St. George and the
English Martyrs.

Saint John Southworth had returned to Westminster.

CHAPTER 23

The Popish Plot and the Revolution

THE Declaration of Breda (April 1660) which preluded the Restoration undertook 'that no man shall be disquieted or called in question for difference of opinion in matter of religion,' but this, and other concessions, were qualified by the provision that the king would accept the guidance of Parliament in carrying out the agreement. Catholics were hopeful that they would enjoy a greater measure of liberty, and they assumed that, out of gratitude for their sacrifices in lives and property in defence of the royal cause, Charles II would regard them with favour. Gratitude, however, was a sentiment alien to the Stuart temperament.

Under the Commonwealth, Catholics had not been fined or imprisoned to the extent they had suffered in earlier years. It is true they had lost their estates, but so had other supporters of the king. As we have seen only two priests were hanged. This was not a matter of toleration; the fact was that the Catholics (except in Ireland) were no longer regarded as a serious political threat; they formed but a small proportion of the royal forces as they did of the total population. Here, as at other post-Reformation periods, it is not possible to give reliable statistics; for want of precise information, these would be little better than speculative.

There is little doubt that the repressive measures following the Gunpowder Plot, the imposition of the James I oath, followed by the exclusion of Catholics from public life, had led to many conforming, and so to a decrease in the number of Catholics.

While they dared not hope for complete toleration under the restored king, Catholics could reasonably expect to be left in peace or to be simply ignored provided they remained quiet. They were to be disappointed. The early years of the reign were fully occupied with a general resettlement and Parliament had no time to spare for Catholic problems. A more urgent need was to work out some kind of agreement between Anglicans and Puritans. The latter were regarded with suspicion; they were the living reminders of Cromwell's victories and rule and could be expected to be discontented and ready to cause trouble. Charles made an attempt to bring together Anglicans and Presbyterians and hoped they would be willing to allow Catholics their worship in private, but neither the Anglican bishops nor the leaders of the Presbyterians were prepared to move from their entrenched positions. A synod at the Savoy was a failure and the Anglican Church resumed its sway with the bitterness resulting from its suppression under the Commonwealth.

A series of Acts, known as the Clarendon Code, was deliberately intended to keep the various sects down; Catholics were not specifically mentioned but as 'Papist dissenters' they were directly affected. The Corporation Act (1661) required all officers of corporations to take communion according to the Anglican rite. The Act of Uniformity (1662) brought back the Book of Common Prayer as the required form of worship; ministers who refused to use it were deprived; some two thousand were thus driven out of the re-established Church. The Conventicle Act (1664) made it unlawful for more than four persons other than members of one family to assemble for worship not in accordance with the Prayer Book. Finally, the Five Mile Act (1665) debarred any non-conforming minister from coming within five miles of his former parish nor could he act as a schoolmaster unless he took an oath of non-resistence. These repressive measures failed to eliminate Puritanism. Here we can see the beginnings of the powerful Nonconformist movement of later times. All these Acts indirectly affected Catholics.

The Elizabethan and Jacobean penal laws were still on the statute book. The Commonwealth Act of 1650 does not seem to have been specifically abrogated, but there was no reimposition of the requirement of weekly attendance at the parish churches. There are some isolated cases of fines being exacted for non-attendance at church but they are so few as to suggest that this old penalty was being allowed to lapse, nor did all such cases involve Catholics, other dissenters were included. The larger recusant fines were still exacted from the gentry and others who had property worth penalising. Parliament from time to time urged that the penal laws against 'Popish Priests and Jesuits' should be enforced and several proclamations banished priests, but the need for this repetition suggests that they were not effective.

Anti-Catholicism was not much in evidence under the Commonwealth, though this was probably because most folk were preoccupied with their own problems. The Fire of London in 1666 showed that the feeling against Papists only needed some occasion for demonstration. A scapegoat for the Fire had to be found and Catholics proved a convenient one. The Monument, two hundred feet high, was erected two years later where the fire had begun. It bore the following inscription:

'This pillar was set up in perpetual remembrance of that most dreadful burning of this Protestant city, begun and carried on by the treachery and malice of the Popish faction in order for the carrying on their horrid plot for extirpating the Protestant and old English liberty, and introducing Popery and slavery.'

This inscription was removed in James II's reign, but replaced in William III's reign and not finally removed until 1830. Alexander Pope's lines are well-known.

'Where London's column, pointing at the skies,
Like a tall bully, lifts the head and lies.'

A new element came into the situation when James, Duke of York, was converted to Catholicism about 1668. His first wife, Anne Hyde, was received in 1670 but this was not revealed until her death a year later. It was at Easter 1673 that James publicly admitted a fact that had been widely rumoured. John Evelyn's comment was typical of how sober people regarded the matter. He went to the Royal Chapel on 29th March.

"I stayed to see whether the Duke of York did receive the Communion with the King, but he did not to the amazement of everybody. This gave exceeding grief and scandal to the whole Nation, that the heir of it, and the son of a Martyr for the Protestant religion, should apostatise. What the consequences of this will be, God only knows, and wise men dread.'

The year 1670 saw the signing of the Treaty of Dover between England and France, but there were also secret understandings between Charles and his cousin Louis XIV which would have raised a storm of protest had they become known. On his part Charles promised to declare himself a Roman Catholic as soon as it was felt safe politically to do so. In return, Louis promised to supply Charles with funds to keep him free of Parliament. In the course of the next eight years Charles received nearly a quarter of a million pounds. Though these facts were not known, there were all kinds of rumours including the belief that Charles himself was a crypto-Catholic and was hand in glove with France.

Two years later, while Parliament was not sitting, he issued a Declaration of Indulgence suspending the penal laws; this exercise of his prerogative (as he interpreted it) may have been meant to impress King Louis, but Charles must have known that it would not be supported, though Parliament's response was probably more extreme than he feared it might be. The Test Act of 1673 was the direct result. It was aimed at the king's two or three Catholic councillors as well as against all Catholics and other dissenters and, obliquely, at the Duke of York. All who held office under the Crown had to take the oaths of allegiance and supremacy, to receive communion according to the Anglican rite and make a declaration denying transubstantiation. The Mass was described as 'superstitious and idolatrous'. This was an echo of Article XXXI of the Prayer Book where 'the sacrifices of Masses' were (and are) declared to be 'blasphemous fables, and dangerous deceits.' The Act further deprived those who refused the oaths of the right to inherit. As a result the Duke of York resigned his offices. In the following year he married a Catholic Princess, Mary of Modena, as his second wife. This gave further impulse to the movement against him. His two daughters by his first marriage, Mary and Anne, had, by the king's orders, been brought up as Protestants, and in 1677 Mary married William of Orange, himself a grandson of Charles I.

The Act of 1673 was followed by a renewed drive to exact fines for recusancy, and a second Test Act (1678) prohibited Catholics from sitting in either Houses of Parliament. Under the Elizabethan Act of 1563, Catholics were excluded from the Commons (but not from the Lords) if they refused to take the oath to the Supremacy. This provision may have fallen into obeyance. The exclusion of Catholics from the Lords was new.

The fear of a Catholic king succeeding Charles was wide-spread; there was the additional fear that James might now have a son by Mary of Modena. People noted the number of Catholics at court and it was thought that the war against the Dutch was really being fought at the behest of France. All this combustible material only needed a spark to set it alight. This was struck by an unbalanced Anglican clergyman, Dr. Israel Tonge, who saw Jesuits everywhere. He found a ready tool in a thoroughly un-scrupulous scoundrel Titus Oates who was also in Anglican orders. They laid their first information of a plot, Jesuit of course, with Sir Edmund Godfrey, a Westminster magistrate.

This was in September 1678; a month later his dead body was found on Primrose Hill. The mystery of his death has never been solved, but it was popularly attributed to the Jesuits and anti-Catholic feeling rose to fever pitch. Oates testified to a Popish Plot, which, he declared, had been unearthed by Tonge and himself. After Oates had been questioned by the Council, the King said, 'For my part I call the fellow a lying knave,' but neither then nor during the terror that followed did Charles raise a finger to protect the many innocent victims of one of the most disgraceful episodes in our history. Macaulay's account cannot be bettered.

'One Titus Oates, a clergyman of the Church of England, had, by his disorderly life and heterodox doctrine, drawn on himself the censure of his spiritual superiors, had been compelled to quit his benefice, and had ever since led an infamous and vagrant life. He had once professed himself a Roman Catholic, and had passed some time on the Continent in English colleges of the order of Jesus. In those seminaries he had heard much wild talk about the best means of bringing England back to the true Church. From hints thus furnished he constructed a hideous romance, resembling rather the dream of a sick man than any transaction which ever took place in the real world. The Pope, he said, had entrusted the government of England to the Jesuits. The Jesuits had, by commissions under the seal of their society, appointed Catholic clergymen, noblemen and gentlemen, to all the highest offices in Church and State. The Papists had burned down London once. They had tried to burn it down again. They were at that moment planning a scheme for setting fire to all the shipping in the Thames. They were to rise at a signal and massacre all their Protestant neighbours. A French army was at the same time to land in Ireland. All the leading statesmen and divines of England were to be massacred. Three or four schemes had been formed for assassinating the King. He was to be stabbed. He was to be poisoned in his medicine. He was to be shot at with a silver bullet. The public mind was so sore and excitable that these lies readily found credit with the vulgar. . . . The capital and the whole nation went mad with hatred and fear. The penal laws, which had begun to lose some of their edge, were sharpened anew. Everywhere justices were busied in searching houses and seizing papers. All the gaols were filled with Papists. London had the aspect of a city in a state of siege. The trainbands were under arms all night. Preparations were made for barricading the great thoroughfares. Patrols marched up and down the streets. Cannon were planted round Whitehall. No citizen thought himself safe unless he carried under his coat a small flail loaded with lead to brain the Popish assassins.' (*History*, ch. 2.)

As a result of this manufactured plot, ten Jesuit priests, five seminary priests, three Franciscans, one Benedictine and four laymen were hanged. Oates was supported by an equally unscrupulous gang of informers and perjurers who would not have received any credit in ordinary circumstances. To these numbers of victims must be added an unknown but large number of people who were imprisoned at a word from Oates or one of his underlings. The trials could be described as farcical had they not been so tragical. The Lord Chief Justice, Sir William Scroggs, bullied and vilified the prisoners and often prevented them from bringing witnesses in their defence. At an early stage he declared that no statement made by a Catholic was trustworthy. At one point he exclaimed, 'They eat their God, they kill their king, and saint the murderer.'

One act of bravery should be recorded. On 13th June 1679, five Jesuit priests were in the dock. Oates had claimed to have been present at a 'General Consult' of Jesuits in London in May 1678, when, he averred, it was planned to 'contrive the death of the king.' The Jesuit prisoners called witnesses to prove that on that very day, Oates had been living at their college at St. Omer. These witnesses were sixteen students who had dared to come over to England to give their testimony; this was that Oates had been at the college from December 1677 to June 1678. They had all, they declared, seen him there with their own eyes. Scroggs dismissed their evidence by saying, 'Your religion does not allow you to believe your own eyes.' Perhaps the very boldness of their action saved these young men from immediate imprisonment, but as they left Westminster Hall, they were reviled by the mob for slandering the 'Saviour of the Nation' — for such was Titus Oates reputed to be. His evil power at this time was at its height, or, more properly, its depth. A contemporary wrote, 'Whoever he pointed at was taken up and committed, so that people got out of his way as from a blast. The very breath of him was pestilential and, if it brought not imprisonment or death, over such on whom it fell, it poisoned reputation, and left good Protestants arrant Papists and something worse than that, in danger of being put in the Plot as traitors.'

At the height of the Plot, Roger L'Estrange, licenser of the press and pamphleteer, reprinted St. John Southworth's 'Last Speech.' L'Estrange was sceptical from the first of the existence of any Plot and, to get out of Oate's range, withdrew to Scotland. Why did he republish this dying speech of a popish priest? It will be recalled that in it Southworth proclaimed his loyalty as well as his priesthood. 'If any Catholic work against the Government, let them suffer.' L'Estrange may have hoped, though in vain, that the loyal opinions of a priest on the scaffold might bring a little sanity into public affairs.

The last Englishman to suffer was William Howard, Lord Stafford, grandson of St. Philip Howard. Oates and his professional liars gave evidence that would not have been accepted by any unbiassed jury. On the scaffold, 29th December 1680, Stafford declared his innocence of any designs against his king and country. Some of the onlookers called out, 'We believe you, my lord; God bless you, my lord!'

There was to be one more victim, an Irishman, Archbishop

Oliver Plunket, primate of Ireland. If one case can be described as more scandalous than another in this infamous series, this was the most scandalous. The Test Act had meant increased repressive measures against the Catholics of Ireland. The Archbishop, often in personal poverty, led a hunted life. Oates's foul slanders reached out to Ireland and the Archbishop was brought to London after attempts to get him condemned in Ireland had failed. The whole proceeding was one of doubtful legality. He was imprisoned in Newgate for seven months and was so destitute that he had to appeal for relief. At his trial he was accused of plotting to bring a French army to Ireland; the so-called evidence was derisory but was sufficient to condemn him. He was hanged at Tyburn on the 1st July 1681, the last of the Plot victims and the last Catholic priest to be hanged in England. The Earl of Essex, who had been lord-lieutenant of Ireland, had known Plunket and was convinced of his innocence. He appealed to King Charles who replied, 'I cannot pardon him, because I dare not.'

Before that date the national hysteria had worked itself out and men were beginning to be ashamed of what had been done in the name of religion.

The Popish Plot had focused attention on the Duke of York. One of the early victims was Edward Coleman, secretary to the Duchess. He had been in correspondence with Jesuits and others to further the Grand Design of bringing England back to the Catholic Church. James had been aware of this correspondence and, when Oates began his campaign, he urged Coleman to destroy the letters, but he foolishly kept some and they were sufficient to condemn him. To his credit, he kept silent on the part James had played in this foolish business. The king saw the danger to his brother and sent him abroad early in 1679. During his absence a Bill to exclude him from the throne was debated in the House of Lords and passed its second reading with a substantial majority and would undoubtedly have become law had not Charles first prorogued and then dissolved Parliament. He later relegated James to Scotland where he remained until 1682. During his absence another Exclusion Bill was debated; it was defeated by a powerful speech by the Earl of Halifax, who, though no friend to James, argued persuasively in support of the principle of hereditary monarchy.

Charles II died on the 6th February 1685. On his death bed he received the last sacraments from Fr. John Huddleston, the Benedictine monk who had helped to save Prince Charles after the battle of Worcester thirty-four years earlier.

James II came to the throne with the good-will of the people and for the same reason that they had insisted on Mary Tudor succeeding her brother — hereditary right. Even had the Exclusion Bill become law, once the fever of the Popish Plot had died down, the nation would have insisted on the succession of King Charles's heir by birth. The fact that he was a Catholic told heavily against him, but the laws on religious observance were strict, and, provided he observed them, there should be no serious trouble. Such a feeling ignored the new king's cast of temper and intellect, of which, it is true, most people would be ignorant. He lacked the quick mental powers and political acumen of his brother; Charles knew when to yield and was a master of expedience. For twenty-five years he had skilfully steered his course through dangerous waters that more than once threatened to swamp the ship of state. Such finesse was alien to the humourless James; he regarded every compromise as a defeat. Moreover he had a far more exalted notion of the rights of a king than his more cynical brother had had. James despised Parliament; indeed, if the portrait of him as king is a true portrayal, his habitual expression was of haughty disdain. To this must be added the well authenticated fact that after his residence in Scotland, a change had come over his mental powers; this may have been due to physical causes, but the fact is indisputable. He became more rigid, even narrow-minded, in his outlook and became incapable of sensing public opinion.

A Catholic king could rightly looked forward to easing the plight of his fellow believers. A prudent, very cautious policy over the years (he could have reigned for sixteen or more) might have brought some relief to Catholics, though it must be admitted the hope of carrying Parliament with him was small. It was here that James failed tragically. He ignored sound advice from Rome, and, unfortunately relied too much on the unstable and unscrupulous Sunderland, and was too much under the influence of Fr. Edward Petre, S. J., who to everyone's dismay, he made a Privy Councillor. Fr. Petre was totally unversed in political affairs and had little appreciation of the strength of the Protestant feeling in the country, still less of the anti-Catholicism that had become ingrained. It might have been thought that the experience of the Popish Plot would have warned him and his master of the need for moving with the greatest circumspection. But both closed their eyes and went forward on what inevitably proved to be a disastrous course.

There would be no point here in detailing what can only be called James's foolish and perverse provocation of a Protestant nation. A bare list of his actions must suffice, all crowded into less than three years.

The building up of a standing army officered by Catholics.

The appointment of Catholics to the Council.

The encouragement of the opening of Catholic chapels and schools.

The appointment of Ecclesiastical Commissioners.

A public reception of the papal nuncio.

The intrusion of Catholics into the universities.

The Declarations of Indulgence followed by the trial and acquittal of the seven bishops.

The remodelling of the magistracy and the corporations.

Interference with the judiciary.

These and other rash measures could not fail to swell opposition until it found expression in open rebellion, and resulted in the English Revolution. When James fled in December 1688, he left a country that was more determinedly Protestant than ever before.

CHAPTER 24

The Vicars Apostolic

THE one benefit English Catholics gained from the reign of James II was that they had a system of government established under vicars apostolic; this lasted from 1685 until the restoration of the hierarchy in 1850.

We have seen that Bishop William Bishop, who was put in charge of the English mission in 1623, died in the following year, but, in this brief time he had set up a Chapter of canons with archdeacons and rural deans. He was followed in 1625 by Richard Smith who claimed the full powers of an ordinary, that is the bishop of a diocese, which, in fact, he had not been granted. When proclamations were issued against him, he went to live in the French embassy until he left England in 1631 and later resigned. No successor was appointed to Bishop Smith. The Chapter, however, filled the gap as far as practicable though it had no official standing in Rome; it repeatedly petitioned for the appointment of a bishop rather than a vicar apostolic.[1] Philip

[1] A bishop in ordinary has full powers of jurisdiction in his diocese. A vicar apostolic (with the title of a bishop *in partibus infidelium*) exercises his authority in the name of his superior. The English vicars apostolic, who were on an equality of footing one with another, came under the Sacred Congregation for the Propagation of the Faith (known as 'Propaganda') which controlled affairs in non-Catholic countries; the vicars apostolic reported to the Cardinal Prefect of Propaganda.

The four Districts of the Vicars Apostolic

Howard, who has been mentioned in connection with St. John Southworth, was a Dominican monk and he came to England as senior chaplain to Queen Catherine of Braganza, and, in 1669, Rome proposed appointing him vicar apostolic for the whole of England; the Chapter, while welcoming him, urged that he should be a bishop with the usual faculties, but before this problem was settled King Charles II refused his consent, so the proposal was dropped. Philip Howard was threatened under the law so he left the country in 1674. He was made a cardinal in the following year and, for the rest of his life, he kept a careful watch over English affairs and became known as the Cardinal of England. He joined his advice with that of the pope to King James II to follow 'slow, calm and moderate courses', but this advice, as we have seen, was ignored.

With the accession of James, the prospects brightened for the restoration of full episcopal jurisdiction and the Chapter again urged that an 'absolute ordinary', not a vicar apostolic, should be appointed, but Rome, in spite of James's support of the Chapter, decided that a vicar apostolic was preferable and Dr. John Leyburn, a former President of Douay, was selected. He arrived in England in October 1685 in the company of the papal nuncio, Archbishop d'Adda. With Dr. Leyburn's arrival, the Chapter[1] ceased to have any effective function outside the normal sphere of a bishop's chapter.

Dr. Leyburn divided the country into four districts each with a vicar-general as his deputy. He had a tremendous task before him as, apart from the Chapter, there was no working Catholic organisation for him to take over. He was indefatigable in touring the country to confirm the many thousands who had not been able to receive that sacrament; for instance, in one visitation to the north in 1687 he confirmed over twenty thousand Catholics. He saw the urgent need for funds; many a priest was existing on a pittance and the greater liberty given to Catholics

[1] It became the Old Brotherhood of the Secular Clergy. On the death of a member, the Brotherhood co-opts a successor. Its work is now mainly charitable.

made it possible to plan the building of chapels and schools. The Orders were soon active. The Benedictines, Franciscans and Jesuits re-established themselves in London and dared to walk the streets in their habits. Mass became available to all. Inevitably this sudden freedom went to the heads of some who became over-zealous and even provocative. Looking back from our distance of time and knowing what was imminent, we may feel critical of the demonstrativeness, yet, at the same time, we can appreciate the enormous sense of relief that seized on the Catholic community. Dr. Leyburn was closely in touch with the king and added his voice to that of others in urging moderation, but his words were ignored. One of the more foolish of James's actions was the intrusion of the Catholic Dr. Bonaventure Giffard as President of Magdalen College, Oxford, in March 1688; the College was on the way to being transformed into a Catholic seminary when the Revolution brought an end to this interference with the rights of the university. The reign lasted long enough for vicars apostolic to be appointed to the four districts into which the country was divided, and to make their preliminary arrangements. Bishop Leyburn became vicar apostolic of the London District; Dr. Giffard of the Midland; Dr. James Smith, another former President of Douay, of the Northern, and a Benedictine, a convert, Dom Michael Ellis, of the Western District. The king insisted on the consecrations being carried out with full publicity and with elaborate ceremonial. Dr. Giffard was consecrated in the Banqueting Hall at Whitehall, Bishop Ellis in St. James's Palace, and Bishop Smith at Somerset House; the last of these three was on 13th May 1688, only six months before the landing of William of Orange.

The four vicars apostolic issued a Pastoral Letter; one paragraph now seems almost pathetic. It reads:

'His Majesty has been graciously pleased not only to favour you with his royal protection, but moreover to honour many amongst you with a share of the government under him. He has admitted you to employments both civil and military, from which by the severity of our laws you have formerly been excluded; he has placed you in circumstances of manifesting to the world that it was neither want of loyalty nor ability that occasioned your former exclusion; he has capacitated you hereby to remove the prejudices which in former reigns your religion and persons have lain under.'

It proved a false dawn.

At the Revolution Bishops Giffard and Ellis were imprisoned in Newgate and Bishop Leyburn in the Tower; they were released and banished in 1690 but only Bishop Ellis left the country to become eventually an Italian Bishop. Bishop Smith was able to remain free; it was far easier for him in the Catholic north to evade arrest. Bishops Leyburn and Giffard began a vagabond life, moving from lodging to lodging to evade informers; they were not unduly harassed by the government who kept an eye on them. It was still a capital offence to be a Catholic priest. The Elizabethan statute was not repealed, but an Act of 1689 condemned any priest convicted of exercising his functions to life imprisonment.

The Declaration of Rights and the subsequent legislation ensured that only a Protestant could come to the throne. A Toleration Act eased the position of Protestant dissenters (non-conformists) but did not affect Catholics. An Act of 1700 permitted Protestant next-of-kin to dispossess the Catholic heirs to estates, and Catholics were forbidden to buy or inherit land; all title deeds had to be enrolled. There were a number of regulations such as not being allowed to own a horse worth more than five pounds or of holding commissions in the army and navy or of entering the professions. Parents could also be fined if they sent their children abroad for a Catholic education. In George I's reign, Catholics had to pay a double land-tax. While it is true that such laws were intermittently enforced, the threat of being indicted always hung over Catholics who were at the mercy of informers. There was, too, the inevitable link in the public mind between Catholicism and Jacobitism; this was justified but it was by no means true that every Catholic was a Jacobite. The rising of 1715 found considerable support among Catholic landed families, and the government took measures to imprison many and to deprive all of arms and horses. Loyalty to the Stuarts came naturally to those who came to regard James II as their deliverer from the penal laws. The position in 1745 was rather different. The Hanoverians had reigned for nearly a generation and Jacobitism among Catholics was on the wane. The vicars apostolic did what they could to restrain those over whom they had influence. Catholics at once came under suspicion and the inevitable house-searchings, confiscations and imprisonments followed. Within the next generation catholics came to accept the Hanoverian monarch as *de jure* as well as *de facto* their king. The refusal of the pope to recognise the Young Pretender as Charles III when the Old Pretender died in 1766 marked the end of Catholic Jacobitism except as a romantic sentiment.

This note on Jacobitism has taken us ahead in chronology. Bishop Leyburn lived quietly in London. He died in 1702 at the age of seventy-eight. Deep as his disappointment must have been at the sudden destruction of his hopes, he had the satisfaction of knowing that he had laid the foundations for a more satisfactory way of conducting Catholic affairs. He was succeeded by Dr. Bonaventure Giffard who, as has been noted, had been forced on Magdalen College. He was academically qualified for the position of its President as he had completed the twelve-year course for the degree of D.D. at the Sorbonne. He came of a long-established Staffordshire family. His life in London was to be far more troubled than that of his predecessor. This was partly due to the Jacobite threat but more because of the activities of informers who hoped to receive the £100 reward if they secured the conviction of a priest. Giffard served four terms of imprisonment but was released through the influence of Catholic nobles. In 1714, when the Jacobite invasion seemed imminent, he had to change his lodgings fourteen times in four months to escape arrest. In 1726 he wrote, 'I have twice been stripped of all I had in the world. No less than £600 was taken from me at the first time. At the second, all my fine ornaments [i.e. vestments, altar vessels, etc.] and whatever belonged to my office, taken away.'

The four vicars apostolic could rarely meet for consultations with one another; one of them visiting London would be able to discuss problems with its vicar apostolic but anything like a regular council was impracticable. Their correspondence, among themselves, or with Rome, was always liable to be opened by the authorities, so caution had to be used in mentioning names. This led to a system of code-words; thus the pope was 'Mr. Abraham', Rome was 'Hilton', Queen Anne was 'Mrs. Hobbs' (which sounds a little disrespectful!). The writers did not sign their own names; Bishop Giffard, for instance was 'Cousin Bona' and, later on, Bishop Challoner signed himself 'J. Fisher.' Catholics avoided using the word Mass even among themselves; it was simply 'prayers', or 'high prayers', and to go to confession was 'at duty.'

It is impossible to give absolute figures of the Catholic population during the eighteenth century. One fairly reliable estimate in 1780 put their number at 56,000 out of a population of about seven millions. London alone accounted for some 25,000 with 60 priests; the Irish were already beginning to look for work in London; they seem to have tended to become porters and to have monopolised the business of sedan-chairmen. In the whole country there may have been up to 350 priests, secular and regular. Outside London the Catholic population centred mainly on such towns as Bristol. We have noted the part played in the countryside by the landed gentry. Unhappily their number declined during the century. The pressure of the laws, especially those affecting property and professional occupations, gradually wore down the constancy of some of the great families who were, at that period, the natural leaders in public life; this avenue was barred to Catholics. Not that there was any social ostracism; the Catholic gentry shared in the social and sporting life of the countryside. One curious result of their exclusion from public life was that they gave more attention to the care of their estates than their neighbours did. It was the younger sons who were hardest hit. Some enlisted in foreign armies especially in that of Austria, but for others there was little alternative but a country life on whatever allowances their fathers could spare. Among those who conformed were five dukes— Beaufort, Bolton, Norfolk, Richmond and Shrewsbury. In addition the Marquis of Powys and Viscount Montague of Cowdray gave up the struggle. Other families who conformed were the Shelleys, the Ropers and the Swinburnes. Each of these defections meant the breaking-up of a Catholic household and the loss of a Mass centre for the neighbourhood. There is no record of how many of these dependants and local residents were lost to the faith. What is clear is that by the middle of the eighteenth century, Catholicism in England had reached its nadir.

There is not space here to follow in any detail the histories of the four Districts each of which had its special problems. It will be more profitable to give a brief account of the life and work of the greatest of the vicars apostolic, Richard Challoner, as this will bring out many of the difficulties that faced the Church of his times. Two subjects, the Relief Act of 1778 and the Gordon Riots, will be dealt with in the next chapter.

Richard Challoner was born on the 29th September 1691 at Lewes of a middle-class Sussex family. His parents were Protestants. The father died when his son was a boy and the widow found employment with the Gages of Firle in Sussex, still a Catholic family. After a few years she went as housekeeper to the Holmans of Warkworth, Oxfordshire. Lady Anastasia Holman was the daughter of Bl. William Howard, Viscount Stafford. The chaplain was the well-known apologist Fr. John Gother. The dispensation needed for a convert[1] before he could be consecrated stated that Richard Challoner

---

[1] He was to be the second convert to become a vicar apostolic; Bishop Ellis of the Western District was the other.

had been converted when he was about thirteen; this points to John Gother as the instrument. The boy felt a call to the priesthood and John Gother arranged for him to go to Douay where he was admitted on 29th July 1705 'on one of Bp. Leyburn's funds.' A boy training for the priesthood spent eleven years at the College. Challoner was ordained priest on the 7th March 1716 and remained at Douay as a professor and later as vice-president. He took his D.D. at Douai University in 1727. Three years later he left for the English mission and was stationed in London. He lived in the district north of Red Lion Square, Holborn. Catholics favoured this part of London as it was near the Sardinian Embassy Chapel in Lincoln's Inn Fields. Some of the embassy chapels, such as the Sardinian and the Bavarian in Golden Square, were deliberately built larger than was necessary for the embassy staffs so that Catholics could hear Mass in comparative security except at times of renewed persecution, as during the Jacobite Risings when attenders might be arrested. Like Bp. Giffard, Challoner had to move from lodging to lodging when informers got on his track; for instance, he used several houses in Gloucester Street. He said Mass at the Sardinian Chapel, at the Ship Tavern in Little Turnstile, in stables in Whetstone Park, in Clare Market and other places. Except for the Sardinian Chapel, these places were hidden from public notice and after Mass all signs of Catholic use were hidden away again. At the Ship Tavern, for instance, a garret was used; passwords ensured that only Catholics were admitted; a chest of drawers served as altar and also to hold the vestments and vessels. The tradition was that each man present had a pot of beer so that the assembly could quickly assume the appearance of a club meeting; it was said that there was some competition to have the privilege of drinking the bishop's beer!

Richard Challoner kept in touch with Catholics by visiting and he set up a charitable fund to help those in need. He liked to be at his lodgings in the evenings to hear confessions or give advice on the difficulties that Catholics had to face. This was the kind of life he lived for fifty years in London but he ceased to be an ordinary priest in 1741 when he was consecrated Bishop of Debora on being made co-adjutor to Bishop Benjamin Petre, the vicar apostolic of the London District who had been selected by Bishop Giffard as his co-adjutor in 1721. Bishop Petre was a member of a noble and wealthy family of Essex; he was not distinguished for learning but he was very devout; his retiring nature was a serious handicap; his chief claim to notice is that he insisted on having Richard Challoner as his co adjutor with right of succession. Bishop Giffard died on the 12th March 1734 at the age of ninety-one. His had been a remarkable life going back to the days of Charles I; the halcyon interval of the reign of James II was followed by nearly fifty years of a hunted life in London; he would not give up, and refused to spend his last days in comfort at Douay. His patient endurance was a wonderful tonic to all priests. He died at the convent at Hammersmith which had been founded by Queen Catherine of Braganza; the nuns dared not wear the habit;[1] they conducted a school where many daughters of Catholics were educated.

At the time of Bishop Giffard's death, Bishop Petre was in his sixty-eighth year and in poor health. It was then that he sought to have Richard Challoner as his co-adjutor. In his petition to the pope, Bishop Petre wrote:

'He has scarcely reached his forty-ninth year, but by his many remarkable gifts of mind, his great humility and gentleness, by his assiduous fidelity in reclaiming sinners to the way of life taught by the Gospel and to the truths of our religion, by his marvellous power of preaching, in instructing the ignorant and in writing books both spiritual and controversial, he has won not only the esteem but the veneration of all who have either heard him preach or who have read his books.'

It is interesting to note the word 'veneration' used in this quotation; in later years Richard Challoner became known

[1] The only other convent was the Bar, York.

among his people as 'the Venerable Bishop Challoner.'
Others, besides Bishop Petre, were equally anxious to secure
the services of Challoner. When Dr. Robert Witham,
President of Douay, died in 1738, there was a determined
effort made to bring Challoner back to Douay as President,
but Bishop Petre's appeal was successful. There can be no
doubt that Catholics gained far more in England than was
lost by the students at Douay. Bishop Petre consecrated
Richard Challoner in the chapel of the Hammersmith
Convent on the 29th January 1741. The vicar apostolic then
retired to his family estates in Essex and no longer took an
active part in the administration of the London District
although he lived for another twenty years. He left his co-
adjutor a completely free hand, and, in effect, Bishop
Challoner was vicar apostolic from 1741 until his own death
in 1781 in his ninetieth year.[1]

Soon after his appointment, Bishop Challoner set out on
a visitation of Surrey, Sussex, Hampshire and Berkshire.
The notes he made have been preserved. Thus he visited
Cowdray and confirmed 116 candidates; at West Grinstead
he confirmed 100 and at Arundel 50. These numbers are
evidence of how rarely Catholics could receive confirmation.
Later visitations were to other counties in the extensive
London District — Buckinghamshire, Essex, Kent and
Surrey.

It will be noted that Bishop Petre referred to Richard
Challoner's 'books both spiritual and controversial.' There is
no way of assessing a priest's influence on the spiritual lives of
those to whom he ministers; contemporary tributes made it
clear that Bishop Challoner exerted a profound moral power
over all with whom he came in contact as a priest. We can
be more precise in giving an account of Challoner's considerable literary work. Let it be admitted at once that his style
was somewhat pedestrian; clarity was his aim and that he
achieved without any of the rhetorical graces of many a
less influential writer of his day. Through force of circumstances, Catholics at that time lacked the means of develop-

[1] The longevity of the vicars apostolic is an interesting phenomenon.

ing a community sense among themselves; a few could get to Mass from time to time, but the greatest discretion had to be used; they had become, as it were, a secret society. The individual Catholic, therefore, was thrown very much on his own resources; even in London, frequent contacts with priests were difficult, and many must rarely have enjoyed regular ministrations. Out in the country, now that so many of the great Catholic families had fallen away, it was far more difficult for the isolated Catholics to maintain their sense of belonging to a Church, for a Church must be a visible community as well as a spiritual one. It was with the needs of such people that Bishop Challoner carried out his apostolate of the printed word.

His first book was written at Douay in 1728 with the pleasing title of *Think well on't*. This was a simple set of meditations for a week and presaged the kind of writing he preferred to do. He followed this with several expositions of the Catholic faith; these showed his distinctive skill in plainly-written aids to understanding the teaching of the Church. He thought of his readers as ordinary folk and shaped his words accordingly, and the number of reprints (well into the nineteenth century) of his first book and of his explanatory and catechetical writings showed that he achieved his purpose. Challoner wrote a few controversial books; he was never abusive but gave his adversary the credit for being reasonable. He turned from such work to the kind he regarded as more important. The faith had, of course, to be defended, but the urgent need was to provide Catholics with ways of strengthening their spiritual lives in the enforced privacy of their own homes. One way of doing this was to bring some of the great spiritual classics within their reach. His translation of the *Imitatio Christi* under the title *The Following of Christ* was first published in 1737 and was frequently reprinted for over a century and was used as the basis for later translations. It is interesting to note that, in the previous year, his great contemporary John Wesley had published his translation with the title *The Christian Pattern*. A translation of St. Augustine's *Confessions* appeared in

1739; this was probably made while Challoner was at Douay for a time when he was threatened with arrest, but the most important fruit of that leisure was *The Garden of the Soul* published in 1740. This might be described as a vade mecum for Catholics; its ancestor can be traced back to the Primers of Catholic days and its descendants to the Small Missals of recent times. The handy book contained a brief summary of the faith, the Gospel lessons of Mass, an English version of Vespers and Compline, the Penitential Psalms, as well as various prayers and devotions. Included was a translation of the ten meditations from the *Introduction to a Devout Life* by St. Francis de Sales, for whom Challoner had a lifelong devotion. Challoner himself revised *The Garden* from time to time, as the demand was so great. With further adaptations it survived into this century.

Richard Challoner undertook the great task of revising the Rheims-Douay Bible. He realised that much of its vocabulary had become out-dated; to this he gave close attention and he did not hesitate to borrow from the King James Bible just as the translators of that had borrowed from the Rheims-Douay version. In this work he was assisted by Fr. Francis Blyth of the Carmelites, so it is impossible to distinguish one reviser's work from the other's. The notes were all by Challoner. The New Testament was published in 1749 and the Old Testament in the following year. It is this version that is known by Catholics as the Douay Bible. Challoner would certainly have approved of a further revision in the next century, but it was not until 1954 that the problem was faced and this time by a completely new translation by Mgr. Ronald Knox.

Of his vast output two further books call for mention. *The Memoirs of Missionary Priests* was published in 1741–2. This was a collection of narratives of the martyrdoms of the priests, secular and regular, and layfolk from 1577 to 1684. Challoner used contemporary documents that had been sent to Douay or otherwise preserved. This was fortunate as some of these important papers were destroyed during the French Revolution. As usual with the bishop's work, there is no lush sentiment; all is plainly factual. So carefully was the work done that historians since have not been ab le to fault him except on a few minor details. His aim was to make Catholics aware of their great heritage and so further strengthen their resolution in their own troubles. The book is a standard work and cannot be superseded. The second book of special note is *Meditations for Every Day of the Year* first published in 1753 and kept in print until recently. As with some of Challoner's other devotional books this was found helpful by some outside the Catholic Church. A few years ago an old lady, an Anglican, wrote to tell me that she had long used Challoner's *Meditations*.

From these few notes on some of his books, it is clear that Bishop Challoner's influence extended far beyond his personal ministrations in the London District. By the printed word he defended and explained the faith; he fortified the faithful and gave them the means for deepening their faith. At one time it was customary to speak a little condescendingly of 'Garden-of-the-Soul' Catholics as a way of marking members of the old Catholic families of the eighteenth and early nineteenth centuries. They had to nourish their spiritual life at home without frequent contacts with priests and without the strengthening that comes from regular common worship. They had none of the exterior and more demonstrative devotions that were customary in Catholic countries. They were strict in morning and evening prayer and in the observation of fasts and abstinences; preparation for confession and communion was long and thorough and the thanksgiving lasted for days afterwards. The result was a sober and firmly based religion which owed much to the guidance of Richard Challoner.

The precarious position in which priests could find themselves was shown in London during the decade after 1765. It is not clear why this outburst of persecution came just then; perhaps it was that the possibilities of earning £100 had come to the knowledge of some seekers after easy money. The leader was William Payne, known as 'The Protestant Carpenter.' He first of all nosed out where Masses

were being said and in the first six months of 1767 'private
mass houses' were suppressed at Saltpetre Bank, Kent
Street, Blackdown Court (St. Giles), and the Park, Southwark. A priest, John Baptist Maloney, was arrested at Kent
Street and at the assizes was condemned to life imprisonment; after four years he was banished. Payne received
the £100 reward. When priests were arrested Bishop
Challoner at once provided for their defence and for their
support in prison awaiting trial; he was constantly engaged
in finding safe lodgings for his priests. The trial of Fr.
Maloney and those that followed led the judges under Lord
Chief Justice Mansfield to formulate a mode of procedure
in such cases, and they laid it down that, in future, evidence
of ordination to the priesthood must be produced in court.
As this was in practice all but impossible, the number of
cases brought to court quickly fell. Mansfield further pointed
out that Payne was almost illiterate and knew no Latin
and therefore could not recognise the Mass if he heard it
said. Mansfield was to pay for all this during the Gordon
Riots. Payne was not yet defeated; he aimed higher. When
Bishop Challoner became vicar apostolic in 1758 he petitioned that a co-adjutor should be appointed. He was then
sixty-seven years of age and in poor health (actually he
lived for another twenty years) James Talbot, a brother of
the Earl of Shrewsbury, was consecrated Bishop of Birtha
and became co-adjutor. His was the last appointment for
which the approval of 'James III' was sought. Here was
a great opportunity for the Protestant Carpenter. Bishop
Talbot was indicted three times; on the first two occasions,
technical errors in the indictments saved him; on the third
occasion, the trial at the Old Bailey in February 1771,
no witness could establish the needed evidence of ordination and the case was dismissed. It seems strange that Bishop
Challoner escaped the attentions of this persistent informer.
We have seen how, in earlier, years Challoner had gone
to Douay for a time to get out of the way. The bishop's
frequent changes of lodgings may have baffled the informers
but his chaplains and his many devoted friends probably

did all they could to shield him especially when he was saying Mass.

An account of his work would be incomplete without a brief reference to his interest in education. There could be no openly Catholic schools, so, here too, great discretion was necessary. There was a school at Twyford near Winchester which had had Alexander Pope, the poet, as one of its pupils. The confused situation after the '45 led to the closing of this school. In 1749 the bishop found an alternative property at Standon Lordship in Hertfordshire; this school survived until 1767 when the property was bought by a non-Catholic. A new home was found at Hare Street, also in Hertfordshire. Bishop James Talbot, who had funds at his disposal, then purchased Old Hall Green nearby; this eventually became the St. Edmund's College of to-day. Bishop Challoner founded another school at Sedgeley Park in 1763; its descendant is Cotton College, near Wolverhampton.

CHAPTER 25

The Gordon Riots

IF, at the beginning of 1778, a Catholic had been asked if there was any prospect of an amelioration of the penal laws, he could only have voiced his despair, yet, within six months, the first Relief Act was on the statute book. There was, indeed, little that Catholics could do to further their own cause. The vicars apostolic were proscribed persons and could not be recognised by the government. There were no Catholic peers in the Lords nor Catholic members in the Commons. The sudden change came about not as part of a sentiment for toleration, but through the exigencies of the political and military situation.

The American War of Independence broke out in April 1775; the surrender at Saratoga in October 1777 showed the precarious position of the British; moreover England was on the verge of war with France and Spain. The general defeated at Saratoga, Sir John Burgoyne, had a part in the story of Catholic relief. He and General Conway in 1770 called the attention of the Commons to the position of Catholic privates in the army; when enlisted they perforce had to take the oath of allegiance contrary to their religion, but, some of them at least had managed to get to Mass. Burgoyne wanted this anomalous situation remedied but the Commons showed no interest in the problem. When, however, the need for more soldiers became urgent, the government considered the possibility of enlisting the Scottish Highlanders most of whom were Catholics. Contact was made with Bishop George Hay, vicar apostolic of the Lowland District of Scotland. The bishop wanted the government's limited relief to be extended to all Catholics, and he urged that Bishop Challoner should be consulted. The aged bishop, he was now eighty-six, was at first cautious. After nearly fifty years of life in London, he was well aware of the temper of the people and of the anti-papist feeling smouldering underneath. Nevertheless he was willing to give his support to a measure of relief; he wanted the complete repeal of the penal laws and also of Hardwicke's Matrimonial Act of 1753 which had added yet another burden on Catholics by making legal only marriages solemnised according to Anglican rites.[1] When, however, the bishop discussed the problem with some of the leading laymen, they convinced him that it would be hopeless to ask for so much that would call for Parliamentary time; they felt there might be a chance for a more moderate demand that could be dealt with speedily. The three bishops, Challoner, Talbot and Hay, then agreed to leave the matter in the hands of the lay leaders and to be content, for the time being, with 'a free toleration of Religion in private, without any mention of particular Grievances.' Consequently a Committee of laymen was formed to study the best way of proceeding. Lord Petre was the chairman; the most energetic of the members was William Sheldon of Gray's Inn, who urged that the business should be carried through independently of the clergy, a course that was followed. It was probably a wise policy at that time, but it was to lead to serious difficulties in later years. An Address was presented to the king on the 1st May 1778 and was graciously received. It was an expression of loyalty at a time when the country was in serious danger; it was not a petition for the easing of the penal laws. On this astute move, Edmund Burke commented:

[1] Quakers and Jews were the only exceptions.

'In that hour of our dismay, from the bottom of the hiding places into which the indiscriminate rigour of our statutes had driven them, came out the body of the Roman Catholics. They appeared before the steps of a tottering throne, with one of the most sober, measured, steady and dutiful addresses that was ever presented to the crown. It was no holiday ceremony; no anniversary compliment of parade and show. It was signed by almost every gentlemen of that persuasion, of note or property, in England. . . . The address showed what I long languished to see, that all the subjects of England had cast off all foreign views and connexions, and that every man looked for his relief from every grievance, at the hands only of his own natural government.'

The favourable reception of this Address with no sign of public disapproval when it was published, paved the way for specific proposals. It was decided to limit the measure to the repeal of the Act of William III, the Act that rewarded informers, that condemned Catholic priests and schoolmasters to life imprisonment, and imposed severe restrictions on inheritance and landownership. The key problem was the framing of an oath of allegiance to which Catholics, in conscience, could subscribe. The Committee drew up a form of oath in consultation with the government, and it was only then that Bishop Challoner was consulted. He made one or two verbal changes, and then he shrewdly advised that the Bill should be introduced as soon as possible. He noted that Rome, if consulted, would probably make difficulties but would accept a *fait accompli*; no doubt he also had it in mind that negotiations with Rome would drag on for months.

The Bill was introduced to the Commons by Sir George Saville on the 14th May 1778 and passed six days later; the Lords made one or two amendments before passing it on the 2nd June and on the following day it received the Royal Assent. All done in three weeks! This astonishingly rapid success is difficult to explain; there was no serious opposition in Parliament and yet there certainly was, as events tragically proved, considerable popular resentment at what was regarded as a sleight-of-hand. Perhaps the slowness of communications made the passing of the Act possible. To-day the introduction of such a measure would be known to the whole country within hours, to be followed by press and broadcast comments and, perhaps, demonstrations. Life went more leisurely in the eighteenth century, but the reaction or backlash could be all the more violent.

The Act was limited in its scope; its real importance was that it broke the log-jam of penal legislation. As Bishop Challoner noted, 'all other particulars can afterwards be considered and decided at leisure.' Briefly the Act meant that Catholics who took the oath could inherit and buy land; that priests were freed from the attentions of informers, and were no longer liable to life imprisonment. The Act speaks of 'Popish Bishops, Priests or Jesuits, or Persons professing the Popish Religion and keeping school.' Technically the Elizabethan Acts remained in force as they had not been specifically repealed, but it was safe to assume they had become obsolete and probably unworkable. The fundamental freedom given to priests was the basis of all that followed. The criticism was made at the time that the landed gentry had taken good care of themselves; there is a grain of truth in this, but without their efforts, nothing could have been achieved.

The oath is of interest. As we have seen, it was the stumbling block in early Stuart times, and it was again to give trouble in later extensions of Catholic relief. The first part of the oath was a plain statement of allegiance to George III his heirs and successors; this was followed by an abjuration of the claims of the person 'said to have assumed the Stile and Title of *King of Great Britain* by the name of *Charles III*.' Only dyed-in-the-wool Jacobites could object to this part of the oath. The oath next dealt with the power of the popes to depose princes and to dispense Catholics from oaths not approved by Rome. This seems nonsense to us, but it was taken quite seriously at that time. The language follows fairly closely that of the obnoxious James I oath, but it was carefully pruned of such offensive terms as 'impious and heretical', and 'damnable doctrine' and of the claim that excommunicated princes could be murdered. Even so, this part of the oath must have seemed rather quaint to many at the end of the eighteenth century.

Bishop Challoner wrote of the oath, 'I am fully convinced that it contains nothing but what may be taken with a safe conscience both by priests and people.' The response from both clergy and laity was immediate. Thus William Mawhood, Bishop Challoner's friend, a woollen-draper of Smithfield, noted in his diary:

'*Tues. 23 June.* Self was at Westminster Hall, Common Pleas, took the oath to King George 3d.'

It was proposed to have a separate Act for Scotland and it was this that sparked off the anti-papist disturbances. Riots broke out in Edinburgh and other Scottish cities; the magistrates made little attempt to protect Catholic property. Provocative sermons were preached and dozens of venomous pamphlets were circulated. A Committee of Protestant Interests led to the setting up of the Protestant Association; branches were soon established in most cities in England. Its manifesto argued that 'to tolerate Popery is to be instrumental to the perdition of immortal souls' and calculated to bring the wrath of God 'on our fleets and armies and ruin on ourselves and our posterity.' The unstable-minded, thirty-year-old Lord George Gordon accepted the Presidency. As a Member of Parliament he had excited ridicule by his eccentric behaviour and foolish speeches. It was decided to present a monster petition to the House of Commons; many thousands of signatures were quickly obtained and it was arranged that Protestants should gather in St. George's Fields, Southwark, on Friday the 2nd June 1780 and carry the petition in procession to Westminster. Some thousands (estimates vary wildly) assembled and marched in three divisions in orderly fashion to the Houses of Parliament. Lord George Gordon took his seat in the Commons where it was being debated when the petition should be dealt with. Every so often he dashed out and reported to his followers how things were going; his reports became more and more provocative. Meanwhile hooligan elements had joined the crowd and peers and members were roughly handled. The crowd became more and more unruly and eventually the soldiers were called in to clear the approaches. The mob then set out on what must have been a prearranged plan to attack the Embassy Chapels in Golden Square and Lincoln's Inn Square; both were gutted and looted.

Bishop Challoner's chaplains and friends were greatly concerned for his safety. They knew that the organisers of this anti-Catholic crusade would seek him out. He was now in his ninetieth year and very frail. He was then living in Gloucester Street in a house taken in the name of his housekeeper Mrs. Mary Hanne. His friend William Mawhood had a country house at Finchley and it was there that the bishop found a refuge for nearly three weeks until all risk of further disturbances had gone.

The main attack on the Saturday was on the chapel in Moorfields; this had the appearance of a small warehouse, but the informers were well aware of its true nature. Other chapels at Wapping and East Smithfield were also wrecked and their contents burned in the street. The Old Ship Tavern, where the bishop said Mass and preached regularly, was demolished. Sunday was comparatively quiet, but on the Monday there were further attacks on the houses of Catholics and on those who had supported the Relief Act. One of the puzzles of this affair was the inactivity of the City authorities who might have been expected to suppress attacks on property. The explanation probably was that, as in Edinburgh, the magistrates sympathised with the anti-Catholic sentiments of the day. When it was later put to them that they should have called in the troops from the Tower, the reply was that they understood (quite wrongly) that military action could only be taken after the reading of the Riot Act. In fact no magistrates were willing to take the risk of doing so.

On Tuesday the 6th June a new phase opened. The mob took control, and the London mob was a dreadful phenomenon. Catholic houses were still being attacked, but the rioting became general. Langdale's brewery in Holborn (he was a Catholic) was stormed and before long many rioters were lying in a drunken stupor in the streets. The Newgate prison was forced and the prisoners set free. Lord Mansfield's house in Bloomsbury was gutted and his great library burned; it will be recalled that it was he who had frustrated the informers. An attack on the Bank of England was repulsed with difficulty.

By now it was clear that unless stern action was taken there might well be another Great Fire of London. The king and his council met and instructed the military to restore order at all costs; it was made clear that the reading of the Riot Act was unnecessary. Within a short time, peace was restored but not before 458 rioters had been shot; 59 of the prisoners taken were sentenced to death, but more than half were reprieved. Lord George Gordon was sent to the Tower but was later acquitted of a charge of treason.[1]

These anti-Catholic riots were not confined to London. Emissaries from the Protestant Association went down to Bath and stirred up the mob there. The Catholic chapel and the vicar apostolic's[2] house were burned and he lost his library and the records of the District.

Richard Challoner died on the 12th January 1781. He was buried in the family vault of his friend Briant Barrett at Milton, Berkshire; the body was transferred to the Chapel of St. Gregory and St. Augustine, Westminster Cathedral, in 1946.

[1] Charles Dickens used contemporary records as the basis for his vivid account of the riots in *Barnaby Rudge*.

[2] The vicar apostolic was Dr. Charles Walmesley, O.S.B., a noted astronomer and mathematician who was elected F.R.S. in 1750. The government consulted him when the Gregorian calendar was adopted in 1752.

CHAPTER 26

Emancipation

IT was greatly to the credit of Parliament that the Gordon
Riots were not followed by the repeal of the Relief Act
of 1778. Catholics were rejoicing in their new-found freedom
but the anti-papist agitation warned them not to be too
demonstrative and some drew back into their shells. The
Committee that had so successfully negotiated the Act
dissolved itself in June 1782 and a new one was elected for
five years. Lord Petre was chairman, and the most active
members were John Throckmorton and Sir Henry Engle-
field, but the real leader was the secretary Charles Butler,
a conveyancer,[1] who was the first Catholic lawyer to be
called to the bar since 1688. The Committee worked
independently of the vicars apostolic and this inevitably
caused friction. Since the 1778 Act they were as free as
other priests and could openly carry out their functions, one
of which unquestionably was to deal with relations with
Rome. The attitude of the Committee from the beginning
was that direction from Rome should be reduced to a
minimum and that the Catholic Church in England should
have the same control over its affairs as France had long

---

[1] Conveyancing was the only form of legal practice open to a Catholic.

317

had; this Cisalpinism or Gallicanism[1] was contrary to the policy of the clergy. The first move of the new Committee was to propose the setting up of a full hierarchy in England which would be less dependent, as they thought, on Rome than the vicars apostolic were. This suggestion was based on an inadequate knowledge of the Roman system; the laity could certainly not lay down the terms on which the Church in England was to be governed. The opposition of the vicars apostolic and a lack of enthusiasm among the gentry lessened the influence of the Committee.

Its inactivity was mainly due to the fluctuating state of political affairs; a further set-back was the marriage of the Prince of Wales to the Catholic Mrs. Fitzherbert in 1785; the subsequent fuss made Catholics keep as much out of notice as possible. When William Pitt had consolidated his position as Prime Minister, it seemed possible to move forward again. He was known to be favourable to emancipation and he had some prominent friends who felt as he did. The Committee now issued an Address to Catholics once again impugning the system of vicars apostolic, even going so far as to say that it was an infringement of the statutes of Praemunire and Provisors. Nothing followed from this Address which was issued without the full approval of the vicars apostolic; the prospects of further relief brightened and left the Address in the air. Approaches had been made to William Pitt and he was sufficiently sympathetic as to ask for some assurances as to the pope's dispensing powers. With this encouragement, Charles Butler drafted a new Relief Bill. Again the vicars apostolic were not consulted, but when they scrutinised the draft they took serious exception to some of its provision. The preamble of the Bill used the term 'Protesting Catholic Dissenters'; to say the least this was a clumsy form of words. To ordinary folk 'Protesting' at once suggested 'Protestant', though that was far from the framers' intentions. Those

---

[1] Cisalpinism was the policy of keeping papal control to a minimum as it had been in France before the Revolution. At the other extreme were the Ultramontanists who welcomed strong papal influence.

who took the oath would be known by this strange designation, while those Catholics who refused the oath would be
'Papists.' The most serious objections were to the terms of
the new oath. It is not clear why the Committee was not
content with the oath of the 1778 Act. They had previously issued a Protestation which was designed to meet
anti-papist prejudices, and perhaps they thought that a
more comprehensive oath would be a further safeguard
against popular misrepresentation. What they produced
was not so much an oath as a manifesto. The most surprising
feature was that the Committee seem to have taken the James
I oath as a model. It has already been noted that in the 1778
oath, care had been taken to avoid the obnoxious wording
of the earlier oath which had been condemned by Rome.
Now the Committee actually brought back such terms as
'impious', 'heretical', 'damnable doctrine' and the reference
to the legitimacy of murdering excommunicated princes.
To this, quite gratuitously, was added a new protestation;
'I acknowledge no infallibility in the pope.' At the time papal
infallibility was not a dogma; Catholics held that the Church
was infallible and by implication the pope himself. The
design of the Committee seems to have been to minimise
the extent of papal authority over the Church in England.
Indeed it would not be unfair to say that the Committee
came near to being more antipapist than the anti-papists
themselves.

It is no wonder that the vicars apostolic were dismayed
when they read this proposed oath. But what could they
do? The Bill was about to be introduced to Parliament
and it was too late to get alterations. They turned for help
to a priest, Dr. John Milner, who was in charge of the mission
at Winchester. He was a man of vigorous mind, of wide
interests, and a voluminous writer. His career was unfortunately marred by an intolerance of opposition that led
him to excessive and even abusive language in his controversial encounters, and they were many; he was always
something of an intriguer. Milner eagerly responded to the
appeal. He at once sought interviews with leading politicians

such as William Pitt, Charles James Fox, and William Wilberforce, who were sympathetic to Catholic claims. He explained the objections of the vicars apostolic to the proposed oath and pointed out that, in its present form, the oath would split the Catholic community in two. Milner also saw several of the Anglican bishops and, in addition, he circulated a printed statement of the case. The Bill was introduced on the 1st March 1791 and passed its third reading on 20th April. The few amendments did not touch on the real objections made by the vicars apostolic. So the struggle was transferred to the Lords. Here an unexpected ally was found in Dr. Samuel Horsley, Bishop of St. David's. As a result of his persuasions, the oath in the Bill was deleted and, in its place, the oath prescribed in the Irish Relief Act of 1774 was substituted. This had been enacted by the Irish Parliament (Protestant in membership) to meet the very serious threats of the overwhelming Catholic majority in the population. The oath of allegiance in the Irish Act was less argumentative than that proposed by the Committee and the obnoxious phrasing of the King James oath was avoided; it was, in fact, similar to the oath in the English Act of 1778 which might just as well have been used. The Act received the Royal Assent on the 10th June 1791 and came into force a fortnight later.

This new measure made legal the erection of chapels and churches which were registered and served by priests who had taken the oath. The buildings were to be without steeples or bells and were not to be locked during Mass, which could now be celebrated with full publicity and with legal protection from disturbance. No ceremonies could be carried out except within the churches. No clerical habits were to be worn in public.

Friction between the vicars apostolic and the Committee did not end with the passing of the new Act; feelings had run too high for an immediate reconciliation. The vicars apostolic had asserted their rightful position as leaders in Catholic affairs; the gentry had eventually to accept this, though not without some grumbling; the sign of their acceptance was that they dissolved themselves in April 1792 and established a Cisalpine Club (the name was indicative of their attitude) but it did not receive the support of all the members of the old Committee and it gradually lost influence.

The new Act did not provoke the public outcry that led to the Gordon Riots after the 1778 Act. This was in part due to the effects of the French Revolution on public attitudes towards Roman Catholics; the arrival in this country of refugee priests led to a more tolerant attitude towards their religion. The first French priests and nuns arrived in September 1792. They had refused to accept the Civil Constitution of the Clergy which made them servants of the state and, in effect, cut them off from Rome. These fugitives continued to arrive for several years. At first some antagonism was shown but this was soon swept away by a wave of sympathy that followed the increasing terrorism of the regime and the execution of the king in January 1793. Considerable funds were raised by voluntary subscriptions and the government added to these as well as supplying accommodation; for instance, six hundred priests were lodged in the King's House, Winchester, a large building begun in the reign of Charles II but never completed or occupied. Altogether about five thousand priests were given aid. Some of them, when they had sufficient knowledge of the language, were able to supplement the work of English priests, and even to establish new chapels. Thus the Abbé Carron built a chapel in Somers Town near St. Pancras, and the Abbé Morel built one in Hampstead. No less than eight French chapels were opened in London. This infusion of French Catholicism stimulated and encouraged Catholics in England at a time when they were just emerging from the mists of penal times. Most of the priests were able to return to France in 1801 when Bonaparte, as First Consul, negotiated a concordat with Pius VII.

A more permanent influence was the flight to this country of monks and nuns and seminary students and priests from the many English establishments in France and the Low

Countries. The students at St. Omer and Douay suffered imprisonment but were eventually allowed to leave for England. The religious communities were given hospitality by the Catholic gentry, and, save for the English Convent, Bruges, remained in this country. Many of our existing monasteries and convents can trace their origins to foundations made abroad during the seventeenth century. So after more than two and a half centuries, monastic life was restored in England. Some of the Douay students went to the school at Old Hall Green, Ware, and there formed St. Edmund's College. Others of them went north and began a new seminary at Crook Hall, near Durham. This became Ushaw College. So St. Edmund's and Ushaw are the heirs of Douay. The Jesuit school at St. Omer found a refuge at Stonyhurst near Blackburn. This Elizabethan mansion was given to the Jesuits by a former pupil, Thomas Weld, one of the wealthiest of the Catholic gentry; he had kept aloof from the work of the Committee. At his home at Lulworth, he entertained George III with whom he was on friendly terms, and it was there too that he sheltered many French priests and monks. When the French entered Rome in 1798, the English and Scots Colleges were occupied and the students allowed to travel to England, It was not until 1815 that the English College could be reopened in Rome, and among the first group of students was Nicholas Wiseman who had been educated at Ushaw.

It was providential that the Relief Acts of 1778 and 1791 had been passed before the coming of these refugees and fugitives. A large measure of relief had been obtained; the essential freedom of worship had been won, but there were still a number of restrictions imposed on Catholics that called for removal. That it took so much legislation to bring full liberty, religious and civic, is an indication of the ramifications of the penal laws; they affected almost every part of Catholic life.

Some years had to pass, even a generation, before Catholics became accustomed to the light after living for so many years in obscurity and uncertainty. The picture drawn by

Cardinal Newman in his sermon 'The Second Spring' conveys the position of Catholics at the end of the eighteenth century.

'No longer the Catholic Church in the country; nay, no longer, I may say, a Catholic community, but a few adherents of the Old Religion, moving silently and sorrowfully about, as memorials of what had been. "The Roman Catholics" — not a sect, not even an interest, as men conceived it, not a body, however small, representative of the Great Communion abroad, but a mere handful of individuals, who might be counted, like the pebbles and detritus of the great deluge, and who, forsooth, merely happened to retain a creed which in its day indeed was the profession of a Church. Here a set of poor Irishmen, coming and going at harvest time, or a colony of them lodged in a miserable quarter of the vast metropolis. There, perhaps, an elderly person, seen walking in the streets, grave and solitary, and strange though noble in bearing, and said to be of goodly family, and "a Roman Catholic." An old-fashioned house of gloomy appearance closed in with high walls, with an iron gate, and yews, and the report attaching to it that "Roman Catholics" lived there; but who they were, and what they did, or what was meant by calling them Roman Catholics, no one could tell — though it had an unpleasant sound, and told of form and superstition.'

The new phase in the struggle for full emancipation opened with the Act of Union with Ireland in 1800. William Pitt had promised that full citizenship would be given to all Catholics in Great Britain by a new Act of Emancipation. He found an obstinate opponent in George III who maintained that any further concessions to Catholics would violate his coronation oath. Pitt then resigned. Henry Grattan, one of the leaders of the former Irish Parliament, was elected to Westminster in 1805 and he concentrated on the problem of emancipation. Year after year he introduced resolutions in favour of further legislation without success but with slowly growing support. He died in 1820.

The vicars apostolic of England were no longer fighting a lonely battle. They now had to work with the Irish bishops and it was not always easy to reconcile their points of view. The Committee was replaced by the Catholic Board in 1807; while this was predominantly a lay association, the vicars apostolic and the clergy were in constant consultation and the old tension was relaxed. The 1791 Act released the energies of Catholics. Churches were built and a more active, because a more open, development of Catholic life became possible. The revival of monasticism was hastened by the return of communities from the Continent; for the same reason seminary training and education were quickened.

Grattan was succeeded by William Plunkett, member of Parliament for Dublin University, and a future Lord Chancellor of Ireland. He brought in an Emancipation Bill in 1821 which passed the Commons by a narrow majority but was thrown out by the Lords. This Bill proposed a clause that was to be the subject of much controversy; a commission would certify the loyalty of anyone nominated as a Catholic bishop and also that any papal communications were of a purely spiritual character. The Irish bishops rejected this proposal outright mainly because it would put decisions in the hands of the English .government. The Catholic Board and the vicars apostolic were prepared to agree to some kind of veto on appointments; in this they had the support of Rome; a similar but more far reaching condition had been part of the French concordat.

A new protagonist now entered the field; this was Daniel O'Connell who organised a remarkably successful Catholic Association in Ireland; ultimately it wanted the repeal of the Union, but, as a first step, campaigned for complete emancipation from the penal laws. A similar Association, but inevitably on a much smaller scale, was set up in England. Another Emancipation Bill introduced in 1825 failed to secure a majority. The crisis came when O'Connell was elected to Westminster for Clare in 1828. As a Catholic he could not take his seat. The wide-spread agitation that followed convinced the Prime Minister, the Duke of Wellington, that there was need for action, otherwise there would be even more serious trouble in Ireland which was becoming ungovernable. Emancipation was one of the keys to the problem. It was with some difficulty that he persuaded George IV to agree to a further measure of emancipation — though no one imagined that the former Prince Regent was troubled with religious scruples.

Sir Robert Peel[1] introduced the Bill to the Commons on 5th March 1829; it had its third reading three weeks later with a majority of 178; it passed the Lords on the 10th April with a majority of 109, and received the Royal Assent on the 13th April. There can be no doubt that it was the great prestige of the Duke as well as his determination once he had made up his mind, that gained the support of the Lords. A contemporary quip was that he said, 'My Lords! Attention! Right about face! Quick March!' It could be claimed that the Emancipation Act was a matter of expediency; certainly without the Irish crisis it might have been some years before a purely English Act could have been gained, though public opinion was gradually, after much discussion, turning in favour of further Catholic relief, but the House of Lords would probably have proved an obstacle for some years.

The Act gave the elective franchise to all Catholics including the right of election to Parliament; they could now hold all civil and military offices and belong to any corporation. The government did not claim to have any say in the appointment of bishops nor to have the right to scrutinise papal correspondence. As Peel put it, 'the Secretary of State [i.e. Home Office] should have no more to do in the way of interference with the spiritual affairs of the Romish Church than he has to do with the internal discipline and regulations of the Wesleyan Methodists.'

There were a few remaining restrictions. Catholics could

---

[1] He had lost his seat as M.P. for Oxford University because he advocated emancipation, but was soon returned for Westbury.

not present to Anglican livings of which they owned the advowsons; this was to be done by the Archbishop of Canterbury. Nor could they hold the offices of Regent, Lord Chancellor of Great Britain, Lord Chancellor of Ireland, or Lord Lieutenant of Ireland.[1] As soon as the Act came into force the Catholic peers at once took their seats in the House of Lords, and at the General Election in 1830 five Catholics entered the House of Commons.

At the time of the passing of the Act, James Yorke Bramston[2] was vicar apostolic of the London District. An extract from the pastoral he issued on New Year's Day 1830 may fittingly close this record of the struggle for emancipation.

'While you may with all virtuous propriety accept of any office, place, trust or dignity to which your talents may seem to entitle you, you are earnestly exhorted to remember ever, and now more than ever, that it is your greatest glory and highest interest to be members of the one fold of the one Shepherd, Jesus Christ our Lord, and to exhibit in your sentiments, expressions, and conduct your gratitude to Heaven for having called you to profession of the one holy Catholic and Apostolic Church established by our Divine Saviour. In one word, you are earnestly exhorted to remember that you are by the blessing of Almighty God *Roman Catholics*, and that your first and highest ambition should be to show forth in your lives and conversation every Christian virtue; for the practice of every Christian virtue your holy religion both inculcates and absolutely commands.'

[1] It is sometimes said that according to the Emancipation Act, a Catholic cannot be Prime Minister. This is not so. When the Act was passed the designation 'Prime Minister' had no statutory authority. It was, so to speak, a courtesy title, used since the days of Robert Walpole, and did not get official recognition until 1905. So, in 1829, in the eyes of constitutional law, there was 'no such person.'

[2] He was the second convert to be vicar apostolic of the London District, the first having been Bishop Challoner.

CHAPTER 27

The Restoration of the Hierarchy

AT the time of the Emancipation, there were about 250,000 native born Catholics in England and Wales out of a population of about 18,000,000. To this should be added perhaps as many Irish immigrants; this flow of immigrants became a flood by the middle of the century, and it is only necessary to glance down the lists of priests in any diocese to-day to realise something of what the Church in this country owes to the Irish. No one has yet made a study of the influence of the Irish on English Catholicism, but it has been, and is, considerable, not only giving us over the years many priests, but Irish Catholicism helped to break down some of the austerity that had marked English Catholicism as the result of the centuries of proscription. As the Catholics had always been in the great majority in their own country, they had led a more normal religious life than was possible here. They brought warmth and a more open enthusiasm especially through their devotion to Our Lady.

The Irish were for a generation or more a poor section of the community they joined; indeed the Catholics of England were themselves far from affluent. We shall have to record the amazing achievements in meeting the charitable

Roman Catholic Dioceses in 1850

and material needs of the emancipated Church; there were a few wealthy benefactors, such as the sixteenth Earl of Shrewsbury, though they tended to concentrate their generosity on the building of churches; it was, however, the shillings and pennies of the ordinary Catholics that provided the greater part of the funds needed for the less pretentious churches and for the schools that were essential if the Church was to go forward into the new era of Catholicism.

There is no record of the number of converts who came into the Church during the years immediately following Emancipation. It is well to bear in mind what conversion entailed in those times. The convert was often ostracised by his family and neighbours; his motives were misrepresented; he cut himself off from the past and had to venture into a strange country. It called for greater moral courage than in our days when a declaration of religious faith is more likely to be regarded as an eccentricity than as a betrayal of national and family traditions.

A few outstanding names call for mention. Ambrose Phillipps,[1] the son of a wealthy landowner in Leicestershire, was a precocious boy who early became fascinated by Catholic ritual which led him to study the teaching of the Church, and to his conversion. He founded the Cistercian Abbey of St. Bernard in Charnwood Forest and laboured unceasingly for the reunion of the Anglican with the Roman Church. He was of sanguine temperament and unwittingly led some Catholic leaders to expect the speedy conversion of England. At Cambridge he came to know another and older convert, Kenelm Digby, later the author of a once influential, but now forgotten book, *The Broadstone of Honour*, a somewhat romantic view of chivalry. These two used to go every Sunday from Cambridge to St. Edmund's, Ware, for Mass, a distance of twenty-five miles. A third Cambridge convert was an Anglican clergyman, George Spencer, the brother of Lord Althorp. He became acquainted with Ambrose Phillipps and was converted in 1829. In Rome he met Fr. Dominic Barberi, the Italian Passionist, whose order

[1] On inheriting the family estates he added the name de Lisle.

Spencer later joined. An even more important meeting was with Nicholas Wiseman, the erudite young rector of the English College who seemed to have before him a brilliant career both as scholar and as ecclesiastic. Spencer told the twenty-eight-year-old rector that he should be more concerned with the crying needs of England than with scholarship. Wiseman had made a reputation as a preacher by the sermons he gave to English residents and visitors in Rome. He was agent for the vicars apostolic in Rome and was therefore well aware of the problems they had to face. He noticed that, apart from his old tutor Dr. Lingard, the Church in England lacked intellectual distinction, and for a revival of religion there would have to be priests who could meet Protestant apologists on the same level of learning and mental ability. The vicars apostolic were doing a great work but were inevitably absorbed in the administration of the large Districts for which they were responsible. Perhaps two other visitors to Wiseman in 1833 helped to stimulate his growing concern for England. They were John Henry Newman and his friend Hurrell Froude; the conversation made little impression on Newman but it depressed Froude to discover that there could be no compromise with the decrees of the Council of Trent. A way was soon to be opened for Wiseman to serve the Church in England.

Peter Augustine Baines, a Benedictine of Ampleforth, became vicar apostolic of the Western District after six years as bishop co-adjutor to Bishop Collingridge, O.F.M. Bishop Baines was a man of bold ideas but of an imperious nature who created more problems that he solved. His long dispute involving Ampleforth and Downside cannot be discussed here, but it was one more example in the eyes of Rome of the quarrelsomeness of the English clergy. When he became vicar apostolic, Bishop Baines bought Prior Park, a magnificent mansion near Bath. Here he proposed to establish a school, a seminary and, ultimately a university, and it was in connection with this last project that he sought the help of Wiseman, who, for this purpose, came to England. The attempt to co-operate soon broke down, as Baines resented all criticism, and the two men found it impossible to work together. Wiseman set out on a tour of England to get a better knowledge of the Catholic position and later took duty in London at the Sardinian Chapel while the chief chaplain was away. In addition to carrying out the normal duties of a priest, Wiseman gave a series of Sunday afternoon lectures which attracted large audiences many of whom were Protestants. His purpose was not controversial, but to expound the truths of Catholicism. The lectures were so successful that they were repeated at the large church at Moorfields and later published in book form. Wiseman was also one of the founders of *The Dublin Review* which was directed at the educated public that read the *Edinburgh* and *Quarterly* Reviews. This year's work had a tonic effect on Catholics though some still clung to the old, less demonstrative ways and shook their heads at this open advocacy of their faith. Such was his impact that many began to hope that Wiseman would find his true apostolate in England. He made occasional visits in the following years. Thus in 1839 he visited Oscott College, which had been rebuilt, and he preached at the opening of the new church at Derby.

The architect of both was Augustus Welby Pugin who was also busy on the plans for the St. Chad's Cathedral at Birmingham, besides being engaged in numerous other building projects. Pugin was a notable figure in the forward movement of the Church. Into an architectural life of only twenty-five years he crowded an enormous amount of work, all inspired by his undoubted genius. This was combined, not always happily, with aggressive views on such matters as liturgy and vestments. He was obsessed with the idea that the Gothic style, in spite of St. Peter's, was the only genuine Christian form of architecture; one example of his extremism was his contention that the chancel should always be separated from the nave by a screen.[1] One shudders to imagine what he would say about the churches now being built!

[1] Most of his screens have been removed.

Meanwhile the vicars apostolic were considering how best to organise the work of the expanding Church. Their desire was for a normally constituted hierarchy of bishops with the functions and powers exercised in other countries. There was some reluctance in Rome to concede this desire. Were the English capable after an interval of three centuries of making effective use of such a hierarchy? They had lost the habit, so to speak, of episcopal rule. This situation had resulted from the years of repression under the penal laws and the impracticability of central administration. The proposal for a hierarchy was opposed by Cardinal Acton at Rome who was regarded as the authority on English affairs although his experience in England had been very limited. His contention was that the English clergy were 'factious and not to be entrusted with more and more independent power.' In view of this, it was decided in 1840 not to proceed with the establishment of a full hierarchy but to double the number of Districts and vicars apostolic. A further decision was that Wiseman should go to England as co-adjutor to Bishop Thomas Walsh of the Midland District and as president of Oscott College. He was consecrated Bishop of Melipotamus on the 8th June 1840 and arrived at Oscott that autumn.

Wiseman was fully alive to the significance of the Oxford Movement, 'the religious movement of 1833', as Newman called it. This was designed to bring out the implications of the article in the creed, 'I believe in one Catholic and Apostolic Church'; stress was put on the apostolic succession. Wiseman himself unwittingly had played a part in Newman's progress towards Rome. In an article in the *Dublin Review* of July 1839, Wiseman had pointed out similarities between the position of the Donatists in the time of St. Augustine and that of Anglicans in the nineteenth century. He effectively quoted St. Augustine's saying, 'Quapropter securus judicat orbis terrarum bonos non esse qui se dividunt ab orbe terrarum in quacumque parte orbis terrarum.'[1] Wiseman's

[1] 'Wherefore, the entire [Christian] world judges with assurance that those men are not good men who separate themselves from the world anywhere.'

carefully reasoned article was admitted by Newman to be 'a most uncomfortable argument.' Wiseman was very tactful in his dealings with the Oxford men. By contrast Ambrose Phillipps had rushed in and put Newman's back up; Phillipps lived in a dream world of his own and had a vision, for which there was not the slightest justification, of the speedy submission of the Church of England to the Church of Rome. There is no doubt that he seriously misled Wiseman who consequently became impatient at Newman's delays, due to a spiritual agony that no born Catholic could appreciate. The two men met in Oxford in 1841 but neither of them ever revealed the nature of their conversation.

Wiseman was well placed at Oscott for keeping in touch with Oxford, indeed providentially so, for some of the vicars apostolic were far from sympathetic to this Anglican development. Several of Newman's disciples were received before he himself submitted to Fr. Dominic Barberi on the 9th October 1845, and on the 31st he went to Oscott to be confirmed by Bishop Wiseman. Few could have shown more considerateness than Wiseman to these Oxford converts; indeed he was soon to be accused of 'cockering up the converts.' He offered them the old Oscott College as a temporary residence until they could decide on their future course. He almost at once came up against a problem that was to continue to worry him, and, indeed, is still a matter of concern — what of the former Anglican clergymen who were married? The unmarried men who had vocations could be absorbed in the Church as priests. He recognised their value in his desire to raise the standard of scholarship among the Catholic clergy and he wanted to use these converts in apologetic work and as preachers.

Many Anglicans from Oxford and Cambridge followed Newman into the Church, but it was soon clear that there was not to be that general influx that Ambrose Phillipps had predicted. Wiseman himself was disappointed but his hopes had been raised too high.

The vicars apostolic were as intent as ever on having a hierarchy established in England. Rome did not appreciate,

333

nor did Wiseman at first, the handicaps that hindered the vicars apostolic. They had neither the men nor the means to employ staffs for themselves; it was not easy to arrange to meet together as they were on the move most of the time doing work that would normally be delegated. This led to delays in correspondence with Rome, delays that were often misinterpreted. The death in 1846 of Pope Gregory XVI postponed the problem, and the death of Cardinal Acton in the following year eased the situation. The coming of Pope Pius IX made it possible to reopen the question. Here perhaps it is not irrelevant to note that the real work of Pius IX has been obscured by concentrating on the political situation in which he found himself; his pastoral work was of far more importance to the Church.

The vicars apostolic decided in 1847 to send Bishop Wiseman and Bishop Sharples of Lancashire to Rome to put before the pope their views. The matter was delayed by two events. Dr. Griffiths of the London District died in the August, and Wiseman was at once appointed to succeed him as pro-vicar apostolic, a curious title chosen to indicate the stop-gap nature of the arrangement. The second event was that Wiseman was sent back to England to seek the government's support in the threatened intervention of the Austrians in the papal states. Wiseman saw Palmerston and convinced him that there was need for diplomatic intervention; this proved successful. The pope had meantime consented to the drawing up of a scheme of dioceses in England for the consideration of the vicars apostolic. Twelve dioceses were envisaged; several problems at once arose — geographical boundaries, titles, the legal safeguarding of ecclesiastical property, and, not least important, the right person to be archbishop. As Wiseman was busy with his new duties, the vicars apostolic chose as their emissary to Rome the newly appointed vicar apostolic of the Western District. He was William Bernard Ullathorne, O.S.B., who was to play an important part in the development of the Church until his death in 1889. A descendant of St. Thomas More, he came of an old Catholic family. As a boy

334

he ran away to sea, but the call to the Church had come to him and he entered Downside in 1823. He always regretted his lack of a sound early schooling but he studied diligently and he was all his life a reader of the Early Fathers. He was ordained priest in 1831 and volunteered for the Australian mission. He did a great work there for ten years and his revelations of the horrors of the transportation system helped to bring about its abolition. On his return he was appointed to Coventry and built up a vigorous Catholic Community; it was with reluctance that he left there to take up his duties as vicar apostolic.

Earlier visits to Rome in connection with his work in Australia had made him well-liked and his forth-right way of negotiating was appreciated. His guidance was welcomed but he could not persuade Propaganda to drop its suggestion that the aged Bishop Walsh should be transferred to London as the first archbishop of a restored hierarchy. There was some doubt as to the expediency of appointing Wiseman; he was still under fifty and there were those who criticised him; it was suggested that he was too much under the influence of the gentry, that he was too rash in his financial commitments and that he showed too much favour to the converts. It was decided that when Dr. Walsh left the new Central District, Ullathorne would take his place. He returned to England at the end of July and was formally received at the new St. Chad's Cathedral, Birmingham on the 30th August. Dr. Walsh had moved to London where he died a few months later.

There was a further delay owing to political events in Rome. A revolutionary uprising forced the pope to leave the city in November; he remained at Gaeta until the French had driven out Mazzini and Garibaldi. The pope re-entered Rome on 13th April 1850. A month later Wiseman received a letter from the Cardinal Secretary of State to tell him that the pope proposed making him a Cardinal. This would mean, as Wiseman assumed, that he would have to reside in Rome. If he had his detractors, he also had his warm advocates, and they were alarmed at the prospect of

England losing his services. The Pope reconsidered the position and decided that Wiseman should become the first Cardinal-Archbishop of Westminster. The Papal Brief restoring the hierarchy was dated 29th September 1850, and in the next month Wiseman received the red hat. On the 7th October he sent to England the manuscript of his Pastoral and four days later, in high spirits he set out on his return journey. The Pastoral was couched in that exuberant kind of language that was one expression of the writer's personality. The Papal Brief, with its formal phrasing, had not roused any excitement, but this paean of rejoicing created a storm of vilification. The Prime Minister himself, Lord John Russell — who had long known of the proposed restoration — led the hue and cry and he had the influential and inflammatory support of *The Times*. It is an old story now and there is no point in describing the scenes in which the Pope and Wiseman were burned in effigy. All that came out of the uproar was the Ecclesiastical Titles Act[1] which imposed a fine of £100 on any person assuming a title to a 'pretended' see. The Bill was opposed by Gladstone in one of his finest orations and also by John Bright — an Anglican and a Quaker. The later declared that 'the noble lord has drawn up an indictment against ten millions of his countrymen.'

By the time this foolish measure became law, the storm had blown itself out. This was largely due to Wiseman's vigorous response. The first warning of the tempest came to him in Vienna as he was making his way leisurely across Europe. He hastened his journey after sending off a letter of protest and explanation to the Prime Minister. At home there was consternation; had England reverted to the mood of the Gordon riots? Many influential Catholics were in favour of advising Wiseman not to come to England for the present and this message reached him in Brussels; he had no hesitation in continuing his journey and arrived in London unexpectedly on the 11th November. No doubt during those

[1] It was dead from the beginning. Gladstone's government repealed it in 1871.

anxious days of incessant travel he had thought out the main lines of his defence, but Ullathorne had also been aware of the need. He, with the help of his convert friend Edgar Estcourt, collected material that might prove useful, such as previous statements made by the Prime Minister and other statesmen on religious toleration. Wiseman had these notes by him when he sat down to write his *Appeal to the English People;* this thirty-one page pamphlet was completed within four days and was published in full in five London daily papers — in itself a sign of a lowering of the temperature. Within a few days 30,000 copies of the pamphlet had been sold. It was a magnificent piece of polemic that commanded the serious attention of all but the most bigoted fanatics. What had seemed to be a *débâcle* was turned into a powerful vindication. He dismissed as absurd misrepresentation the idea that Roman bishops were trying to oust Anglican Bishops from their sees; the Westminster for which he himself would be responsible was not the Abbey but the slums that came close to its walls where destitute people were crying aloud for spiritual as well as material sustenance. His direct appeal to the English sense of fair play was undoubtedly effective. Newman wrote, 'He [Wiseman] is made for this world and he rises with the occasion. Highly as I put his gifts, I was not prepared for such a display of vigour, power, and judgment and sustained energy as the last two months have brought.'

The suddenness with which the anti-papist demonstrations died out was as remarkable as the suddenness of the explosion itself. During the rest of the century there was little organised opposition to Catholics; there were local sporadic outbursts here and there; priests would be abused; there might be some stone-throwing; but even these minor attacks faded out. This was in part due to the fact that the extreme Protestants were soon hunting other game; they were engaged in a running battle with the ritualists, as they were called, who became known as Anglo-Catholics, and were, according to their opponents, trying to introduce Roman practices by the back door. In this warfare, the Roman Catholics were left much to themselves.

CHAPTER 28

The Second Spring

In 1848 Newman established the Oratory at Old Oscott, renamed Maryvale, while Wiseman was still at Birmingham. When the bishop moved to London, he would have liked the Oratory to be transferred there, but Newman felt that the Papal Brief fixed him at Birmingham. However, a year later, one of his Oratorians, Fr. Frederick Faber, with some of the younger men set up a branch Oratory in London. A number of difficulties developed between the mother-Oratory and her offspring; these need not concern us here; eventually in 1856 the London Oratory became a separate house.

Another but smaller influx of converts came into the Church at the period of the restoration of the hierarchy. This was the result of a decision of the Judicial Committee of the Privy Council to compel a bishop to induct a clergyman, G. C. Gorham, to a living to which he had been appointed by the Lord Chancellor. The bishop had objected to Gorham's theological views and his objections had been upheld by the ecclesiastical courts, but now reversed by a civil court. Many saw in this judgment an unwarrantable control by a lay court in a purely ecclesiastical and theological question. For some it was the final impulse that turned

338

them to Rome. Among them was Henry Edward Manning Archdeacon of Chichester. He was received on the 6th April 1851. Wiseman alarmed his friends and some at Rome by the precipitancy with which he ordained Manning. On 14th June he became a priest and left to study at Rome. Once again Wiseman was to pitch his hopes too high; he talked of the new priest bringing 'thousands and tens of thousands into the one true fold of Christ.' Manning was indeed to be the means of converting many, but not on the scale envisaged by the Cardinal. Was Wiseman, in effect, saying that he was disappointed with the results of Newman's conversion? The two were never on easy terms with one another but this may have been that one of Wiseman's exuberant nature could not appreciate the far more sensitive nature of the former Anglican leader.

In the spring of 1850 Newman[1] gave a series of lectures in London on *Certain Difficulties felt by Anglicans in Catholic Teaching;* they attracted considerable attention from Protestants and led to a number of conversions. Wiseman was among the most appreciative of Newman's listeners. As soon as the anti-hysteria had died down, Newman gave some lectures at Birmingham *On the Present Position of Catholics in England.* The fifth lecture referred to the immoral life of an ex-Dominican, Dr. Achilli, who was touring the country and scandalising the Church he had forsaken. Newman based his account on an article by Wiseman in the *Dublin Review.* This disclosure had gone unchallenged but in November 1851 Achilli took proceedings against Newman for libel. Newman assumed that Wiseman had the documentary evidence on which he had based his own attack but when the Cardinal was asked to produce it he was unable to find the papers. It was therefore necessary to send to Italy to get the evidence and to bring over witnesses. At the end of the long drawn-out proceedings, the judge expressed the opinion that Newman's character had deteriorated since he had

[1] It is a temptation, hard to resist, to dwell at greater length on Newman's life and works. Of the many books about him, my own preference is for Wilfrid Ward's *Life* (1912), and, most perceptive of all, Louis Bouyer's *Newman* (1958).

become a Catholic. *The Times* referred to the proceedings as 'indecorous in their nature, unsatisfactory in their result, and little calculated to increase the respect of the people for the administration of justice.' Newman was fined £100 but his costs came to £12,000. A subscription brought contributions from all parts of Great Britain and from other countries. The sum was so large that Newman was able to build with the surplus the Church on St. Stephen's Green, Dublin. This was evidence of a swing round of public opinion within two years of what had been called the Papal Aggression.

Newman had been called to Ireland to establish a Catholic University. How this project was frustrated is no part of the story of Catholics in England. The important outcome was Newman's influential work *The Idea of a University*.

The first Provincial Synod was held at Oscott in July 1852. It was a memorable occasion; for the first time for three centuries the leaders of the Catholic Church in England met together and legislated for their own community without fear of prosecution. It was at this Synod that Newman preached the moving sermon in which he used the phrase 'the Second Spring.' Much necessary business was carried through, but there was much more to be done before things could work smoothly; the concord of that first Synod was not to be repeated during Wiseman's lifetime. This was in part due to Wiseman's assumption of an authority that was not his. His position as Archbishop, even as Cardinal, did not give him supremacy over the other bishops; he was their head in the eyes of the government, but he had no power to override the wishes of the bishops. His failure to accept the limitations of his authority was to lead to disagreements. All this, however, may be regarded as the growing pains of a hierarchy that had to discover its function by experience.

Wiseman had hoped to go some way towards solving the problem of the lack of priests especially in the poorer districts by the co-operation of religious communities. With his encouragement Redemptorists, Passionists, Marists and Oratorians as well as a number of Orders of nuns were established. The work he hoped they would do included preaching, the care of young boys and girls leaving school, confessors to convents, retreats for the clergy, Advent and Lent courses of sermons and special missions. His hopes were only partly met as the rules of the Orders did not allow them to carry out all the work he wanted. It is curious that he had not known this when he urged their establishment. He was again disappointed when Manning founded the Oblates of St. Charles in 1857. Wiseman found that, as Superior, Manning had the last word on how the Oblates should be used. While in Rome, Manning had formed a friendship with Herbert Vaughan who was his junior by twenty-four years; Vaughan became vice-president of St. Edmund's College in 1855 and, when the Oblates were established, he and two of his colleagues joined Manning's community though they could not live with them. This created a difficult situation; the seminary was under the control of the bishops but the Oblates were under the control of their Superior. Wiseman had earlier caused some discord when he made W. G. Ward Professor of Moral Theology at St. Edmund's. W. G. Ward had been among the most vociferous followers of Newman at Oxford where he had been deprived of his degree on account of his religious views. The choice of a married layman, a convert of five years' standing, for such a key position in the training of future priests shocked some Catholics. Ward's intellectual power — though exercised on a narrow front — undoubtedly strengthened the work at St. Edmund's, and his pupils were to bear testimony to the stimulus of his teaching. His position seemed to many to be anomalous.

The question of the control of the seminaries was bound to arise as the hierarchy gradually became more organised. The point was — were the three Colleges, St. Edmund's, Ushaw and Oscott, to be governed by the bishops in whose dioceses they were situated, or by all the bishops who sent students from other dioceses? Wiseman held strongly to the first view but he was opposed by the bishops and, much to his chagrin, Rome eventually decided against him.

Wiseman felt the desirability, once the anti-papist agitation had died down, of making the Church more widely known to the public; every effort was, of course, directed towards the conversion of those outside the Church, and this work was fruitful, but it was also necessary to let people see that Catholics were not a race apart. It was with this in mind that he used his gifts as a popular lecturer. It was an age of lectures of all kinds as there were few other ways of spreading general knowledge. At first his lectures were given in Catholic churches and halls and were on religious subjects; later he received many invitations from Protestants to lecture in public halls on a variety of subjects, such as, the Education of the Poor, Recollections of the Last Four Popes (later made into a book), Self-culture, a National Gallery of Paintings and so on. No one to-day would dare to give two-hour lectures on such an assortment of topics; our experts know more and more about less and less, but Wiseman interested his listeners out of his well-stored mind. This policy of going out to the people did something to break down prejudices; no doubt many went to the lectures for the thrill of seeing a real, live cardinal, but they often came away with a more friendly feeling towards Catholics.

From about 1854 Wiseman's health began to fail bringing intermittent energy and impaired judgment. Day-to-day affairs were being neglected and his unbusinesslike habits led to confusion. He decided to ask for a co-adjutor with the right of succession. With the approval of the Chapter, he put forward the name of George Errington, then Bishop of Plymouth. They had been at school and college together and Errington had been Wiseman's vice-rector at Rome. Two men, both over fifty, could hardly have known each other more thoroughly. So Errington was made Archbishop of Trebizond. Rome assumed that he would carry out the normal duties of a bishop leaving Wiseman free to devote himself to wider interests. Unfortunately Wiseman did not give his co-adjutor a free hand and interfered with his decisions. Thus they differed on the position of W. G. Ward at St. Edmund's; at Errington's suggestion, Ward resigned, but Wiseman reinstated him. This was not the only instance of how Wiseman reversed Errington's decisions, whose position became impossible. He wanted to resign and the matter was eventually taken to Rome. Errington was released from office; he later refused preferment and spent his remaining twenty-six years in pastoral and professorial work.

Errington had also found it difficult to work with Manning of whose career as a priest something must now be said. When he returned from Rome in 1857 as Superior of the Oblates of St. Charles, he was also the newly appointed Provost of the Westminster Chapter. Many had been dismayed at the speed with which Wiseman had ordained Manning; this appointment of a convert of only six years, half of which had been spent in Rome, to an important position over the heads of experienced clergy, gave further cause for doubting Wiseman's judgment. He had good reasons for making full use of Manning's great abilities which counterbalanced his own limitations. The Cardinal was a man of bold conceptions and was fertile in ideas for building up the Church in this country, but he was not a good administrator nor a patient executive, and he had little financial sense. Here Manning was able to supply the application to detail and the staying power so necessary if paper schemes were to be realised in fact. In addition to building the church and house for the community at Bayswater, he was responsible for new churches and schools in Pimlico and Notting Hill; seven schools for the poor were established and the position of Catholic children in reformatories and workhouses was safeguarded. The last achievement bore out Wiseman's recognition that Manning had the entrée to Government circles that would be denied to other Catholic representatives. To this must be added Manning's reputation as a preacher, and to quote Wiseman, 'the gift of converting others.'

Manning went to Rome to combat compaints against his Oblates' connection with St. Edmund's.[1] An earlier association with Mgr. George Talbot was strengthened. Talbot,

[1] Rome decided that the Oblates must be withdrawn from St. Edmund's.

himself a convert, had gained the ear of Pius IX who accepted his version of the state of the Church in England of which Talbot had small first-hand knowledge. Manning kept up an indiscreet correspondence with Talbot, informing him of what was going on behind the scenes and giving his impressions of the persons involved. The letters are open to the criticism that they displayed a spirit of uncharitableness towards those whose views were disliked by the writers. All this, in his gossipy way, Talbot passed on to the pope. Talbot is mostly remembered for a remark he made in a letter to Archbishop Manning in 1867.

'What is the province of the laity? To hunt, to shoot, to entertain. These are matters they understand. . . . Dr. Newman is the most dangerous man in England, and you will see that he will make use of the laity against your Grace. You must not be afraid of him.'

The regrettable discord between Newman and Manning cannot be ignored. It was in part the result of conflicting temperaments. Manning was all black and white; he was impatient of intellectual difficulties. Their attitude towards potential converts illustrates this divergence of attitude. Manning was dominating; as in his sermons, so in private instruction, he gained acquiesence by reiteration. Newman was acutely aware of the intellectual difficulties of those who sought his guidance; he insisted that the enquirer must fully count the cost of becoming a Catholic. His vast correspondence fully witnesses to the infinite trouble he took to resolve problems of conscience as well as of mind. In later years Manning became more and more rigid in his views and his extreme ultramontanism, encouraged by W. G. Ward, inevitably led to greater estrangement from Newman.

Newman himself had to suffer many adversities. The collapse of the Irish University project has been noted. A proposal that he should supervise a new translation of the Bible was frustrated by Wiseman's failure to give continued support. When he was delated to Rome for heresy, Wiseman again failed to act, and so for years Rome frowned on

Newman. He was involved in trouble with the hierarchy over *The Rambler*, a journal conducted by convert scholars who were not sufficiently in line with official views. In this matter Sir John Acton and Richard Simpson were concerned; admittedly both were difficult men to handle but the suppression of their opinions was not to the credit of the hierarchy. All these and other smaller annoyances made Newman feel, as Wiseman once said to him, that 'he was on the shelf.' One of his consolations during this desolate period was the growth of a close friendship with Bishop Ullathorne.

The period of Newman's apparent eclipse ended with the writing of his *Apologia* in 1864. It was provoked by Charles Kingsley's rash questioning of Newman's integrity and, by implication, that of all Catholic priests. In reply, Newman, in much anguish of spirit, gave the 'history of my religious opinions.' The book, it has been said, 'carried the country by storm.' Some six hundred priests signed addresses to him in which they recognised that in defending himself, he was defending them.

Nicholas, Cardinal Wiseman, died on the 15th February 1865. Two months later Henry Edward Manning succeeded him; so the Anglican Archdeacon of 1850 became the second Archbishop of Westminster fifteen years later. The appointment surprised many and dismayed others, some of whom would have preferred Ullathrone, and that would have been a good choice. Manning met with no serious opposition and there was a welcome for his resolute policy of bringing more order and discipline into the Church after Wiseman's haphazard ways. Manning began his rule with clearly defined objectives. These were the more efficient use of the seminaries for education of the priesthood, provision of adequate schooling for the poor and middle classes, increased public usefulness of laymen, and provision for foreign missions. The greatest danger, he considered, was 'tame, diluted, timid or worldly Catholicism' which could be combatted by 'downright, manly and decided Catholics, more Roman than Rome, and more ultramontane than the Pope himself.' Pius IX had written to him urging greater

M   345

discipline among the clergy and greater control over the regular clergy.

Outward signs of the direction in which Manning was moving may be noted. He insisted on Roman vestments being used, and on altars being dressed in Roman fashion; the Italian pronunciation of Latin was introduced. The Roman collar[1] was to be worn, and a secular priest was to be known as 'Father', a title previously limited to the regular clergy.

Manning's failure to appreciate the conservative spirituality of the old Catholic families was a weakness. Thus in his dealings with St. Edmund's he made no allowance for the heroic Douay tradition that was there treasured. The difficulties with the regulars were troublesome. They had through penal times and sometimes by papal dispensation acted independently of episcopal authority. This was a position that Manning and the bishops could not accept, and it was not until the Papal Bull of 1881, *Romanos Pontifices*, that the problem was at last resolved to the satisfaction of the bishops. The concern for schools that Manning had shown under Wiseman was continued when he himself became archbishop. He established the Westminster Diocesan Education Fund in 1866; this was to be used for the elementary schooling of Catholic children. In its first year of the Fund, twenty new schools were started. The other dioceses followed this example. We cannot here go into the problems raised by the 1870 Act and the question of rate aid, with the cry 'Rome on the rates.' It was a long struggle, that indeed goes on, to secure that every Catholic child should be brought up in a Catholic school. The cost to the Catholic community has been enormous, but it has been met, and is still being met, by the contributions of Catholics throughout the country. Manning's one failure in his education programme was his attempt to set up a Catholic University in Kensington; it failed partly because he insisted on full

[1] Anglicans later adopted the collar, and some the 'Father'. It is curious that nonconformist ministers also adopted the collar, though some have now given it up.

control under himself and did not seek the advice of those with experience of the practical problems, but the main cause of failure was that parents did not respond to the idea. The hierarchy had ruled against Catholics going to Oxford or Cambridge; some parents ignored the rule even though their sons could not take degrees. This prohibition meant that a generation of young Catholics was deprived of higher education.

Manning's attitude towards St. Edmund's had not changed; he thought that it was not a diocesan seminary as decreed by the Council of Trent. He had hoped that through his Oblates, especially Herbert Vaughan, he would have more influence there, but their withdrawal frustrated this plan. When he became Archbishop, he set up a diocesan seminary, St. Thomas's, in the old convent at Hammersmith, and withdrew the theological students from St. Edmund's.

Events in 1860 in Italy posed a difficult problem for Catholics. In October Garibaldi with his army from the south and Victor Emmanuel with his army from the north met near Naples and before the end of the year the whole of Italy, except the Patrimony of St. Peter, was united under a king. The Patrimony would have been annexed but for the presence of French troops, and for diplomatic pressure. What would be the fate of the pope? Public opinion in this country welcomed the freedom of Italy from Austrian control and the expulsion of the Bourbons from Naples. Catholic opinion was divided. The extremists such as Manning and Ward regarded the loss of the Papal States as a disastrous blow to the papacy; if the Patrimony also went, how could the papacy survive? More moderate opinion was expressed by Newman who hoped that the Patrimony could be saved but thought that the loss would not be catastrophic; the Church would endure. Those who held such moderate views were denounced by the neo-ultramontanists, such as Ward in this country and fanatical journalists such as Veuillot in France as traitors to the Church. Ward called them 'low type, insular Catholics.' This injected into Catholicism a poison that did much harm. But worse was to come. One of the subjects before the Vatican Council of 1869–70 was that of Papal Infallibility. Manning and Ward and their supporters such as Vaughan wanted infallibility defined so comprehensively that almost any papal utterance would have to be accepted without question. Newman's opinion was that any such pronouncement would be inexpedient; he and many bishops in other countries, as well as some in this, were labelled 'Inopportunists.' Ullathorne and others were prepared to accept a carefully guarded definition. These diverse opinions called for calm discussion but, unfortunately, some of the infallibilists took up a truculent attitude to those who differed from them. Eventually the dogma as defined by the Council and afterwards interpreted in accordance with the pope's understanding, was far from being as extreme as Manning hoped; it came close to the moderate view of Ullathorne and Newman.

Manning's great contribution to the Church did not lie in these controversial matters; his opinions have been largely superseded. We must look elsewhere for his achievements. Among his primary cares, as we have seen, was the care of poor Catholic children and on their behalf he carried on a ceaseless advocacy to ensure not only their material but their religious welfare. It was no doubt his concern for children that turned his eyes to the social conditions of their lives. A long list could be made of his many activities in this field; it would include the conditions of agricultural workers, the industrial slums, social justice, shop hours, Sunday observance and temperance. He was a member of the Royal Commission on the Housing of the Working Classes in 1884, and he intervened effectively in the Dockers' Strike of 1889. On these and other social questions he frequently spoke in public, often sharing the platform with the clergy and leaders of other denominations. This work of his was by no means welcomed by all Catholics; many criticised him for interfering in what they regarded as political questions; some even called him a socialist. The seal was put on his work by Leo XIII's Encyclical of 1891,

Rerum Novarum which committed the Church to the cause of social justice.

In March 1875 Manning received the dignity of Cardinal from Pius IX. Four years later Leo XIII conferred the same honour on Newman. There was one shadow over an event that was generally applauded; Manning was too ready to interpret some hesitation expressed by Newman to mean refusal, but Bishop Ullathorne and the Duke of Norfolk intervened successfully.

John Henry, Cardinal Newman died on the 11th August 1890 in his ninetieth year. Two years later, on the 14th January, Henry Edward, Cardinal Manning died in his eighty-fourth year. Bishop Ullathorne had died in March 1889; he was the last of the vicars apostolic. The deaths of these three great prelates marked the end of an epoch.

In a record of this kind it is inevitable that attention is largely given to the leaders and outstanding personalities as they so greatly influenced developments. It must however be remembered that what was happening in Westminster Diocese was being done, to varying degrees, throughout the country. Churches and schools were being built, missions established, and the religious orders and lay societies were at work in increasing numbers. The achievement of the second half of the nineteenth century was astonishing, especially when it is realised what vast sums of money had to be raised; these were contributed by a section of the community that was not rich or even well-to-do. No one can estimate the extent of the sacrifices Catholics of all classes made to ensure the continued growth of the Church.

At the end of the century the Catholic population of England and Wales was about 1,300,000 out of a population of 32,500,000. This considerable increase owed much to the great Irish immigration of the middle of the century. Indeed, Manning once wryly remarked, that he had 'given up working for the people of England, to work for the Irish occupation of England.' The continued influx of converts was an important contributory factor but there are no precise records of the number. This Catholic population

349

was not evenly distributed; the greatest concentrations were in London and the south-east, the industral region of the Midlands, Lancashire and the West Riding of Yorkshire with lesser concentrations in Glamorgan and Newcastle-upon-Tyne. Broadly speaking, this remains the picture of distribution.

When we compare the state of the Catholic Church in England at the death of Manning with what it was at the beginning of the century, the contrast is startling. Richard Challoner, at a time when the Church was at its nadir with a population of only some quarter of a million, predicted, 'There will be a new people.' His prediction had become fact.

CHAPTER 29

The Twentieth Century

'THERE were giants in those days.' It was not to be expected that leaders of such high qualities as Wiseman, Newman, Manning and Ullathorne would be followed by a similar group of outstanding personalities. The second half of the nineteenth century had, under their guidance, brought the Catholic Church in England out of the shadows into the broad daylight. A period of consolidation was needed though there is always the danger that consolidation can mean petrification. Happily this was avoided and the Church continued to build on the firm foundations laid down since Emancipation.

The appointment of Bishop Herbert Vaughan (*b.* 1832) as Archbishop of Westminster within two months of Manning's death, did not come as a surprise. He was the outstanding bishop of his generation. It has already been noted that he and Manning met in Rome when both were studying at the Accademia Ecclesiastica, and that subsequently Vaughan became an Oblate of St. Charles while vice-president of St. Edmund's. The two were very close in friendship though not always in full accord in policy. After he had left St. Edmund's, Vaughan became filled with the desire to do something for missionary work, and, with

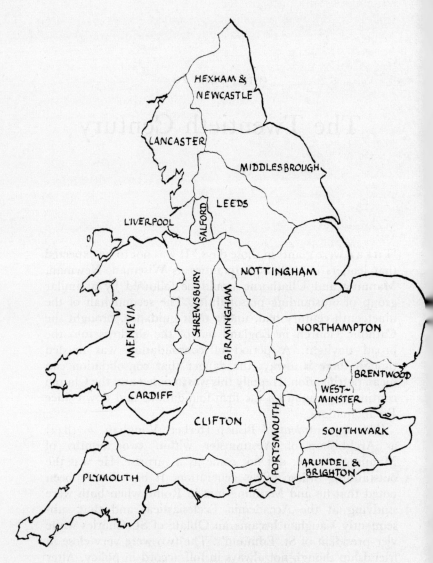

Roman Catholic Dioceses today

Wiseman's approval, he set out to obtain the funds to establish a missionary college. With this in view he toured North and South America and on his return he was able to found the College of St. Joseph at Mill Hill in 1866. This proved a success and missioners from St. Joseph's have worked, and are working, in many parts of the world. In 1872 Vaughan became Bishop of Salford; he established a diocesan seminary and also St. Bede's College for Catholic boys. His activities were over a wide field; diocesan synods were held regularly, a Rescue and Protection Society was established with seven homes, and a Voluntary Schools Association was formed. His twenty years' work at Salford showed Vaughan at his most effective as a truly pastoral bishop.

There was, however, another side to Vaughan's character. He was not a scholar, nor, indeed, an intellectual; as a member of one of the old Catholic families, he was brought up to accept without questioning the teaching and policy of the Church. He was, as we have seen, among those neo-ultramontanists whose leaders were Manning and Ward. Vaughan was able to support them through *The Tablet* which he bought in 1868 and which remained under the control of Westminster until Cardinal Hinsley sold it in 1936. In 1878 Vaughan also acquired control of *The Dublin Review*. One thing was certain — there were to be no more 'dangerous thoughts' in the leading Catholic journals which became rigidly orthodox and dull.

Cardinal Vaughan (he received the red hat within ten months of becoming Archbishop) reversed Manning's policy in two directions. He wished to set up a central seminary to which all theological students could go from the southern dioceses. This he considered would make the greatest use of the best qualified teachers. So Oscott became the central seminary. The second reversal was in Manning's attitude towards Oxford and Cambridge. It had become clear that the Catholic University at Kensington was not going to attract many students; its lack of status in the academic world was its chief drawback. It was only slowly that Vaughan came to accept the realities of the situation, nor were some of the bishops inclined to withdraw the prohibition; in the end they came round to Vaughan's opinion, and Leo XIII agreed that Catholics could go to Oxford or Cambridge provided there were resident chaplains to safeguard their religious welfare.

Among Vaughan's earliest concerns was the building of Westminster Cathedral; this had been designed as a memorial to Cardinal Wiseman. The project had the support of Manning but he made it clear that, in his mind, the urgent needs of Catholic children must come first. Funds were generously subscribed, but, beyond buying a site, Manning refused 'to pile up stones and bricks.' Vaughan felt that, quite apart from the tribute to Wiseman, a cathedral was essential as a focus for the Church in England. He decided that there should be no suggestion of rivalry in appearance with the Abbey or St. Paul's, so a Byzantine style was chosen and he was fortunate in finding in John F. Bentley an architect of genius. The foundation stone was laid in 1895 and the main fabric completed by 1903. By then both founder and architect were dead. Bentley died in 1902 and the Cardinal a year later.

During Vaughan's eleven years at Westminster many societies and institutions, now so familiar to us, were established with his encouragement. Perhaps the one closest to his heart was a continuation of his predecessor's campaign for helping deprived children. The Crusade of Rescue, for which Vaughan was responsible adopted as its policy, 'No Catholic child who is really destitute, or whose faith is in danger, and who cannot be otherwise provided for, is ever refused.' Mention may also be made, among other societies, of the Catholic Truth Society, the Converts' Aid Society and the Catholic Social Union.

A troublesome matter arose in 1894 when the question of the validity of Anglican Orders was put to Rome. This was due to the initiative of Lord Halifax, the leading Anglo-Catholic layman, and the Abbé Portal, who had conceived the idea of the Anglican Church being reunited to the Roman

Church. The Abbé, who had no conception of the ethos of the Anglican communion, came to England but he did not see the Cardinal who was kept in the dark until inquiries came from Rome. The outcome was the declaration of the invalidity of Anglican Orders in the Bull *Apostolicae Curae* of 1896. Vaughan had no wish for the question to be raised, but once it had come into discussion he saw to it that he was represented by the best qualified scholars.

During the last years of his life, Vaughan was perturbed, as many others were, by what came to be called 'modernism', an unfortunate term that became objurgatory. More must be said of this presently. Meanwhile a Joint Pastoral of the hierarchy in 1901 did little to elucidate the genuine problems that called for serious discussion; the Pastoral was rigidly conservative without giving positive guidance; it reflected Vaughan's own chilly attitude towards intellectual probings.

Francis Bourne, Bishop of Southwark was appointed to follow Vaughan in August 1903 at the age of forty-two. His main priestly training had been at St. Sulpice in Paris; the austere system there was the foundation of a life of deep spirituality. He was ordained priest in July 1884 and, after five years of parish work, he was chosen to be the first rector of Wonersh, the Southwark seminary; there he remained until 1897 when he became Bishop of Southwark. As Archbishop he reversed Vaughan's central seminary policy and the Westminster theological students returned to St. Edmund's, where he also developed the secondary school. Bourne wished the theological students to have their basic formation in England and then go abroad for higher studies; he did not favour their having their whole training at, for instance, the English College in Rome. One of his hopes was that a Catholic Theological Faculty could be established at one of the older universities; this he was unable to realise, but it may be noted that he sent Ronald Knox to the Oxford chaplaincy.

The Catholics of England had to face the effect of proposed education legislation on their own schools for which they had striven so hard, at such sacrifice. Bourne was unremitting in his efforts to secure equitable treatment by the State. The Education Act of 1902 had provided for the maintenance of the voluntary schools and when the Liberals came into office in 1906 it was with the understanding among their Nonconformist supporters that neither Catholic nor Anglican schools should remain 'on the rates.' By the Bill of 1906, accordingly, voluntary schools, unless entirely self-support-ing, were to be transferred to the local education authorities and only 'undenominational' religious teaching would be permitted. Before the Bill was published, but while its trend was a matter of common knowledge, Bourne began to mobilise Catholic opinion. His Lenten Pastoral plainly set out the issues and declared that, if necessary, 'we shall be prepared, to the extent of our power, to continue the struggle of the past rather than sacrifice our children.' A crowded meeting at the Albert Hall made the Catholic case known to the public; as *The Times* noted, 'this remark-able protest could not be ignored.' The Irish members in the Commons gave their support but this would not have been enough if the Anglicans had not been fighting for the same principle. The Bill did not become law, nor did three later attempts of the Liberals to 'solve' the religion-in-schools problem.

Bourne also clashed with the Government in connection with the Eucharistic Congress of 1908. For the first time for three centuries a Papal Legate was to come to England. This in itself made the event a landmark in the history of the Church in this country, but the presence of seven Cardinals and over a hundred archbishops, bishops and abbots added to the significance of the occasion. It had been planned that, on the last Sunday of the Congress, a procession of the Blessed Sacrament should pass along streets near the cathed-ral. The Archbishop, with his usual thoroughness, had made careful preparations and had sought and obtained the approval of the police authorities. This proposal roused the antagonism of some fanatical Protestants and threats were made that the procession would be attacked, but the police were confident that they could deal with any trouble. A few days before the procession, the archbishop received indirectly a message from the Home Secretary, H. H. Asquith, suggesting that the plan should be abandoned as 'provocative to Protestant sentiment.' The Archbishop wrote to the Prime Minister saying that he would of course obey an official order but not a private communication 'and I shall give the matter the fullest publicity in order that my action may be amply vindicated.' After some shuffling Asquith gave the official order and the procession was cancelled, but the Government had a bad Press.

During Bourne's early years at Westminster, the so-called modernists (there was no organised movement) continued to give grave concern to the Church. Among the English writers was the Jesuit priest George Tyrrell. He was anxious, as other thinkers were, that the Church should face up to the progress in knowledge of the times and restate its theology in terms of the day. This particularly affected the official attitude towards Biblical criticism. The leader in France was Alfred Loisy who tried to bring Catholic teaching in line with what was sound in Biblical studies. One of his close supporters was Baron Friedrich von Hügel[1] who was also a friend of Tyrrell. The Jesuits expelled Tyrrell from the Society in 1906 and he was later excommunicated. Bourne had no part in this as it was a Jesuit concern, but it was through his influence that there was no condemnation of von Hügel, nor of Wilfrid Ward who had been appointed editor of *The Dublin Review* by Bourne in 1906, a post he held with great distinction until 1916. He was not an extremist like his father W. G. Ward and he was not out to shock the hierarchy; he saw that the 'modernists' were troubled with serious problems which could best be dealt with by equally serious discussion. The correspondence between the cardinal and the editor throws light on the characters of both. In his letters Bourne postulated that the freedom he allowed the editor was conditional on its always being made clear that

[1] Von Hügel's father was an Austrian diplomat who married an Englishwoman. From 1876 Friedrich lived in England and was naturalised in 1914. He died in 1925.

the opinions expressed were those of the contributors and were not authoritative. He had to suffer some criticism by his refusal to bring Ward to heel.

The 'modernists' were condemned in 1907 by Pius X in a decree *Lamentabile* and in the encyclical *Pascendi*. Further measures were the setting up of vigilance committees in all dioceses to report suspects; in addition an anti-modernist oath was exacted from all priests. Moreover Pius saw that the membership of the Biblical Commission set up by Leo XIII in 1902 was restricted to the most conservative theologians; the statements it issued could not unfairly be described as fundamentalist. These draconian and panic measures set back the Church intellectually for a generation and it ceased to play a meaningful part in the study of the Scriptures and in theological inquiry. It was not until the issue of Pius XII's encyclical *Divino afflanti spiritu* in 1943 that the strait-jacket was loosened.

One inevitable result of these restrictions was a dearth of theological writing and of Biblical investigation. This stagnation was to some extent compensated by the work of two laymen, Hilaire Belloc and G. K. Chesterton, both persuasive writers with a wide appeal. Belloc's historical work was unfortunately open to attack from reputable historians since he allowed his bias to influence his use of facts and his reiterated 'The Faith is Europe, and Europe is the Faith' will not stand up to close examination. G. K. Chesterton was not converted until 1922 but long before that his writing tended towards Catholicism. Much of his controversial writing now dates and he will be best remembered for such impressionist studies of personalities as his *St. Francis of Assisi*. Both writers did great service to the Church and kept its claims before the greater public.

In 1908 Catholic affairs in this country ceased to be under the direction of the Congregation of Propaganda and at length the hierarchy was given the powers that are normal in a Catholic country. Following this increased responsibility, a change was made in 1911 when ecclesiastical England and Wales was reorganised into three Provinces, with Liverpool and Birmingham as metropolitan sees in addition to West-minster. Wales became a separate Province in 1916 with an archbishop at Cardiff and Menevia as a suffragan see. Brentwood became a separate see in 1917, and in 1924 the diocese of Lancaster was formed.[1] These changes were necessitated by the increase in the Catholic population. When Cardinal Bourne died in 1935 the Catholic population was estimated at 2,350,000 out of a total population of forty millions. In 1850 the number of Catholics had been about 680,000 out of a population of eighteen millions, and the number of priests did not exceed 800; by 1935 their number had increased to 4,500. In 1875 there were about a thousand Catholic churches; in 1935 the number was 2,400. With the creation of additional archbishoprics it was necessary to define the position of the Archbishop of Westminster. He is the president of the meeting of bishops and he represents Catholics for official purposes, but has no over-ruling authority over the bishops; his position is one of honour rather than of superiority. His being a cardinal makes no difference to this position save that his opinions carry more weight due to his relationship with the pope.

There was no obvious successor to Cardinal Bourne in 1935. The appointment of Archbishop Arthur Hinsley came as a total surprise. He had been rector of the English College, Rome, and then Apostolic Delegate to Africa. At the age of sixty-nine he was a canon of St. Peter's, a position of virtual retirement. It was therefore with some misgivings that he went to Westminster and some asked 'Why send us this old man?' He very quickly won the loyalty and affection of the priests of Westminster and he was a devoted pastoral bishop. He was created a cardinal in 1937. It was the Second World War that made him a national figure such as his two predecessors had not been. His broadcasts for this country and for foreign countries were stimulating and popular. He wanted, however, to bring the other churches into closer association with his work for victory and peace.

[1] Southwark became a separate Province in 1965 with Arundel & Brighton as a suffragan see.

In December 1940 he joined with the two Anglican Archbishops and the Moderator of the Free Churches in sending
to *The Times* a declaration of the principles that should be
the framework of national policy and social life. This had
followed his setting up an association called 'The Sword of
the Spirit' designed to bring Catholics and others together
to co-ordinate Christian effort for justice in peace and war
in a campaign of prayer, study and action. Many ways were
devised, such as lunch-time sermons, addresses to gatherings
of members, retreats, study circles and public meetings,
and the inevitable pamphlets. At one notable three-day
conference in May 1941, at the time of the London blitz,
the Stoll Theatre was packed to overflowing to hear the
Catholic and the Anglican Archbishops and other leaders.
Similar meetings were held in many parts of the country.
The sense of fellowship among all who called themselves
Christians was notably strengthened. There was, however,
one condition that proved a set-back. The movement was
under the control of the Catholic bishops and only Catholics
could be full members. This undoubtedly led to a cooling
off among some who had assumed that this was a fully
ecumenical association. With our knowledge of what has
happened since the war, we can see Cardinal Hinsley's
effort as foreshadowing the ecumenical movement that
we now associate with Pope John XXIII and the Second
Vatican Council.

In 1938 an Apostolic Delegation was set up in London
with the Cardinal's approval; the one stipulation he made
was that the Delegate should be of British nationality. The
first Delegate was Mgr. William Godfrey who had succeeded
Hinsley as rector of the English College. The appointment
is not a diplomatic one; the Delegate represents the Holy
Father to the clergy and laity.

When it was known that the coalition war-time Government was contemplating a new education Act, the Cardinal
at once made known the views of the Church; they were,
of course, the same as those for which his three predecessors
had striven. Catholic schools must remain Catholic. The

Cardinal pleaded for fair play for Catholic children so that they could be educated in their own schools in the atmosphere of the Faith. In Cardinal Bourne's day, the Anglican Church had also fought to retain its own schools, but under the proposed scheme, the Anglicans were willing to accept full State control with religious instruction based on a non-committal Agreed Syllabus. Catholics were left to fight alone.

Cardinal Hinsley did not live to see the passing of the 1944 Act; he died in March 1943. He was Archbishop of Westminster for only eight years, yet in that time he had became a much respected national figure. *The Times*, in a leading article, stated that 'he leaves a happier relation between his communion and the national church than has been known since the reformation.' It could have added with equal truth, a happier relation with all the churches and with the people at large.

Epilogue

THESE pages have recorded the history of the Roman Catholic Church in England and Wales from the earliest times until the Second World War, a period of some eighteen centuries. Much interesting detail has had to be omitted and it has not been possible to enlarge on some topics that merit more extended treatment. In spite of these unavoidable limitations, it is hoped that the reader has gained an impression of the continuity of the Church. The watershed was the Reformation and we have seen how Catholics were proscribed for three centuries, but a determined remnant clung to the Faith until the coming of the Second Spring.

> 'God would leave a remnant of our race surviving, leave us a foot-hold on this holy ground; some gleam of hope our God would afford us, some breath of life in our bondage.' (Ezra, 9, 8).

* * *

It would be unwise to attempt an assessment of events since the Second World War; they are too near us for a detached judgment. Note should, however, be made of the problem that faced the Church when the 1944 Education Act became law. The hierarchy took the bold decision not only to preserve existing Catholic schools but to increase their number. This has meant an inordinate strain on the financial resources of the Catholic people; the struggle continues.

For the Church as a whole the accession of Pope John XXIII in 1958 unexpectedly proved to be a land-mark in its history. A man of seventy-eight is not usually regarded as a possible innovator. His call for renewal, for rejuvenation and new vigour was followed by the Second Vatican Council (1962–5). The most evident outcome has been the adoption of the languages of the peoples in place of Latin in the Mass.

Sufficient time has elapsed for this innovation to be seen as justified. Pope John was also determined 'to broaden the frontiers of Christian love.' Out of this has come the ecumenical movement. Before he became pope, Cardinal Roncalli, had frequently voiced his longing for closer fellowship with other churches. Thus he had said, 'I have been careful, mindful of moral principles and of the Catholic faith, to concentrate not on those factors which separate and cause conflict, but on those which unite.' He died in 1963 before the Council had completed its work, but the spirit with which he imbued it lived on. It would be difficult to exaggerate the importance of this Council not only to Catholics but to all Christian communities. To understand its achievement and to appreciate the present outlook of the Church, the reader must study the remarkable documents that record the findings of the Council.[1]

Inevitably there have been misunderstandings and some have pitched their hopes too high; there were none of those dramatic scenes, so beloved of reporters, at the Council which was a grave consultation on subjects deeply affecting the life of the Church. It was also inevitable that extravagant opinions have been put forward that have caused alarm to some Catholics. Questions have been raised, for example, on the celibacy of priests, on the method of appointing bishops, and on other controversial matters with which the Council did not deal. The questions are ones of discipline and order, not doctrine. Here again the undue prominence given to these problems in newspapers and on radio tends to give the impression that the Church is in a state of turmoil. So too, when priests defect from the Church the spot-light is momentarily turned upon them so that the true state of affairs becomes distorted. Those who know something of the history of the Church — and it is hoped that these pages will add to their numbers — are aware that there is nothing new in these disturbances; for instance, throughout the life of the Church, priests have left it for one reason or another

[1] Published by the Catholic Truth Society in a series of pamphlets, 'Council Documents.'

ROMAN CATHOLIC CHURCH, ENGLAND AND WALES

without the glare of publicity. So, too, many kinds of intellectual and disciplinary problems have been raised, argued and determined. The Church is never hasty in reaching decisions on disputatious matters for they affect the faith of millions of ordinary folk. This patience is part of the strength of the Church.

The barque of St. Peter has weathered many a stormy sea, and we know that it will always do so, for Our Lord has said, 'I am with you all through the days that are coming, until the consummation of the world.'

There is a famous passage in Lord Macaulay's essay on the History of the Popes that is as true to-day as it was when he wrote it in 1840.

'The Catholic Church is still sending forth to the farthest ends of the world missionaries as zealous as those who landed in Kent with Augustine. . . . Nor do we see any sign which indicates that the term of her long dominion is approaching. She saw the commencement of all the governments and of all the ecclesiastical establishments that now exist in the world; and we feel no assurance that she is not destined to see the end of them all. She was great and respected before the Saxon had set foot on Britain, before the Frank had passed the Rhine, when Grecian eloquence still flourished at Antioch, when idols were still worshipped in the temple of Mecca. And she may still exist in undiminished vigour when some traveller from New Zealand shall, in the midst of a vast solitude, take his stand on a broken arch of London Bridge to sketch the ruins of St. Paul's.'

A note on further reading

MANY of the books mentioned below are out of print but should be available in any good Public Library. Most of the books contain bibliographies.

For the pre-Reformation period, the first four volumes in Macmillan's *History of the English Church* provide the most detailed account.

1. *From its Foundation to the Norman Conquest.* William Hunt.

2. *From the Norman Conquest to Edward I.* W. R. W. Stephens.

3. *Fourteenth and Fifteenth Centuries.* W. W. Capes.

4. *From Henry VIII to the Death of Mary.* James Gairdner.

These were published at the beginning of the century and more recent work modifies some of the views expressed, but not to a great extent. Reference to the relevant chapters in the volumes of the Oxford History of England will provide corrections.

There is a good translation of Bede's *Ecclesiastical History* in the Penguin series. Margaret Deanesley's *The Pre-Conquest Church* (1960) is excellent.

For monasticism, the reader should consult, Dom David Knowles, *The Monastic Order in England* (1941), and *The Religious Orders in England* (3 vols. 1948–59).

For the Reformation, *The Reformation in England* (3 vols. 1950–4) by Mgr. Philip Hughes is a reliable authority; it is particularly good on those theological questions that most historians evade. The same author published a one-volume abbreviated version of his main work. His earlier *Rome and the Counter Reformation in England* (1942) carries the history on to 1632. A well-balanced Protestant account is given in A. G. Dickens, *The English Reformation* (1964). The most recent Catholic view is given in J. M. Todd, *Reformation* (1972).

A. O. Meyer, *England and the Catholic Church under Queen Elizabeth* (1910), was reprinted in 1967; the author was a Lutheran historian but the translator was a Catholic.

J. H. Pollen, *The English Catholics in the Reign of Queen Elizabeth* (1920), is by a Jesuit historian. J. E. Neale, *Elizabeth I and her Parliaments* (2 vols. 1953, 1957) is of great value.

For the period since the Reformation there is Archbishop David Mathew's *Catholicism in England, 1535–1935* (1936), which is described as a 'Portrait of a Minority, its Culture and Tradition.' *Roman Catholicism in England from the Reformation to 1950*, by E. I. Watkin (1957), is a good short survey.

Basil Hamphill, O.S.B., *The Early Vicars-Apostolic of England, 1685–1750* (1954), leads to a series of volumes giving a detailed history from 1691 to 1850. Canon Edwin Burton wrote *The Life and Times of Bishop Challoner* (2 vols. 1909), a fine biography. The other volumes were written by Bishop Bernard Ward, the son of W. G. Ward and brother of Wilfrid Ward. The titles are:

The Dawn of the Catholic Revival in England 1781–1803 (2 vols. 1909).

The Eve of Catholic Emancipation, 1803–1829 (3 vols. 1911).

The Sequel to Catholic Emancipation, 1830–1850 (2 vols. 1915).

Denis Gwynn's *The Second Spring, 1818–1852* (1942) gives an excellent account of this phase of Catholic history.

The English Catholics 1850–1950 (1950) is a collection of essays commemorating the centenary of the restoration of the hierarchy. It contains valuable material not easily accessible elsewhere. In his Foreword Cardinal Griffin wrote, 'if we are to learn from this record of a hundred years and, indeed, from the whole history of the Church since the coming of St. Augustine to this country, then we shall have before our eyes a lesson that will call forth apostolic zeal.'

General history can be supplemented by biographies and some readers may find this a congenial approach. Public Library catalogues should be consulted for subjects and authors; librarians are always glad to give advice on what is available. The articles in the *Dictionary of National Biography* provide reliable accounts especially of many secondary figures of whom no full biographies have been written.

Index

Wilberforce, William, 320
Wilfrid, St., 25, 27, 32–3, 37, 41, 45
William I, the Conqueror, 51, 74–9
William II (Rufus), 89–93
William III, 266, 285, 297
William of Orange (1584), 243
William de Corbeil, (C), 97, 105
William of York, St., 105–6
Willibrord, St., 37–8
Wiltshire, Earl of, 194
Winchcombe, 81
Winchelsey, Robert of, (C), 151
Winchester, 41, 54–5, 61, 137, 157; College, 155; Council (1076), 83
Windebank, Sir Francis, 280
Windsor, synod of (1072), 78
Wini, Bp., 31, 33
Winter, Robert and Thomas, 263
Winwaed Field, 25
Wisbech, 242, 250
Wiseman, Nicholas, Cardinal, 322, 330–1, 333–6, 339–42, 351
Whitham, Robert, 304

Wonersh seminary, 355
Wolsey, Thomas, Cardinal, 176–8
Worde, Wynkyn de, 160
Wright, Christopher and John, 263
Wright, Peter, 275
Wulfred, (C), 52
Wulfhelm, 61
Wulfhere, (Y), 58
Wulfstan of Worcester, St., 60n, 67, 75, 84; (C), I, 60; II, 69, 72
Wyatt, Sir Thomas, 212, 214
Wycliffe, John, 150, 161
Wykeham, William of, Bp., 155, 165

Yates, Lawrence, 276
Yelverton, Sir Henry, 272
Yevele, Henry, 158
York (ecclesiastical), 11, 23, 28–9, 32, 41, 58; and Canterbury, 17, 42, 77–8, 97, 122, 130; and Worcester, 64
Young, Richard, 248

Zacharius, Pope, 43